MY FIRST LIFE
Becoming a Man on the Colorado Frontier
1880-1905

A Newly Discovered Memoir by
Frederick Frank Blachly

Transcribed by Sat Hari Khalsa

Edited by Peter M. Blachly

SHEEP ISLAND PRESS

My First Life
Becoming a Man on the Colorado Frontier
1880-1905
A Newly Discovered Memoir by Frederick Frank Blachly

© 2021-2025 Sheep Island Press
Published by Sheep Island Press

All rights reserved. No part of this book may be used or reproduced by any means without the written permission of the author except in the case of brief quotations embodied in critical articles and reviews.

Transcription: Sat Hari Khalsa
Editor: Peter M. Blachly
Book Design: Book Savvy Studio, Ashland OR
Cover Paintings: Peter M. Blachly

Library of Congress Control Number: 2025902182
ISBN: 978-1-7372280-4-2
First Edition
Printed in the United States of America

To the memory of my parents

Andrew Trew Blachly

and

Mary Adelle Bradley Blachly

Editor's Note

WHEN I WAS A SMALL CHILD, my older siblings and I would sometimes sit at our grandfather's feet—on the rare occasions that he came to visit us—and beg him to tell us stories about the old West. The world he described was full of adventure, wild horses, cattle, poverty, and hardship. Regretfully, I never got to know my grandfather well. I was too young to truly understand the epic role he played in his early life, and to me he was just a kindly old man with a green visor who wrote academic books on subjects I could not comprehend.

A dozen years ago, while clearing out my father's apartment, I came across a 1966 letter from the University of Colorado Press describing a book that my grandfather had submitted (the manuscript was "worthy of being published" but the University was short on funds). Intrigued, I asked my aging father about it, but he had no idea where the original manuscript was. His younger sister, my Aunt Daphne, with whom my grandfather lived for the last ten years of his life, remembered the manuscript but could not remember where she had put it, or if she even still had it. Only after she died in December 2016 did her daughters, my cousins Carol and Barbara, discover it while clearing out their mother's house, tucked away under a stairway in the garage. They also found the 50+ photographs that my grandfather had intended to be included. Carol eventually passed the entire package along to me. My daughter, Sat Hari Khalsa, took on the task of transcribing the memoir from hand-typed onion-skin pages, and has helped me enormously with organizing and editing the complete work. For her help I am deeply grateful.

My First Life, documents my grandfather's first 25 years as a cowboy and farmer on the western slope of the Colorado Rockies

(1880—1905). His father, a part-time banker, was shot and killed in 1893 in a daring robbery in Delta, Colorado by members of the notorious McCarty gang, leaving my grandfather at age 13 to provide for his mother and seven brothers. Their struggles and triumphs were epic, and out of necessity he became a farmer, cattle rancher, and an expert horseman. The memoir ends with my grandfather at 25, jumping a cattle train and heading east on his way to get an education at Oberlin College, which his mother and many other family members had attended. In fact, his grandmothers on both sides had been roommates there and were among the first women in the world to receive a BA upon their graduation in 1845.

Eventually, after graduating from Oberlin at the age of 30 in 1911, my grandfather obtained a PhD from Columbia University, and after a sabbatical following seven years as a full professor at the University of Oklahoma, he and his wife, Miriam Oatman, PhD (Oberlin class of 1912), became Fellows at the Brookings Institution and together authored numerous academic and technical books on politics, government administration, and economics—one of which formed the basis of the Marshall Plan in the rebuilding of Germany after WW II. In 1952, together they co-chaired the New Mexico commission on the restructuring of the state's administration — often referred to as the "Mini-Hoover Commission."

Editing *My First Life* has given me much more than just an understanding of my grandfather's life and character. Getting to know him in this way has been immensely gratifying, but the book also provides an extraordinary and intimate view of frontier life on the western slope of the Colorado Rockies in the years when the threat of Indian warfare still loomed large, and cattle thieves, bank robbers, and other outlaws—as well as mountain lions and grizzly bears—still roamed the land.

— PETER MACDONALD BLACHLY, September, 2021

Contents

Editor's Note v
Foreword ix
I   Early Years 1
II   Melvale Farm 17
III   Life on the Farm 47
IV   School Boy 73
V   Family Tragedy 93
VI   The Elms 119
VII Hauling Coal 141
VIII Poverty Flat 165
IX   Farmer 185
X   Peach Valley 211
XI   Struggle for Water 249
XII Cattlemen 265
XIII Tough Winter 297
XIV Hitting Bottom 315
XV Transition 335
Appendix I 345
Appendix II 347
Appendix III 358
Family Tree 359

Foreword

THIS BOOK IS THE TRUE STORY of my early life on the Western Slope of Colorado. It has seemed worthwhile to tell the story, partly because it touches upon events of historical interest, partly because it deals with a type of frontier living that has nearly gone out of existence with the inroads of modern machinery, and partly because it may help to correct the widespread impression that the early settlers of the mountainous west were of a single type. The happy-go-lucky cowboy with his six-shooter, rope, spurs, chaps, and high-heeled boots, was indeed among the early settlers. But of even greater importance, although not so picturesque, were the persons representing other types.

The following groups, and their major problems, are mentioned here as they touched upon my own experience:

The land-hungry settlers, taking claims on land which earlier explorers had described as "barren deserts fit only for savages to live in," their struggles for water to irrigate such lands, their trials with a long-depressed agricultural economy and with financial panics, their dependence upon the east for capital, which was granted only at outrageous interest rates, their primary markets cut off by the silver policy of the Federal government, and the small returns from distant markets because of high freight rates.

The cattlemen, changing over from scrub stock to well-nigh thoroughbred cattle, their fight against imported cattle diseases and pests, their tribulations during terrible winters, the end of the open range and the development of year-round feeding of cattle for beef, and the warfare between cattlemen and the sheep men.

The fruit raisers, dreaming of wealth from orchards, but

plagued by insect pests, late frosts and nearly impossible marketing conditions; forced to pull out their orchards by the roots, taking heavy losses, and compelled to turn to other types of agriculture, or even to give up in despair.

The many educated and cultivated people, who had found it necessary to come to a high, dry climate for their health; restarting life, but bringing with them and establishing the religious, educational, and cultural institutions to which they had been accustomed.

The bankers and businessmen, operating in the "boom and bust" conditions of the mining camps, trying to cope with the uncertainties and fluctuations of a rapidly changing economy.

These groups of people, in various combinations, were the unsung and unpublicized heroes, who during my lifetime have made a large part of a "dry and thirsty land where no water is" blossom like the rose, have conserved water in hundreds of beautiful lakes, drained alkali flats, built great modern highways, and have developed little towns with paved streets bordered by tall shade trees, with fine schools, churches, public buildings, business enterprises and comfortable homes.

Our family, or members of it, were intimately concerned in the activities of all these classes and combinations in the county and town of Delta, Colorado, and we shared their hopes, fears, tribulations and successes. Since my own life, during its first twenty-five years, was closely tied in with the development of the Western Slope, I believe that this memoir may have more than a personal interest.[1]

The story could not have been told accurately without the assistance of many others. One of my most important sources

---

1 For more information on the economic, political, historical, and social context of this story, please see Appendix II

of information consists of letters from my mother to her own mother. These letters were kept by Grandmother Bradley, and, finally, typed copies came into my possession. They reinforced and at times corrected my own memories, and were particularly valuable as to dates.

My brothers Louis and Clarence have also been of assistance. Louis has done research work among early documents and in the files of pioneer newspapers, and has recorded the tales of many "old timers" on the Western Slope. Clarence has helped to refresh and correct my memory in numerous details.[2]

Several members of the Nutter family have contributed to the story. Charles Nutter gave me first-hand information regarding several events that I have described. His daughters, Anna and Eveline, both of whom served at different times as librarians of the Delta Public Library, gave me valuable information. They also gave me my brother Louis' tape recordings of events in the history of Delta. Similar help was given by their sister, Stella Nutter Fairlamb, whose husband was one of Delta's important lawyers.

Ula King Fairfeild furnished information not formerly available regarding the Radcliffe affair.

I am particularly indebted to Benjamin Laycook, a former classmate in the Delta public schools, for many photographs of persons and scenes connected with the history of Colorado's Western Slope. Most of these were taken by his father, F. M. Laycook, an early photographer in Delta who evidently knew by instinct what photographs were likely to be of historical interest. Elmer Skinner has also furnished several photographs.

Information was provided by many officials of Government

---

2   Louis Blachly's papers are in the possession of the University of Arizona, and Clarence's are preserved at in the library of Grinnell College in Iowa."

departments in Washington: the Library of Congress, the Bureau of Indian Affairs, the Forestry Service, the Geological Survey, and other agencies which have been concerned with activities on the Western Slope. I am particularly indebted to the Bureau of Reclamation, whose economists Edward J. Talbot and Archie B. Goodman made available to me archival materials regarding the Uncompahgre project, the annual reports on the project, and the texts of the different contracts made between the Uncompahgre Valley Water Users Association and the Federal government.

Finally, most of all I am indebted to my wife and research collaborator, Dr. Miriam Oatman, for unfailing interest, constructive criticism, and careful editorial work.

FREDERICK F. BLACHLY, 1965

My First Life

Frederick Frank Blachly
(1880 - 1974)

CHAPTER I

Early Years

I WAS BORN IN A BARN.

This event took place on August 20, 1880, at Salida, Colorado, not far from the continental divide. In order to explain why my parents were at that particular place at that particular time, I must make a brief excursion into family history. Chief personalities involved in this tale are the Blachly and Bradley families.

My grandfather, Eben Blachly, who was a physician and ordained minister, had undergone an experience during the Civil War that gave direction to the remainder of his life. While searching for one of his sons, a Union soldier who had been captured by the enemy, he himself was taken and accused of being a spy for the North. After some sort of field trial, he was condemned to be hanged. As he sat on his horse under a tree with the noose about his neck, he obtained permission to offer a final prayer. He prayed aloud with such fervor and conviction that his captors were forced to believe in his truthfulness and to accept his statement that he was not a spy. They removed the noose and allowed him to go on his way.

Grandfather Blachly had always been a religious person, but he now felt a deepened desire to serve God. He finally decided to do so by devoting himself to the education of former slaves. With the full acquiescence of his family, he sold his property in Dane County, Wisconsin, and purchased about 130 acres of land overlooking a great bend of the Missouri River at Quindaro, Kansas (now a part of Kansas City). This land was improved with several useful buildings, and here he established Freedmen's University. His faculty consisted largely of himself, his wife, and his eldest children by a previous marriage. It was a well-qualified faculty. An important member was Grandmother Blachly, formerly Miss Jane B. Trew, who was a graduate of Oberlin College in the class of 1845, and was thus one of the first few women in the world to earn the B.A. degree. For a long time, Freedmen's University served the intellectual, social, and religious needs of colored students.

Two sons were born of my Grandfather's marriage to Miss Trew. These were my father, Andrew Trew Blachly, and my uncle, Dr. Frank Chalmers Blachly. Andrew Trew entered Washington and Jefferson College; but before he had completed his work for a degree he was threatened with tuberculosis and was ordered to go to a dry climate to restore his health. He moved to Monument, Colorado, where he supported himself by engaging in such work as his strength permitted. Apparently, his health and vigor returned fairly soon.

In 1877, Grandfather Blachly became ill, and word that his death was expected went out to various relatives. One of these was his niece, Mary Adelle Bradley, who became my mother.

Her father, my Grandfather Bradley, was a medical missionary in Siam. The story of Reverend Doctor Dan Beach Bradley has been told in other places, and I shall not outline it here. His second wife was Sarah Blachly, a sister of my Grandfather Eben Blachly. She was also a classmate and roommate of Jane B. Trew at Oberlin, and was graduated with the B.A. Degree in the same year. Hence, there were close bonds uniting the Blachly and Bradley families. Grandmother Bradley prepared all her children to enter Oberlin College, and all except one did so. After the death of her husband,

Grandmother decided to stay in Siam, carrying on the printing business which Grandfather Bradley had established. In 1875, she sent her third child, Mary Adele (known as "Dellie"), to Oberlin. Dellie was pursuing studies in the College and Conservatory when word of her uncle's condition reached her. She started immediately for Quindaro, and arrived a few days before his death.

Meanwhile, Andrew Trew Blachly had started back to Quindaro in the hope of seeing his father once more. But Grandfather was dead before his arrival. Andrew met for the first time his beautiful cousin Dellie, a slender, retiring girl whose help and sympathy gave much comfort to his mother. With her son's advice, Grandmother Blachly decided to retire from teaching, sell her interest in the University, and accompany Andrew to Monument.

Before it was possible for Grandmother to leave Quindaro, however, Andrew and Dellie fell deeply in love with each other. Father pressed for an immediate marriage. This seemed impossible to Dellie. She said that she did not know how to cook or manage a household, but that she could learn these things if she returned to Oberlin and completed her work there, as she felt she ought to do. Her brother, Dan, who had stopped at Quindaro on his way from Siam to Oberlin, supported her position. Father brushed aside all objections. He, himself, he stated, was a good cook and an experienced manager of his own house. He could easily teach Dellie all that she needed to learn about cooking and housekeeping!

Someone raised the question whether first cousins should marry. Much praying was done in hope of obtaining light on this point. Both Father and Mother finally decided that their marriage would be in accordance with God's will. As the laws of Kansas did not permit first cousins to marry, the ceremony was performed in Kansas City, Missouri. The next morning the bride and groom left for Monument, Colorado. They reached the little town at sundown, to find themselves welcomed by several friends and Father's brother Frank, who was a young physician.

Monument contained at the time some fifteen or twenty houses, a church, a schoolhouse, and a saloon, all snuggled against the front range of the massive Rocky Mountains. It was located about half way between Colorado Springs and Denver. To the east were rolling upland plains, covered with short grass and wild flowers, where only a few years before, the Ute Indians had great herds of Buffalo. The town was the center of a rather large farming and stock raising community, and for this reason it carried a station of the lately established Denver and Rio Grande Railway, where Father was employed as a station agent, express agent, and telegraph operator. He also kept the Post Office and operated a small drug store.

Sometime before his marriage, Father had been engaging in a thriving general merchandising and commission business in Husted, near Monument, but as the result of the panic of 1873 the business had failed. Apparently, he was now engaged in multiple occupations as a method of paying debts, and perhaps embarking in another business of his own.

There are various indications that Father was one of the important and progressive men in that little community. His name appears frequently in the *Colorado Springs Gazette* of the period. He was one of the incorporators of the Monument, Bergens Park, and Fairplay Wagon Road Company. He established and edited the *Monument Weekly Mentor*, a newspaper with a circulation of 400 copies. He was named as a trustee and recording secretary of the Monument Academy. After his mother came to live with them, she joined the Academy faculty, and though 64 years old at the time, she was considered "one of the best teachers." Both Father and his brother Frank signed the petition seeking incorporation of the town of Monument. Father was elected corresponding secretary of the Colorado Press Association, and as a delegate from Monument to the El Paso County Republican Convention. Further, he was superintendent of the Sunday school and leader of the church choir.

Although Mother in her early home had been accustomed to several Siamese servants and had never had to cook or do housework, she readily adapted herself to the care of the little home in Monument. Father had a flute, a violin, and an organ, which were put to good use every evening, Father playing the flute or violin and Mother the organ accompaniment.

Father and Mother organized a singing club of 14 members, which met every Saturday night. Mother was the organist and Father the conductor. Mother played the organ at church, taught a Sunday school class, and gave a few music lessons. She also learned how to keep Father's books, and studied telegraphy.

For the first two years in Monument, Mother and Father were very happy. In the latter part of 1878 Arthur Trew, their first son, was born. He was not very strong. An interesting sidelight on a fad that had swept Oberlin and other parts of the country about this time is contained in a letter written by Father to Grandmother Bradley about a year after Arthur's birth, which said in respect to the little fellow: "We are bringing him up on graham bread and milk with a liberal use of flesh brush and he seems to be gaining much in constitution."

During the next year, several events led my parents to consider leaving Monument. Father had been publishing in the *Monument Mentor* articles that upheld "temperance", opposed the drunkenness and lawlessness prevalent in the little settlement, and maintained that the selling of alcoholic beverages should be prohibited by law. This position greatly incensed the saloonkeepers and other rough elements. One day as Mother looked out of an upstairs window, she saw Father standing in front of a little store across the street with a big German, Herman Schwanderbeck, who was holding his fist in front of Father's face and talking in a loud and rough manner. Feeling that Father was in danger, Mother hurried to the kitchen, picked up a heavy stick of stove wood, and ran across the street. She spoke to the man and seemed to calm him down. A few nights after this, however, a great bonfire was made in front of my parent's house. The men who had been drinking in the nearby saloon gathered about the fire, talking violently and threatening to kill Father. At Mother's request, Father reached one of his strong young friends, who brought a gun and sat up all night with my parents. No direct violence was offered that night, but Mother was convinced that Father was in danger. In particular, she feared that some ruffian might push him off the little station platform just as the train pulled in.

Father and Mother went to Colorado Springs to have Herman Schwanderbeck bound over by the court to keep the peace. They were successful, and Schwanderbeck was held for appearance in the district court under a bond of $200. But this did not convince Mother that Father was safe. She urged him to move immediately to some other place, before any threats, which had been made against him, were carried out. In the summer of 1880, he agreed to move if he could find a suitable location.

About this time, after a bitter contest with the Santa Fe Railway for possession of the Royal Gorge of the Arkansas, the Denver and Rio Grande Railway was expanding on the Western Slope.

The two railway companies had fought for this prize through the state and Federal courts, and among some of their representatives and employees, feelings had run so high as to involve actual warfare. In the end, the Rio Grande won control of the disputed area, which was essential to its expansion in Colorado. It began to build lines that ran out of Salida in different directions, serving separate areas before they met again at Grand Junction. One ran north to Leadville, an active mining camp. Plans were under way to extend this line northward until it reached the Grand River (now the Colorado), and to proceed down this stream southwestward until the railway line entered Grand Junction. The other line was to run west, crossing the Rockies at Marshall Pass, and going on to Grand Junction by way of Gunnison, Montrose, and Delta. The mining camps of the San Juan region were to be served by a spur, which joined the line at Montrose. From Grand Junction goods and passengers could be moved by the Rio Grande Western line, which ran to Salt Lake City and Ogden, Utah. Thus, a large agricultural, mining and cattle section of the Western Slope would be opened to commerce.

As Salida was to be an important railway junction, with a round house and shops, and was already the center of cattle country, Father felt that it might be a good place to start a small drug store. There is no doubt that he and those whom he consulted visualized the development of the town as a pleasant residential area with expanding business opportunities.

Father went to look over this location while mother packed his little stock of drugs preparatory to making a move. Evidently, Father was convinced that Salida had possibilities for his undertaking. He asked one of his friends there to find suitable quarters, while he returned to Monument to help in moving the family. They reached Salida at night and stayed at the hotel. The next morning they went to see the place that had been secured for them and were greatly depressed when instead of the house they had expected, they saw a good-sized barn. The front part was large and open to the ceiling, while the back part had a loft. All the back part was partitioned off from the front. Despite this discouraging situation there seemed nothing to do but to make the best of the matter temporarily.

So, Father unpacked his drugs and placed them on shelves in the front room. Grandmother's furniture, as well as the furniture my parents had brought, was placed in the back room. The loft was reserved as sleeping quarters for Mother and Father and little Arthur. This loft was so low that, as Mother said in a letter, they had to "bend when getting about… There was one window sash dreadfully dirty, which when washed showed a stable yard below, and the back of shacks beyond the yard. Very unromantic! I found that the wind blew through the large cracks in the walls, so I took strips of cloth and shoved them in all the cracks. It was tiresome work, for it was August, and the eaves were so low that I had to move with my back bent." My mother was nine months pregnant at the time.

"I think," continued Mother, "that we had been here about two weeks. I had been so busy getting the house (or barn) in shape, that my washing had accumulated, and I resolved to get it all done that day (August 20th). I was strong, young, and ambitious, and I wanted my barn homelike. That night at 9 pm my baby Fred came. Then I became very ill with heat, which brought on trouble with the bowels. I was too ill to remember anything more. When I got about again (I think it was November) I went downstairs with the baby. Little Arthur was so jealous of the baby that he would not even look at it. While I was sick, Arthur had stayed with his grandmother downstairs."

Thus, I was born in a barn

Father's drug business began to prosper, and within a short time, he was able to rent a comfortable house with a place for the drug store in front. Mother wrote me, years later "In those early days, the stores were at the front of the house. These stores were so small, that a good-sized room would hold the stock."

Here, as in Monument, Father and Grandmother continued their church work. Father was made Elder in the Presbyterian Church and the Superintendent of the Sunday school, and Grandmother organized Sunday school classes.

Despite the hopes that had brought the family to Salida, my parents did not remain long. The town failed to develop a substantial permanent population. As the railway construction workers moved out of it, pushing the tracks farther and farther, Salida found, like the other "boom and bust" places, it could not support expanding business enterprises.

There was feverish mining activity on the western slope of the Rockies about this time, and with the prospect of large silver production, many little mining camps and towns were springing up. One of the most important of these, because of its central location, was Gunnison, which had been laid out as a silver mining town in 1879 and incorporated the following year. Long lines of wagons, according to a newspaper report at the time, were pouring into Gunnison and the surrounding mining camps. In August of 1881, the narrow-gauge railroad came into the town from Salida, from where it was gradually extended to Montrose, to Delta, and down the Gunnison River to Grand Junction. Gunnison began to "boom." A hotel costing nearly a quarter of a million dollars was constructed, a large smelter was built, a brick schoolhouse was erected, several churches were organized, and two daily newspapers were telling of the glorious possibilities of this great mining, stock raising, and farming center. Almost simultaneously with the railroad, Father went to Gunnison. After he had sounded out the possibilities of the place, he moved his family there in the fall of 1881. His mother and brother Frank accompanied them.

A little piece of good fortune now came our way. Grandmother Bradley, with the aid of her youngest daughter, was still operating the rather large printing business that had been established by her husband in Siam. She sent to our family a sum of money, which enabled Father to set up a good-sized drug business, and Mother to buy a new piano. Because of booming times, business developed rapidly, and Father became the wholesale supplier of many little drug stores in mining camps all over the western slope.

Father and Mother were very happy with Gunnison, which, though only two years old, had a population estimated at 3000. The climate, particularly in the summer, was delightful, as the town lay at an elevation of about 7,500 feet. There was beautiful mountain scenery in all directions. After living in Salida, the family particularly enjoyed the much wider social and religious life of Gunnison.

As usual, Father became interested in church work and in the musical and educational activities of the place. He was made a member of the school board. Uncle Frank, who had trained as a doctor, was appointed as City Health Officer. Father was soon able to build a comfortable house in which my brothers Clarence and Howard were born.

It was in Gunnison that my first consciousness of the world about me began to develop. One's memories of very early life always consist of a few scattered experiences, which stand out like peaks in a long mountain range seen dimly in the distance. It is not always the events of importance that one remembers, for the mind of the child, just learning to find its way about in its own little world, selects and retains incidents which seem important or interesting according to its own standards.

I think that my earliest memory is of the baptism of my brother Clarence, who is sixteen months younger than I. Probably I was less than three years old when Uncle Dan, who was visiting Mother just before completing his course in the Oberlin Theological Seminary, baptized my baby brother. I remember Clarence's white dress, and the water that my uncle sprinkled on his head.

Several memories return to me from the period when I must have been about four years old. One beautiful clear morning I went to the door, and upon opening, found a little basket full of flowers. I ran into the house and asked Mother if it were mine. The other little boys, Arthur and Clarence, wanted to know if it was not theirs also. "Go and look at the other doors," said Mother. When the boys had done so, they too found lovely little baskets filled with flowers. "It is May day," said Mother, "and these are May baskets".

One morning bright and early, a team of black horses pulling a double-seated buggy drew up at the door. We all jumped in and went for what seemed to me a long ride to a place across the river, and there we had a picnic. These were the first horses I remember. They fascinated me, as horses have done to this day.

The winter that I was four must have been very cold and snowy, for I remember that Arthur and I dug a tunnel in the snow around the house, and built a snow fort. Going through that tunnel seemed a great and dangerous adventure.

Sometime during the winter we went to the church to hear

the cantata "Esther," which was conducted by my father. I can still remember some of it, particularly the chorus: "Haman, Haman, bow down to Haman! He is the favored one, he is the favored one, he is the favored one in all the King's dominions." The singing made a great impression on me. On the way, home I fell out of the sleigh into the snow, but was soon rescued.

Another event that fixed itself in my memory was walking one Sunday afternoon beside the beautiful Gunnison River, and seeing some white sheep and lambs in the soft green grass. My father repeated the twenty-third Psalm.

> *The Lord is my shepherd; I shall not want. He maketh me to lie down in green pastures: he leadeth me beside still waters. He restoreth my soul: he leadeth me in the path of righteousness for his name's sake. Yea, though I walk through the valley of the shadow of death, I will fear no evil: for thou art with me; thy rod and thy staff they comfort me. Thou preparest a table before me in the presence of mine enemies: thou anointest my head with oil; my cup runneth over. Surely goodness and mercy shall follow me all the days of my life: and I will dwell in the house of the Lord forever.*

It may have been because of this occurrence that I never could develop the hatred for sheep and their owners and herders, which my later companions had.

After their experiences in Monument and Salida, my parents found Gunnison almost like the Promised Land to those who came in from the wilderness, so that Mother and Father considered making it their permanent home. Then disaster struck. The anticipated streams of silver and gold from the numerous little mining towns and camps did not materialize. As had happened so many times in mining country, the early "boom" was succeeded almost immediately by a "bust." The smelter went to the wall. The famed, expensive Lewis Hotel (later La Veta) closed for the winter. One daily paper died and another became a weekly. People were leaving the whole region in droves. Business collapsed. By the early spring of 1885, Gunnison was dead.

At this time, Father became seriously ill and his business had to be carried on by a partner. When he recovered sufficiently to go back to work, he was confronted not only by a great business depression in the town, but also by the fact that his partner had mismanaged the business and had evidently robbed him. In an attempt to save his business, Father mortgaged the family furniture as well as Mother's piano. All was to no avail. No comeback was possible with conditions as they were. Worst of all, Father was told once more by his doctors that he must lead an outdoor life. But where?

The "where" turned out to be Delta County, Colorado, about eighty miles from Gunnison. I believe that the choice of this location was influenced by Henry and George Teachout, whom Father had known in Monument and Salida as well as in Gunnison. Father and both Teachouts preempted adjacent homesteads on the former Indian reservation from which the Utes had been driven only four years before. The location of these preemptions was about 15 miles from the town of Delta, on a little creek called Blue Nose.

The last morning that we were in Gunnison, some teams and wagons came, and men began to move our furniture. I was much distressed, particularly when I saw Mother in tears as her piano was taken away. That afternoon we took the train bound for Delta. Father cheered up the little group by saying that we were going to a new home on a farm, where we would have horses, cows, and chickens. I do not remember much about the journey except feeling quite happy in going so fast, and watching the telegraph poles speed by. Howard, who was not more than two years old, carried a little pet rooster in his arms. The conductor told him to hold it tightly, for if it flew out the window nobody could stop the train to catch it. Presently I fell asleep. I was awakened by Father shaking me. We stepped out of the train and found ourselves on the station platform at Delta. Here by the platform was a wagon partly filled with straw, covered over with blankets. It thrilled me to see the team of beautiful black horses hitched to it. We all got into the wagon and in a few moments I was asleep again.

I woke in the morning not knowing where I was. Overhead was a white cloth on which the warm sun was shining. Father explained that it was a tent, and that we would live in it until we could make a new house. It was all very exciting to me, as I had always connected tents with Indians.

After we had eaten breakfast cooked over a campfire, we began to look around to get our bearings. Evidently, we were in a rather long valley through which a little creek ran. Near the tent was a grove of scrub oak trees, which had many possibilities for climbing, as some of them, instead of growing straight up, had interesting crooks and bends. A few went up eight or ten feet and then grew out almost horizontally. There were several cliffs and bluffs to be seen. Just across the creek, a tall cliff ran down from the mesa on the southwest of the valley. To the northeast was a high mesa with steep eroded sides, on top of which were a few scrub cedars. Looking to the northwest, we saw several interesting

CHAPTER I: *Early Years*

The family's view of their new "farm", several miles northeast of the small town of Delta, Colorado. In the distance is Grand Mesa. Only four years earlier, the Ute Inidans had been driven out, and fear of attack plagued the early settlers for many years. (Photo by FF Blachly c. 1934)

features. A large bluff, which Father said was called Deer Mountain, was the first thing that caught the eye.

Beyond this, on the steep side of a high tableland that we learned was called Grand Mesa, we saw a curious formation of white and dull pink sandstone we thought looked like a sailing ship. Above it the rim of Grand Mesa formed a straight line along which trees could be seen. For several years, the little boys played, and half believed, that those dead spruce were Indians marching along in single file.

The creek, we were informed, was called Blue Nose—perhaps from the shape or color of a bluff a few miles up its course, or possibly because some early settler or cowboy had almost frozen there. The "Blue Nose" Valley was about nine miles from the little town of Delta as the crow flies—and 15 miles by land. Our new home, where we were to spend the next five years, was located toward the center of the valley, between the ranches of Henry and Edward Teachout.

Since our parents much disliked the name of the creek, they began almost immediately to call it Oak Creek, a title that it still bears. They named the farm "Melvale."

CHAPTER II

Melvale Farm

Not long after we had eaten our first breakfast in the valley, Mr. Teachout came to help us in the work of erecting a second tent. Skunk brush and grease wood brush were cut in order to make a clearing, the skunk brush emitting a strong unpleasant odor. The tent was set up on its poles, and stakes were driven to hold the guy ropes. We boys watched these interesting operations until we had seen enough. Then we ran off to climb the scrub oak and pick and examine the acorns. We waded in the creek, though there was little water as it was the latter part of August. In shallow pools, we saw tiny minnows. We were entranced by the "water wigglers" which skimmed rapidly back and forth on the surface, or floated idly down the stream for a few feet and then worked their way up again.

I went across the creek and we followed what we called a deer trail over the face of a steep bluff beside the stream. Mother was terrified when she saw me there. She called to me, telling me to sit down and be perfectly still. It was well that I obeyed her for I must have been twenty-five or thirty feet high on a slope that rose at an angle of nearly sixty degrees. Father came and rescued me by crawling on hands and knees along the face of the cliff.

On several occasions, we heard Father and Mother talk about the necessity of building a cabin before the fall and winter set in. One day two or three large loads of spruce logs arrived. They were silvery white, about twenty-five feet long, and eight to ten inches in diameter. I fell in love with them at first sight. They had been cut on top of Grand Mesa, and were the trunks of dead spruce trees from which the bark had peeled off. These trees, so some neighbors told us, had not died a natural death but had been killed as the result of fires started by the Indians in their wrath at being driven from beautiful Grand Mesa.

A few days after the logs arrived, several neighbors from Oak Creek and Tongue Creek came over for what Father called a "cabin raising." The little boys were tremendously excited. Arthur and I acted as water boys. The cabin was to be approximately twenty feet long and sixteen feet wide. A separate room for Grandmother was added to the South.

The men used their sharp axes to cut notches in the logs about a foot and a half from the ends, deep enough to permit the logs to fit together quite snugly. Since the climate was dry, there was no need to fit the corners with great care as a means of protecting the notched portions from decay due to moisture. The men worked fast and hard and within a few days were ready to lay up the ridge pole and the supporting roof poles. The log chosen for the ridge pole ran from end to end of the cabin. It was very thick, so that it would provide for a slant to the roof. Since it was far too heavy for the men to lift, they made a ramp of logs against the side of the cabin on which to roll it up. When the ridge pole was in place, two smaller logs were laid parallel to it, halfway between it and the cabin walls to support the boards for the roof, which was slanted down from the ridge pole and projected over the sides of the cabin. On the roof boards earth was packed to a depth of four or five inches. Then we moved in, although the cabin as yet, had no floors.

About this time, when we were living partly in the cabin and partly in the tents, we had a visit from Aunt Sarah and her children. Our aunt had come on a visit to the United States from Siam, where she lived with her husband, a medical missionary. As I learned later, she was shocked by our situation and immediately alerted all the relatives. Mother's letters of this period indicate that several members of the family sent help of some kind.

One day when Father was in town, it rained very hard. The roof began to leak muddy water. The little boys crawled under the beds for shelter, while all the pots and pans in the cabin were commandeered to hold the drippings. Upon his return, Father was quite angry, for he had been told that the roof construction was adequate in every respect. Within a few days he went to town again and brought back tar paper which he placed over the roof, fastening it down with battens, and packing earth over all. That stopped future leaks.

Father "chinked" the cabin by nailing split quarters of small tree trunks between the logs, then plastering the chinking over with adobe mud, as was usually done in the locality. The cabin was thus made absolutely tight. The first fall we could not afford regular windows, so Father placed raw buckskin over the window openings. The buckskin, dried in this way, became somewhat translucent. For a short time, a blanket served as a door.

Near the house a corral was built from the same kind of spruce logs used for the cabin. This was needed because we had three animals: we had acquired a lumber wagon and two old mares, Dolly and Nellie, and Grandmother had bought a cow, "old Whitey."

While helping to finish up the chinking of Henry Teachout's cabin, Father fell from a height of about eight feet, striking his arm and shoulder on a sharp split log, and injuring it so that he was unable to use it for a month.

Sometime that fall, as we were walking near the creek bank, we discovered large bushes with silvery white leaves, much like willow leaves, and bearing beautiful red berries resembling currents. The neighbors called the fruits "squaw berries", and said they were as good as cultivated currents for making jelly or jam. We picked many of these and Mother put them up. The neighbors also brought us some wild gooseberries and currants from the mountains. This was about all the canned fruit we had during that first winter on Melvale Farm.

Not long after the cabin was built, my brother Hal was born. According to a letter from Mother to her own mother, "Trew worked hard to put a temporary floor on part of the house before my confinement. He succeeded in doing so just before I was taken sick, having worked with all his might; as my bed had to be moved and put back before I should be laid on it. I was somewhat sick all day and it seemed that I waited for him to get through, for in an hour or more I was through with the shortest and most fearful labor I ever had." Thus, was William Harold born, a baby weighing fourteen pounds, without benefit of a doctor. All that we boys knew of this was the fact that early in the afternoon Father had sent us quite a long way from the cabin to one of the hills breaking off from the northeast mesa, with instructions to remain until he called us.

Mother was obliged to remain in bed for six weeks, but was still able to carry on to a great extent. "I managed to have my bureau packed with all I thought I should need for dressing the children, baby and myself, put beside the bed, so that by reaching, I could get sheets, pillow cases, etc., for the bed, or dress the children, which I did altogether. My comb and brush, water pitcher, and wash basin … were where I could get at them, and as Arthur could bring me all the water I wished and empty it too, I felt somewhat independent as I needed no other help in caring for myself. Trew could have done all the housework but he had to put the roof and floor on his mother's room, also had to go to town for several loads of goods, so that his mother, who was living with us, did the housework for him, and I think it was hard for her with all her infirmities to do so."

Mother tells how we spent our first Christmas on the farm:

"The little boys did not know whether Santa could get so far out into the country, as the roads were almost impassable on account of deep mud. We looked for a box from Cornelius (Uncle Cornelius Bradley, a professor of English at the University of California) but could not go to town for it, and I was greatly disappointed on their account, for I feared the great disappointment among the little flock Christmas morning, but the little stockings were nailed up on one of the logs behind the kitchen stove, four in a row. I had made some candy and with a cap each and a pair of mittens which Dan had sent a month previous and I had kept for the occasion, I filled the little stockings. They seemed delighted to find such a lot of good things, as they expressed it and one of the younger boys thought that 'Santa was a good man to send us candy and such good things.' We got up a good dinner for the family and invited 'Grandma Blachly' to join us. After all, we spent a pleasant day thankful that the Lord had brought us thus far through the winter without much suffering."

After the muddy roads had cleared up a bit, the barrel (instead of a box) was secured from Delta. It contained four pairs of boys' shoes, suits of clothes all around, night garments for all, and many other items of clothing. There were also toys. Uncle Dan and Aunt Lillian sent "a dress for <u>Mother</u>, a good warm shirt and hood for myself, caps and mittens for the children, a shirt for Howard, and clothes for Trew." Cornelius also sent "books and reading matter, that Trew and I enjoy the evenings taking turns reading aloud to each other. Though living in a poor little dark log cabin I think I shall be very happy, having Trew near me most of the time, a privilege which this far, had been denied me."

"In regard to food," Mother wrote, "with money Sarah gave us we bought enough potatoes to last until spring, and Cornelius sent us a present of $15.00 which bought us flour and meat. We live just as plainly as we dare to, our expenses are from ten to twelve dollars per month. Our children are very strong, hearty, and happy looking this winter. They go out of doors a great deal and have good appetites for the plain food, and it is good for them. How sorry to make you think that perhaps we have suffered for food and clothing. We have not really suffered. Our food this winter has come to us as the manna did to the children of Israel, a daily supply, as it were. It is hard for us to stand the disgrace of it, and we would gladly hide it from you all, if we had no children to suffer thereby, but had not Sarah come to our rescue our children truly might have suffered this winter from our pride. I cannot bear to borrow, much less beg. 'Pride goeth before the fall.' With me pride follows the fall."

I remember that we lived quite largely on bread and milk that first winter, for Grandmother's cow gave plenty of milk. We often had cornmeal mush and milk for supper and fried mush for breakfast. Father shot a good many rabbits and turtle doves, and at times the neighbors, who were great hunters, would bring in a quarter of venison, for deer were plentiful at that time. Mother made Indian pudding of cornmeal with a few raisins to improve its taste. She had Boston Brown Bread tins in which she cooked the most delicious cornbread. Father would sometimes say that the best diet for growing boys was "bread and milk, mother's love, and kisses." We had plenty of all of these commodities. And when we had cornmeal mush Father might say, "When in the evening's quiet hush, gather we round the pot of mush."

We had a large stove that was adequate for cooking and furnished enough heat for the cabin. Much of our fuel was easily secured from oak trees growing on the place. We also burned cedar wood which we could get by going up Oak Creek a few miles into the mountains. Sometimes we had piñon wood, which burned almost like pitch and gave off a great heat. So rich was the Piñon resin, that one could use it as a torch. Both the cedar and the piñon gave off a fragrance that was very soothing and pleasant.

During the winter, fence posts of cedar were secured from the Grand Mesa, and fencing operations were begun. After the posts had been set and braced at the necessary places, barbed wire was unwound from a reel on the back of our wagon. Every so often, it was stretched tight with a "wire stretcher." Once the wicked barbed wire broke and a long strand started to recoil in the most fiendish way. Luckily, we were not where it could entangle us.

That first winter was a hard one, not only for us but for all the ranchers in the neighborhood. The long-horned cattle would generally live through the winter on dry grass found in and around the cedars on the lower mesas, or on salt weed and sagebrush. Only a few of the cattle were brought into pastures and fed some hay. But the winter was so severe that many cattle died of starvation, although they had eaten sagebrush down to its large stalks and had even devoured cactus. Later we found cattle skulls almost filled with cactus spines.

Before we had our fence quite completed, cattle would often rove freely over our land. One Sunday afternoon when we were taking a walk, a long-horned cow came near us and ran toward

Arthur, striking him fully with her head but not with her horns. Arthur was knocked down, and the cow fell flat from weakness due to starvation. Father rushed up, saying, "My God, my boy!" Luckily, all of us were able to escape before the cow recovered her feet. We found that Arthur was unhurt save for bruises around his chest.

During the winter and early spring we began to clear the land for crops. The land next to the creek, where Father decided to plant the orchard and the garden, was black and rich and covered with scrub oak, sagebrush, and skunk brush. Back of this was some greasewood, which seemed to thrive on adobe soil. Most of these growths had to be grubbed up and burned. The rare perfume of the burning sagebrush gave me a particular sensation of happiness. The greasewood stalks grew to five or six feet in height and to an inch or more in diameter. They had peculiar indentations, and were almost as hard as iron.

The land toward the high mesa northeast of the cabin was almost free of vegetation, save some little sagebrush, but stones of various sizes were scattered all over. Father made a sled of boards on which to haul away the stones. He explained the principle of the lever to us as we used the crowbar to pry stones out of the ground, and showed us the advantage of rolling a stone to the body of the sled instead of lifting it into a wagon. Early in the morning we would drive out to the field carrying the plow in the wagon. While Father plowed, Clarence and I—ages four and five, respectively—would follow the plow around and around the field until we tired of it. Then we might hunt for pretty stones or rest in the wagon. Father harrowed the field that first spring with long spikes driven through a board, since he could not yet afford a harrow.

The sowing of the grain impressed me deeply. I remember watching Father walking back and forth over the field sowing wheat, millet, alfalfa, and sorghum seed from a bag hung over his shoulder. The first evening of the sowing, Father read from the Bible about the sower who went forth to sow.

One day at noon, Father decided that we would ride on the horses back for dinner instead of using the wagon. He placed me on top of old Dolly. I never felt so far away from solid ground in my life. I was scared! Dolly started for home on the run. Father, following on Nelly, yelled, "Hold on!" I grabbed the harness with both my little hands and held on, literally for dear life. As Father's horse could not keep up with Dolly, I arrived before him in front of the cabin, where Dolly stopped. I was terribly frightened, but extremely proud. It was my first lesson in horsemanship.

The creek was rather high that spring. One day after a heavy rain on the steep slopes of the mountain, still covered with snow, a flood swept down the creek carrying logs and all sorts of trash. It did not reach up to our house, but carried off one of our wooden tubs and other articles left near the banks of the creek. The flood waters had a peculiar smell, which, I have since learned, is characteristic of floods in wooded areas. We had to drive down to the mouth of the creek to recover our property.

One day Father went to town and returned with a box about eight feet long and two or three feet square. We were greatly excited and very curious as to its contents. "Here," said Father, as he opened the box, "is the beginning of our orchard and vineyard." The big box contained many little fruit trees, grape vines, and strawberry and gooseberry plants sent by our Uncle John Blachly, who had a nursery in Kansas. We "heeled in" the trees and shrubs by plowing a deep furrow, soaking it with water, and burying them in it above their roots, until we were ready to plant them.

A hole was then dug for each little tree, water was poured into the hole, the trees or bushes were set in place with their roots carefully arranged, and earth was gradually filled in and tamped down. That evening at worship, Father read from the great family bible of the joys one experiences from sitting under one's own vine and fig tree. I have often thought of the moral discipline that comes to farmers through the continuous process of planting in the spring for a harvest that won't be reaped until the fall, of setting out trees and vines that will not bear fruit for several seasons, of breeding animals who may not come into usefulness for years, and of looking forward to many other distant objectives.

The planting of the garden impressed me. It was hard to believe Father's assurance that the little dry seeds would soon be coming out of the ground as plants. Every morning I watched to see the miracle happen. At last, it did so. One small row of corn had started out of the ground! In a few days, row after row of tiny corn blades stood up above the earth. Before long many other vegetables raised their different green heads and started to grow, each according to its own nature.

One morning Father came into the cabin showing signs of excitement, and asked us all to come down to the improvised stable. There beside old Dolly, standing on unsteady legs, was a little bay colt with a white star on his forehead. I think Father and Mother were quite as excited as the little boys to see, as Father said, "the first fruits of our increase."

That spring Mother set chicken and turkey eggs under several hens. I was rather afraid of the cross old "setting hens" and did not disturb their nests, although I was anxious to see the little chickens come from the eggs as Mother said they would. One morning we saw and heard a hen clucking to a whole flock of little yellow chickens. One or two eggs were not yet hatched, but while we were looking at them the shells on these eggs cracked and out came the other chicks. Mother took the chicks into the cabin to keep them warm, and fed them hard-boiled yolks of eggs mashed up very finely. Within a few days the turkeys had hatched, as well. They were much bigger than the chicks but not so pretty. Mother said they were very delicate and required the best of care for a few days. We also took these into the cabin. For several days the cabin was filled with the peep-peep of the new-comers. When we let the little turkeys out, they walked in the adobe mud near the house and got balls of mud on their feet from which we had to free them.

One morning young Frank Teachout came to our land and started to plow, running a furrow only a few yards in front of our cabin. Father went out and asked him what he was doing. He replied that he was going to bring the Teachout main irrigating ditch, which ran along our outer fence at the foot of the northwest mesa, straight down to their place. Father protested, saying that as the slope of the land was rather steep, a ditch would soon become a great gully, not only ruining the land in front of our cabin, but also endangering the little children. He further pointed out the fact that nobody has the right to use another man's land in such a manner, without the owner's consent. Frank became angry and threatened Father. When Father ordered him off the place, Frank said that he was going to get his gun. "And what would you do with a gun, my boy?" said Father. Still threatening, Frank left with his team and plow. The next day Father went to Delta and had Frank bound over to keep the peace and stop intruding upon our premises. No ditch was built, and fortunately, this episode did not destroy our friendly relationship with the Teachout families.

About March or April of that year, Father brought home three or four tiny pigs. One of them, named Ann, was given to the boys.

We gathered grass and alfalfa for the pigs and fed them scraps from the table. Father also bought another cow.

On Easter morning Mother asked us to go out to the chicken coop and gather the eggs. What was our surprise and delight to find six or eight eggs with pretty faces and flowers painted on them. We realized only later that Mother had prepared the eggs and painted them with water-colors.

Both cows birthed calves that spring. We put bells on the cows and took them outside the ranch fence to pasture. Since we let the calves suck after we had partly milked the cows, the memory of their calves at home would generally be strong enough to keep the mothers from going too far away. Sometimes, however, Arthur and I had to search up and down the creek for them. We were always happy when we heard the sound of their bells. If they had wandered on the mesas on either side of the creek it might take an hour to find them. One evening we decided to ride old Dolly to bring in the cows. Arthur "rode the horse before," as the old song went, and I rode behind. As we were going up a very steep hill, I slid off, but only my pride suffered.

One of the pleasures of bringing the cows home was the fact that we passed by a little hill covered with perfumed white flowers we called primroses, for lack of the actual name. They were really a kind of four-o'clock, which opened in the evening. Each stem held a composite flower nearly an inch across, with two or three hundred flowerlets forming a compact dome. I have never smelled anything sweeter, nor have I ever seen the flower except on Oak Creek. The same hill was a favorite place for the turtle doves to spend the evening hours, whether attracted by the perfume, I do not know. The soft call of the turtle doves, together with the sweet fragrance of the four o'clocks, always gave me a feeling of peace and happiness.

We heard a great deal about rattlesnakes and were continually afraid that we might meet one. At times we imagined that the noise of a loud cicada was a rattlesnake. However, we always brought home the cows without seeing the dreaded reptile.

Arthur soon learned how to milk, and I did the same shortly afterward. One evening as we were milking, Arthur started to squirt milk on me from the cow's teats. Though I replied in kind, I was not able to squirt as fast or as far as he. I became angry and poured all the milk I had in the pail over his head. We were sent to bed and had no bread and milk for supper.

One spring afternoon Father and I were out in the garden cultivating it with a shovel plow that Father had acquired. The little bay colt was following along back of us as he always did when we were plowing or when Father drove his mother in the wagon. A sudden thunderstorm came up. We hurried to the shed, leaving Dolly hitched to the shovel plow. A bolt of lightning struck very near us and there was a terrific crash of thunder. Old Dolly started to run, with the little colt following her. The plow suddenly jumped into the air and hit the ground several times. Then tragedy happened. The shovel of the plow struck the little colt, and down he went. The mare stopped. We ran up and saw that the shovel blade had cut the colt's jugular vein and that the little fellow was quickly bleeding to death. Nothing could be done. In horror and grief we watched the light fade from his eyes as he lay there in a growing pool of blood. It was my first experience with death.

About that time Uncle Frank arrived with his wife, Pearl, and built a little shack on our land less than a quarter of a mile from our cabin. I did not know why he had come. Much later I learned that when the town of Gunnison had petered out, he had taken a position as Health Officer for the Southern Utes, on the other side of the San Juan Range at Ignacio. There he became seriously ill. When he was a little stronger, he married the nurse who had taken care of him, and came with her to Oak Creek to regain his health. Apparently, he made a fair recovery, because he soon began to help with our farm work.

The second fall on Melvale Farm was a period of great excitement for us boys as Uncle Frank and Father harvested the grain. Father would swing the "cradle," cutting the grain and laying it in neat rows. Uncle Frank picked it up in small bundles and bound them together with slender wisps. We older boys helped by shocking the sheaves. The shocks were hauled in and made into two small stacks. I was much impressed by seeing how a grain stack was built: layer after layer until the stack ended in a steep peak.

Father tried to engage a threshing machine, but the owner said that the bridge across the lower end of Oak Creek was not strong enough to bear the weight. So we had to thresh part of the grain with a home-made flail, consisting of a wooden staff, to one end of which, attached with a buckskin thong, was a short stout club for beating the grain. A large piece of canvas or a heavy blanket was laid on the ground, and a few sheaves of wheat were placed on it. Then down went the flail time after time, until it appeared that the grain had been separated from the straw. The straw was cleared away, leaving a mixture of grain and chaff. When a strong breeze was blowing, the mixture was tossed in the air. The wind blew away the chaff and the wheat fell back on the blanket. I do not know how much we threshed in this way, but probably not enough to take to the Delta grist mill near the mouth of the Uncompahgre River to be ground into flour. Father secured a large coffee mill and we used it to grind our own flour, or rather wheat meal. I am quite sure that we did not flail out all the wheat, for I remember hearing Father say that the chickens would find the grain when the sheaves were thrown to them for food. We did not attempt to thresh the oats, since the horses could eat both grain and straw. As the winnowing process was going on, Father quoted scripture about the winnowing of the wheat from the chaff. The bible seemed very real to us in all these primitive operations.

The sorghum cane was cut and placed in a large pile. One day a so-called sorghum mill arrived to extract the juice from the cane. The power was furnished by a yoke of oxen, who plodded around and around for several hours, grinding out the sweet juice. This was placed in tubs or half barrels, to be cooked down later until it reached the right consistency, and then stored away for winter use.

That fall an unexpected treat came our way. As Arthur and I were roaming up the creek, we saw bees going in and out of a hole in a large cottonwood tree. We were much excited and ran to the cabin saying that we had discovered a "bee tree." Father and Mother looked at the tree and confirmed our belief. Then Mother in her bee veil took a "smoker" and puffed smoke into the hole until the bees were stupefied. Father cut off the tree, let it down to the ground with a rope, and scooped out the honey into a tub. Although the honey was dark even after being strained, it was sweet and was a great aid to our low sugar rations.

Grandmother conceived the idea of making our own soap. She would run water over wood ash in order to get the necessary lye solution, then pour this over clarified grease from bacon or other fatty materials. The mixture was boiled until it thickened, and then laid out on boards, to be cut into cakes of "soft soap." We also made our own hominy by soaking corn in lye water until the skin came off, then washing it thoroughly to remove the lye.

We had a good garden that year. I remember picking up the potatoes as they were ploughed out of the ground, and looking in wonder at the great yellow pumpkins. Most of the potatoes were placed in a shallow hole and covered over with straw and earth for use during the winter and spring. From time to time, potatoes were taken from the pile and placed in the kitchen for immediate use. The garden corn made quite an impression on the little boys, for it was the native Indian variety—red, yellow, white and blue—and passing sweet. Often, instead of making coffee, Mother would roast wheat in the oven until it was quite brown, then boil it in water. I thought this substitute coffee was very good. Of course, we boys were not allowed to drink real coffee. Quite often, Mother would cook whole wheat and serve it with cream and sugar. The cream was not the carefully standardized bottle variety, but a rich sheet, a quarter of an inch thick, that had risen to the top of shallow pans filled with milk. If there is a much better cereal, I have not tasted it.

We saw many interesting things on walks with Father, or on our own expeditions. Often, on the sunny hillsides we would see chameleons sunning themselves on large rocks, and changing colors as we approached. Toward the edge of our farming lands were prairie dog towns, consisting of groups of hillocks two or three feet high, each mound with several different entrance holes. Burrowing owls would sometimes sit near the tops of the holes. The prairie dogs were the most amazing little people. At times we would go near their mounds when not a prairie dog could be seen. We would clap two small stones together, thus making a noise similar to their barking or chatter. Immediately, some little fellows would appear, and if we were not too near would stand up on their hind legs and chatter at us. As is the nature of boys, we would sometimes throw stones at them, but we were never able to hit them, for they seemed to be able to see the stones coming, and always dodged back into their holes before being struck. In a moment or so they would come back chattering. They seemed to regard dodging stones as a good game.

There were several large ant hills near the cabin, which interested us very much. One was in a rather stony location. It was built up nearly two feet high with little stones about one quarter the size of a pea. On Garnet Mesa, where we moved later, there were similar pebbles in ant hills, but among them were little bits of garnet and other bright stones. I suppose that Garnet Mesa was named because of these small garnets. Another ant hill that I found was very different. It was built in the adobe land covered with greasewood where there were no stones. Here the hill was composed largely of greasewood leaves and small twigs. Evidently, the ants constructed their dwellings with material that was easily available.

One day we saw some hornets making a nest in the back of the stable. Father told us not to disturb them, for it would be interesting to see the results of their labors. Toward the end of the summer they had quite a large nest built. One day, Father's cousin, John Trew, came to visit us. He had a team of very small mules, which he put in the barn. In some way or another, one of the mules must have kicked the hornets' nest; and the fierce insects immediately swarmed over their enemies. The mules broke their halters, ran down into the field and started to roll over and over to kill the hornets. We decided that a mule has good horse sense!

Along the creek where trees grew, there were many grey squirrels. These were particularly noticeable in the fall when the acorns were ripe. We enjoyed seeing them climb, and we liked to see them eating acorns they held in their paws.

Every once in a while, we would see a little horned toad with his strange little body and a face that looked a thousand years old. Some boys kept horned toads inside their shirts, not only as pets but also as vermin exterminators.

There were a few jackrabbits, with their very long ears and large hind legs. They could outrun almost everything. When running they would now and then jump high in the air, whether to get a better view of what was happening or to get added momentum, I do not know. At first old Rover, our dog, would try to catch them, but he could never quite overtake them. Presently he seemed to resign himself to this fact of life, for he would merely sit still and watch them out of the corner of his eye.

Porcupines lived in the valley, and occasionally we would see them. We had been warned not to get too close, as they "threw their sharp quills" which could inflict very serious wounds. I learned later that belief in the throwing of quills is mere superstition. What really happens is that animals or persons are pricked by quills from the body or from the lashing tail when they attack this well protected animal. Lost or molted quills are replaced by new growth. One day old Rover tried to whip a porcupine, but came off loaded with quills in his hide. On another occasion I chased one of the beasts with a shovel, and was chagrined to have him outrun me and escape.

I had two experiences with bees about this time. One day Arthur thought he had killed a bumble bee, and ran after me trying to put it down my neck. As it happened, the bee was not quite dead, and before Arthur could reach me it stung him. It was my view that this served him right. At another time a honey bee stung me directly over the jugular vein. My neck immediately began to swell and turned black and blue. Mother filled a basin with kerosene and soaked my neck with it. Soon the swelling went down.

Occasionally we would find little "hair snakes" with their thread-like bodies six or eight inches long. The Teachout boys maintained that they grew from lone tail hairs of horses, and that if we would place such hairs in water for a few days, they would become snakes. When we went to school, we found that all the boys there also believed in this biological phenomenon, but so far as I am aware no one ever tried to prove it by making the experiment. It was too good a belief to be tampered with.

There were several birds in our neighborhood that are not common in the eastern part of the United States. One was the so-called burrowing owl, which apparently lived with the prairie dogs and shared their holes. I believe that it did not take any part in the burrowing process, but was content with free lodging. The camp robber, a bird much like the blue jay, was the chief petty thief of the region. He was not afraid of people and would pick up any small object left unprotected, such as mittens, rope, toys, or other trifles. When we were camping, we had to hide all our food or it would be stolen by him (or by pack rats).

We often saw magpies with their contrasting colors of black and white. It was claimed that they could be trained to talk if their tongues were split. We never tried this.

During our second year on the farm, a schoolhouse was built in the valley. The men of the neighborhood had decided to place it near the lower end of Oak Creek, so that it would be in a central location for the possible pupils. It is true that the location was fairly convenient, but unfortunately the schoolhouse was built in the most desolate environment imaginable. It stood on a slight elevation, back of which were high bare adobe bluffs with many

Site of the former schoolhouse which served the children of early settlers in the mid 1880s. (Photo by FF Blachly c. 1934)

curious formations. One of these was a little box canyon some eight or ten feet deep, whose sides were almost perpendicular. In front were greasewood lands sloping down to Oak Creek, from which the big boys carried the necessary drinking water in large pails.

Later, as we read Whittier's poem, I contrasted the school pictured therein with our little school house, slightly to the disadvantage of the latter.

> *Still sits the school house by the road*
> *A ragged beggar sunning,*
> *Around it still the sumac grows,*
> *And blackberry vines are running-*

In fact, all aspects of our physical environment were so different from those of New England, where most of the authors represented in our school books lived, that the scenery, birds, flowers, trees and other natural objects described in the poems and "elegant extracts" we studied, seemed quite unreal to us.

Father, the Teachouts, and some men from Tongue Creek and Dirty Gorge Creek, as well as others, joined in hauling logs for the schoolhouse from Grand Mesa. They then organized under Dan Baldwin, an expert carpenter, for a "raising." The primitive desks and benches were made of planed board. A long blackboard ran across the front wall. Toward the center of the room was a large pot-bellied stove, which in cold weather was red-hot, almost cooking those near it, while the children who sat at the sides and ends of the room were uncomfortably cold.

That fall Arthur and I started school. It must have been towards the middle of October, since droves of cattle were coming off the high mountain ranges to avoid the early snows. Every once in a while, we would have to duck under Henry Teachout's barbed wire fence to escape them. We sometimes saw cowboys coming up the creek to drive the cattle back to the higher ranges, where they would have as much pasturage as possible before the real winter set in.

I well remember my first day in school. Arthur and I went that morning with one of the Teachout girls, who was perhaps twelve or thirteen years old. The school house impressed me deeply, for it was much larger than our log cabin. Miss Myers, God rest her soul, was our teacher. According to Mother's letters she had nine years of teaching experience, but I can hardly imagine a person with less understanding of young children. She was rather tall and slim, had large eyes that rolled, and wore glasses. I was trying hard to adjust myself to Miss Myers, the children, and the new surroundings, when she called my name. I had to go to the front of the room, where she lined up all the little shavers in a row for spelling. The first word she assigned to me was "banyan." Of course, I could not spell it, for although I could read fairly well, I had little conception of the way in which letters formed words. As punishment for my failure, Miss Myers made me stand alone in front of the whole school. I was trembling with fright and shame. My complex of fear, whenever I am called upon to spell out loud, must have started that day.

At recess one of the big boys offered me a penny if I would say certain words. I said them willingly enough. Arthur, who was nearly two years older than I and rather more sophisticated, declared that I was swearing and made me give the penny back. Another boy offered me some candy if I would kiss one of the girls. She was considerably larger than I was, and when I tried to kiss her, she slapped me in the face.

During the noon intermission one of the big boys dared me to climb the steep bluff in back of the school house, with him and other larger boys. I went along with them to the top of the bluff, where at one side there was a small canyon or arroyo, cut out by wind and rain. We all jumped down into it. The big boys crawled out and left me alone, like Joseph in the pit. I could not get out and started to cry. Finally, after the young heathen had sufficiently satisfied their sadistic impulses, one of them pulled me out. All afternoon I needed to go to the toilet, but did not know how to ask the teacher, or else I was afraid of her. At last school was dismissed and we started home. I was wearing new boots with red tops and shiny brass toes. Suddenly, to my horror and shame, one of my boots began to fill with water. I went home in the depths of misery, feeling that I had not only disgraced myself but had also ruined my beautiful new boots.

According to a letter that Grandmother wrote at this time, Arthur read very well and I read "less readily" by the time we started school. Grandmother had drilled us in mental arithmetic, but in written arithmetic, writing and spelling, I had received no training. I have little recollection of the school work, except that I really enjoyed it. We read from the McGuffy readers. They contained several poems we had to learn by heart, all of which I do still remember. I filled out several copy books with attempts at writing. Either I did not succeed very well, or else my writing has since deteriorated as the result of trying to take down lectures in college and graduate school.

Late in the season, perhaps in early November of our second fall in the valley, word came up the creek that the Utes were returning to their former hunting grounds and were on the warpath. The neighbors gathered their horses together in our corral and waited all night with rifles loaded, ready for an expected attack. In a few days we learned that the word was merely unfounded rumor. The fear of Indians, however, was very real to the early settlers. There were Indian reservations on three sides of us, all within a radius of about one hundred miles: the southern Utes were at Ignacio, the northern Utes were on the White River Reservation beyond Grand Mesa, and the Uncompahgre Utes, who had been driven out by force from the Uncompahgre Valley country, were now on the Green River Reservation in Utah, no great distance from the Colorado line. The settlers in our region might well have had an underlying fear of reprisals by the Uncompahgre Utes, since their treaty—providing that the Western Slope should be kept by them "as long as the rivers run and the grass is green"—had been violated by the Federal Government.

Only a few years before, in 1879, not far on the other side of Grand Mesa, the "Meeker Massacre" had occurred. In this tragedy all the employees of the Indian agency were killed. Major Thornbush and his men were ambushed and slaughtered, and the agent's wife, another woman, and their children were carried into captivity. South of the Ignacio agency, in Arizona and New Mexico, a bloody warfare had been carried out against the white people by Geronimo and his small band. We boys often heard the grown folks talking of the danger from Indians. Henry Teachout claimed that a few years previously the Utes living at the time in the reservation on Taylor Creek near Gunnison had stolen a large bunch of his horses. Everyone seemed to think that theft or attack by Indians was possible at any time.

That fall I made my first trip to town. Father shook me awake one morning while it was still dark. Mother cooked breakfast while Father and I went out to feed and harness the horses. The stars were shining as they can shine only in a high dry country. There was one star larger than all the others, which Father said was the morning star. Father, looking up into the sky, quoted a verse from the Bible, which I had often heard but never understood, about the morning stars singing together and all the sons of God shouting for joy. I think that was the first time I appreciated the beauty of the heavens and comprehended some part of the meaning of the Bible verse.

Slowly, we went down Oak Creek and Tongue Creek and then turned to drive over the barren adobes. The road was rough, filled with big chuck holes, and very dusty. We finally reached the Gunnison River, which we crossed on a ferry boat that was fastened to a cable stretched across the river. Father tried to explain to me how it worked, and explained that the first investment of Delta County had been a bridge here, but it had been swept away by a flood in 1884.

Delta, which at that time was only five or six years old, was a little village of some 200 people, located about half a mile from the Denver and Rio Grande narrow gauge railroad station. It was

CHAPTER II: *Melvale Farm*

The first building in what was to become Delta was constructed of hewn logs and wattle in 1881. Rifles and other weapons were kept at the ready in fear of Indian attack. (photographer unknown)

situated on a greasewood plain at the junction of the Gunnison and Uncompahgre rivers. Already the alkali had begun to seep out of the encompassing mesas as a result of irrigation, and in many places white alkali crust covered the ground. The town streets were wide but were nothing but dirt with great chuck holes when dry, or seas of adobe mud when wet. Along Main Street, board sidewalks had been built. Most of the buildings were made of logs. The earliest one was built in 1881, just after the Indians had been moved out.

A few of the most pretentious stores had erected false fronts, giving the impression that the buildings were larger and more elegant than they actually were. Water was brought from the Gunnison River in a tank which was hauled back and forth, up and down the streets, dispensing water at 25 cents per barrel. There was, of course, no system of sewage disposal or garbage collection. Chickens and even pigs roamed the streets. There were no trees until the 1890's

During the 1880s Delta, at the junction of the Gunnison and Uncompahgre Rivers, grew into a modest community, with a dozen or so small businesses, including several saloons. (photograph by F. M. Laycook)

Despite these shortcomings, which I was naturally too inexperienced to realize, the place appeared to me as a city of grandeur because of the many stores with large glass windows. In the drugstore windows were immense red, green, and blue bottles, and in other store windows were saddles, boots, boxes of candy, clothes, and other things highly to be desired.

Although this little town impressed me so deeply, I have since learned that "Main Street" consisted of only the following businesses, located on the west side between third and fourth streets: Shield's and Healy's Saloon, Bouldin's Barber Shop, McMurray's Drug Store and Drink Emporium, Steve Bally's Saloon, Jeffer's Dry Goods Store, Ed Meredith's Saloon, Hank Hammond's Livery Stable, Wilson's Harness Shop, and Latham and William's Groceries and Drugs. Toward the north end of the street was Uncompahgre House, a modest hotel, afterward called the Delta House. *The Delta Chief* (later the *Delta Independent*) was the local newspaper. Two or three blacksmith shops flourished in various parts of town. As I was too young to have any memory of the "City of Gunnison," I had no basis for comparison, and the glories of Delta overwhelmed me.

We ferried across the river again toward evening. Soon it began to get dark as we went slowly over the dusty road. I fell asleep and did not wake up until I heard the barking of a dog. When I sat up there was a light in the distance. "That light," said Father, "comes from home." We were soon there. Mother stood in the doorway with all the boys to greet us. After the horses had been cared for, the family sat down to supper. Father lined the boys up in a row after dinner and distributed pieces of candy, starting with Arthur, going down to Howard, and then repeating the process. It may seem strange that I should remember such a small incident. Candy, however, was a very rare treat at the time. It may also seem absurd that an errand to a town only fifteen miles away should take from daylight to dark, but with old horses pulling a lumber wagon over rough, uneven roads, thirty miles in a day was quite a journey.

In the early fall, all of us boys were sent to gather acorns from the groves of oak trees near the place, to be used for fattening the hogs. They had lived most of the summer on alfalfa, which we cut for them from the field that had been sown with it early in the spring, as well as scraps from the table and any other materials available. They had grown quite large and rangy, but were far from fat. The bushels of acorns that we gathered, plus a little corn, put them in pretty good shape by about the first of November.

I think that when the pigs were first purchased, it had been Father's intention to keep the boys' pig, Ann, and another pig as brood sows. He now felt, however, that since we needed money and must sell two or three of the hogs to raise it, the others must be killed to feed us. Mother protested mildly, but as the days began to get cold and frosty and our needs became more pressing, I think she yielded. One morning when we ran out barefoot, our feet were chilled by the frost that lay over the ground. We came in begging for shoes. This incident helped to seal the fate of the swine.

In a few days, with the help of neighbors, all the hogs were killed. The end of them was quite a blow to Mother, as well as to us boys. The next day Father took two of the dressed hogs to market and returned with shoes and boots for the boys. It upset us greatly to see the hogs killed and butchered, particularly our beloved Ann. Yet we did appreciate the good warm shoes and boots, and when Father explained that the only way to get them was by selling the hogs, we were somewhat reconciled.

Father then made a little smoke house to cure the hams and bacon we had kept. After preparing and salting the pieces of meat and hanging them up, he built a low fire of oak chips in the center of the smoke house and kept it going for several days. The odors that came out of that smokehouse made my mouth water. I gradually forgot that the hams and bacon were from our friends, the hogs, and enjoyed the meals made memorable by their sacrifice.

The second Christmas on Oak Creek was quite different from the first. All the people on Oak Creek and Tongue Creek had banded together to make a real Christmas celebration, held in the new school house.

The night of Christmas Eve was exceedingly cold, and the stars shone with splendor. Father piled the lumber wagon half full of hay with several blankets over it, and tucked us in with more blankets. As we entered the schoolhouse, the large stove in the middle was glowing almost red hot. At the front of the room was what seemed to us the most beautiful thing we had ever seen: a great spruce tree that reached the ceiling, all covered with lighted beeswax candles, strings of popcorn and red apples. Soon the entertainment began. Several of the older boys and girls spoke "pieces." Clarence, not yet five, sang "Hang up the Baby's Stocking." E. H. Perkins was to have sung "The Jolly Cowboy," with words composed by Father and set to the music of "So Early in the Morning." Mr. Perkins started the singing, but because of too much Christmas cheer, had forgotten the words, so the song was performed by Will Powers, a young man who was staying in the neighborhood. It ran as follows:

> *I mount my horse at break of day,*
> *And with the wind I speed away.*
> *My heart is light and free and gay*
> *When seated in the saddle.*
> *For I'm a jolly cowboy, for I'm a jolly cowboy,*
> *For I'm a jolly cowboy, the gayest of them all.*
> *Sometimes my horse gets on the buck*
> *And tries to throw me just for luck,*
> *And up and down I go chuck, chuck,*
> *When seated in the saddle.*
> *For I'm a jolly cowboy, for I'm a jolly cowboy, (etc.)*
> *Perhaps someday a maiden fair*
> *With eyes of blue and golden hair,*
> *Will wish to marry me, I declare*
> *When seated in the saddle.*
> *For I'm a jolly cowboy, for I'm a jolly cowboy (etc.)*

Old Santa was there to distribute presents, which hung on the tree or were placed on the floor. Many of them were intended as practical jokes. There was much merriment when Will Kennicott and his wife, who had just been married that fall, were given a beautiful little crib made by Dan Baldwin, with a doll inside. Clarence Mower, who hated swine more than anything else next to sheep, was given a pig's tail. It seemed an age until my turn came and I began to think that old Santa had entirely forgotten me. Finally, my name was called, and I received a Jew's harp and a mouth organ. I was extremely happy, and soon learned to play my new instruments very well—that is, provided a Jew's harp can ever be played well. After the presents were distributed, Charles Mundry presided over a large barrel of red apples, which he, a cowpuncher, proudly announced were of his own raising. He also distributed balls of homemade popcorn to everyone. The perfume of that barrel of apples in the warm schoolhouse, mingled with the smell of burning wax candles, and the fragrance of the spruce tree, I shall never forget. After the celebration we crawled into the wagon under warm blankets and I was soon sound asleep. I remember nothing until the next morning.

CHAPTER III

Life on the Farm

THE YEAR 1887 STARTED OUT VERY WELL FOR US BOYS. The relatives "back east" had sent a barrel filled with warm clothes and toys, as well as skates for Arthur and me. There was a little low place near the cabin, filled with water in warm weather, now with solid ice. Here we learned to skate by pushing a chair in front of us, thus avoiding the usual bruises and bumps from landing too fast and too hard. After a few days of this practice, we were able to care for ourselves on the ice.

We often went to visit Uncle Frank and his wife "Auntie Pearl" in their little shack a few hundred yards from our cabin. One day Clarence and I were told to take them some white bread that Grandmother had baked. It was fresh from the oven and had a wonderful smell. As we had eaten nothing at home for a long time but graham bread, the temptation to taste the fresh white bread was too much for us, and we nibbled until we had picked large holes in each loaf. When we arrived, Uncle Frank examined the bread and winking his eye remarked that he had found some two-legged mice in the valley, and he believed that they had eaten slight holes in the bread. We expected at least a scolding and perhaps a whipping for stealing, but Uncle Frank's manner relieved us a good deal, though we still feared that he would tell Father. We were in terror for a few days, but as time went on, we felt sure that Uncle Frank had kept the faith with two hungry little boys.

I do not think that Uncle Frank attempted to practice medicine while in the valley, as he was recovering from severe illness. However, when I was in Delta a few years ago, Clarence Mower, one of the early settlers in Delta County, told me of at least one professional visit for the delivery of Mower's first son. As the time for the birth was rapidly approaching, Mower awakened Uncle Frank from sweet dreams, gave him barely time to throw on some clothing and pick up his physician's case, and placed him on an unsaddled horse. Then "hell-bent for action" the horses tore down the Oak Creek valley and Tongue Creek valley for about six miles, Uncle Frank hanging to the mane of his horse for dear life. They arrived just in time. The doctor may have been a bit nervous from the journey, but he brought a strapping boy into the world and shared in the general rejoicing.

Uncle Frank was a fine-looking man. He was very scholarly, with a special love for history. I think that he knew Gibbon's *Rise and Fall of the Roman Empire* and Green's *History of England* almost by heart. Often, he would give us a talk on some historical subject, which impressed me not so much for the information which it contained, but because of its long flowing words and beautiful style.

With Aunty Pearl, he remained in the valley for a year or so. Then they went back to the Ignatio Reservation. Shortly after, we heard they had been divorced—a terrible thing for our pious family.

That spring and summer we began to enjoy carving wood with new jack knives which Grandmother Bradley had sent us at Christmas. We had two chief sources of whittling material. Old honey sections that had been broken or used and scraped off clean made excellent material for flat work, such as little men, women and children. For work that required three dimensions we used cotton wood bark that we would pry from the trees. It was as much as five or six inches wide and four or five inches thick, and as it was rather soft and easy to carve, it was perfect for making boats, ships, wagon bodies, and doll furniture. I still have scars on my left hand from the slipping of my knife, but a few cuts were not worth noticing in comparison with the pleasure of carving.

We also manufactured bows and arrows for hunting rabbits, squirrels, prairie dogs, hawks and crows. Although I think we never succeeded in hitting one, we had the thrill of trying to find our prey and shooting at it. Though we were forbidden to shoot at some birds, I am afraid we often disobeyed. But again, no damage was done.

Beside the bows and arrows we had two other weapons. One of these was what we called a bean shooter—these days called a slingshot. It was made with a small crotched stick for a handle, to which were attached two wide elastic rubber bands with a leather strap between them. In the strap we placed little stones or (even better) buckshot, which at times we were able to beg from Father while he was loading shotgun shells. By pulling back the elastic and allowing it to recoil, we shot the "bullet" for quite a long distance. Although we considered this device more deadly than the bow and arrow, we never seemed to be able to get any game with it. A much more powerful weapon, though even less accurate than the other two, was the sling. This was made by attaching two long buckskin strings to a little pouch. By placing a small stone in this pouch, whirling the sling around and around and then letting go of one end, we were able to throw a stone as much as two hundred yards. We liked this implement, partly because of its performance and partly because we knew from the Bible about David and Goliath. This weapon was particularly valuable in scaring off hawks.

We learned a good deal from nature on our hunting trips up and down the creek. We found where rabbits and squirrels were accustomed to stay, how the holes of prairie dogs were arranged, and how to recognize the calls of different birds, such as the blue jay, the camp robber, the flicker, the wood pecker, the black and white magpie, and the king bird. Several of these birds particularly interested me. I regarded the flight of the flicker as one of the most beautiful of all bird movements. It pleased me when a group of king birds or "bee birds," as we called them, would gather around a large hawk and torment him until he was only too happy to get away. Hawks would often circle over our chickens and turkeys. An old turkey gobbler would arch his eye toward the heavens and give a warning cry. All the chickens and turkeys would make for shelter, but at times a hawk would swoop down and catch one. Father always kept the shotgun loaded to shoot at the hawks. They were very hard to hit and usually got away. Some of the neighbor boys had caught a magpie and slit his tongue and supposedly taught him to talk, but we did not try this.

We were often bothered by skunks, which stole our chickens. One night a skunk got under the corner of our woodshed behind the cabin and excreted his vile fluid. Old Rover, our dog, attempted to drive him out and became befouled. The next morning when we boys awoke, we could not endure the smell. We all ran out of the cabin and went up on a ridge of the high mesa to the east, where we sat down in sad contemplation. Old Rover came up and we drove him away. He rolled in the dust, went down to the ditch and wallowed in the water, and tried his best to rid himself of skunkiness. Taking pity on us while we sat on the mesa, Mother brought our breakfast to its foot, and we rushed down to eat it, keeping Rover away. I never saw a dog as much ashamed of himself as Rover was for the next few days.

Very often we would hear coyotes howling at night. Their howls are enough to make a little boy's blood chill. I would almost shiver in my bed when two or three of them would join a chorus. Old Rover always kept them from doing any damage to our chickens, pigs and calves.

Quite often in the spring, cowboys would be seen driving large bunches of cattle past our farm up into the mountains. Once in a while they would stop to ask for a drink of water, or perhaps to get a cow that had broken into our place. How grand they seemed to us with their white sombreros, handkerchiefs fastened around their necks, woolen shirts, leather chaps and high-heeled boots. I particularly admired their horses and saddles. Some of the cowboys prided themselves on the silver ornaments on their saddles and bridles. They appeared to be very jolly, and they loved to tease us. The height of my ambition at this time was to be a cowboy. One of the cowboys whom we knew very well, came to get a calf that had wandered into our field one day. As he stopped to pass the time of day, Mother, who worried lest we boys had been using profane language in saying "you bet," asked him if his expression was really swearing. Without cracking a smile, this expert on the subject said that it surely was, and thereafter we were not allowed to use this profane expression.

It was about this time that some missionaries from Siam came to visit us. I was out in the yard playing. Just a few minutes before the ladies came, I had been climbing a tree and had torn a great hole in the seat of my trousers. Mother called me in to be introduced to the visitors from the Orient. I could not refuse and I saw no way to explain my situation, so I marched in, shook hands and backed out as gracefully as I could. As soon as I was out of the room the missionaries remarked to Mother, so she told me years later, that I was one of the most perfect little gentlemen they had ever seen. "Why," said they, "he has the manners of a prince." Neither they nor Mother knew the reason for such extraordinary manners, but I was all too conscious of it!

That spring Dan Baldwin—who hailed from Winstead, Connecticut—and his partners, the Van Tuyle brothers, started a milk ranch up in the mountains toward the head of Oak Creek. Their plan was to make butter to supply the mining camps of Ouray and Telluride. They built a road up the creek that was so rough and steep that only a light cart could get over it at first. Some of the cowboys swore that the way that Baldwin and his partners churned their butter was simply to haul cans of milk over this road so the jiggling and jarring did the work. As the partners often stopped at our house on their way, we became well acquainted with them. I do not think their venture was successful, for it was soon given up, and the men went into business in Delta. However, we still had the advantage of the road running up into the cedar and pinon country where we could secure wood. Later on, it was used to haul salt up to the salt licks for the cattle. The contacts with these men were presently to prove advantageous to our family.

One evening toward dusk, a man appeared on horseback, leading a pack horse, and asked if he could spend the night. He introduced himself as Captain Spaulding, explaining that he was a surveyor and that he was going up to the lakes on Grand Mesa to survey for a reservoir, so that the Surface Creek Mesa would have water stored for use in the late summer. He was made welcome and was invited to take part in our little evening worship, which he did, joining us in the singing. His outfit of high-laced boots, leather coat with large pockets, bright red shirt and Stetson hat seemed to me almost as imposing as the clothing of the cowboys. His surveys constituted a first step toward the important system of lakes and reservoirs on Grand Mesa which still serves the area.

Later in the summer, we were wading and swimming in a pool in the creek, when suddenly we saw, perhaps a hundred yards upstream, a wall of water about ten feet high rushing down on us. We barely reached the bank in time to escape being washed away. Evidently there had been a cloudburst in the steep hills that bordered the creek several miles about us. Such flash floods were quite common in the western mountain country.

That summer we saw our neighbor boys wearing straw hats, and decided that we must have some. Father said we could not afford to buy them. Grandmother took pity on us and offered to make them if we would get some good long grain straws. We went into the fields and selected many of the best straws that we could find in the wheat that was just beginning to ripen. Grandmother braided the straw into strips, ironed the strips flat, and then sewed them together into hats. We were quite proud of our new head gear.

Since there had been more irrigation water than usual, due to the heavy snow of the previous winter, we had rather good crops that fall. I remembered that we had two stacks of wheat and two little ones of oats. As the bridge over the lower end of Oak Creek had been strengthened, and as we had enough grain to warrant the trip, the owners of the threshing machine consented to come to our place. There was great excitement when the machine arrived. We were filled with wonder as we saw the engine blowing out great billows of smoke, the wide band running from the engine to the separator going round and round, and the sheaves of grain going into the hopper of the separator where they were chewed up, with the straw and grain coming out separately. There were several neighbors to assist, as it was customary for all of them to exchange work at threshing time. Mother had prepared a great dinner, which added to the excitement of this notable day.

There was only one fly in the ointment, and that was the stacking of the straw, a job left to Arthur and me. The straw was borne from the separator by a continuous conveyor and dumped on the ground, instead of being blown out of a long tube as was the case later on. Hence it had to be pitched back away from the carrier and built up into a stack. Our straw contained some rust and much chaff, with which we soon became covered. Our bodies prickled all over from this combination, and we were mighty glad when the work was done. We had never been more tired, for we had climbed around on the straw stack all day, pitching straw as fast as possible in order to keep it from clogging the machine.

That fall, we made a straw barn for the livestock by setting a few poles in the ground, running cross poles in the shape of a shed, and then fastening smaller poles and very small poles and wands to cover three sides and the top. Over all this we placed a thick layer of straw. It made a very warm barn, open on one side to face the sun.

We also used straw for mattresses, after quite an argument as to the respective advantages of straw mattresses versus those made of corn husks. We filled all the bed mattresses with oat straw, as that was considered softer and more pliable than wheat straw.

I do not know how many bushels of grain we raised that year. I do remember, however, that I went with Father when he took a wagonload of wheat to the Delta grist mill to be ground. The mill was run by water from the Uncompahgre River, and the flour was ground between great stones. The miller explained that the flour would not be considered "flour" in the effete east (how the westerners loved that expression!), but that it was very good. "Of course," he said, "you may find an occasional oat or bit of straw in the flour." After giving the miller his share, which I think was ten percent, we returned home that evening with many sacks of flour, perhaps enough for the winter.

During our third spring in the valley we expanded our farming operations a bit. We now had a team of horses and two cows, both of which had calves. According to a letter from Mother, Father mortgaged the farm, as so many homesteaders did, to make improvements; and Grandmother Bradley (Sarah Blachly Bradley) sent $200 in aid from Siam.

Mother bought two hives of bees. By the process of subdividing old hives to make new ones, she had nine hives by fall. One or two hives, however, swarmed before she could subdivide them. We could see the swarming bees leave the hive, circle around and around for a few moments, and them make a "bee line" for parts unknown. Unless we were to lose them, they must be made to alight nearby. As was the custom, we beat tin pans and kettles in order to frighten them into stopping. This seemed to work, and when they had alighted in a great brown and golden ball, Mother, in her bee veil and gloves, smoked them with the smoker until they were somnolent, and brushed them into a hive that Father had brought up. The old colonies made surplus honey, but the new colonies made only enough to last them through the winter, and not always that much—for sometimes in spring we would have to feed them sugar syrup in order to keep them alive. There was an old saying: "A swarm of bees in May is worth a load of hay. A swarm in June is worth a silver spoon. A swarm in July isn't worth a fly." Mother related that she took out 175 pounds of honey that year. We sold the perfect sections of honeycomb, but had the privilege of eating with our meals the honey from all the sections which were not entirely filled or which were partially uncapped.

The previous spring Father had planted several acres of alfalfa, which had done well. In fact, alfalfa was planted on much of the land around us, not only in our valley but on Surface Creek Mesa and Tongue Creek Mesa. It produced three large crops a year and was an ideal winter feed for the cattle. As such, it was in great demand, since the cattlemen now began to feed their cattle for some months during the winter. Hitherto, the cattle had been allowed to spend the cold months in "hustling" for themselves on the lower ranges, which by this time were becoming far from adequate for the number of animals on them.

That summer Mother tried to instill in us some idea of the importance of money and the elements of thrift. She gave the four older boys a hive of bees, each boy to have a fourth interest. From this hive we got 25 pounds of honey and a good swarm of bees, both of which we sold. We also bought a little pig with some of the money that we had previously saved. Each of us also had a hen whose eggs we might sell. A purse was given to each boy in which to keep the profits from his business undertakings. We scraped up a little money and sent it to Uncle John in Kansas for seed, as we had been authorized to use a small plot of ground for our own garden.

Although my parents had planned to send not only Arthur and me to school this fall but also Clarence, this was not to be. The Teachout boys and girls were now all beyond the eighth grade and had dropped out of school, so our family was the only one in the valley with school children. Since other families with children had moved into Tongue Creek and the adjacent mesas, it was decided to move the school house to a site nearer the school population on Tongue Creek. As this location was five or six miles from our home, the move ended school for us, as long as we remained in the valley. For the next two years we had no schooling except Mother's and Grandmother's instruction. They taught us to read and required us to memorize and recite certain poems and Bible verses. Of course, we heard the Bible and other books read aloud and we were able to do a bit of reading ourselves. Arthur began to memorize a great deal of Shakespeare, but I was not interested.

Arthur was ten years old on the eleventh day of November, 1888, and Mother tells of his birthday party. "I asked three of his school friends over and made a little dinner for him. I always remember their birthdays with a cake (often made of flour, home-ground in a coffee mill)—but it is a cake—and some little trifle. This time I got Arthur a nice book, for I wished him to remember his tenth birthday."

Mother says at this time in a letter to her own mother: "I live just for Trew and the boys. I am shut out from the rest of the world and limited to these, but if we can send six good men into the world to help it to become better, that is all I ask...... We are frequently pleased by strangers remarking about our fine boys. Yesterday an old gentleman said that in all his travels he had not seen so fine a lot of boys, and a gentleman from Chicago also said the same a few months ago."

In writing the above letter Mother seemed to feel that the mention of Arthur's tenth birthday gave her a good opportunity to describe the six boys to her mother. She wrote as follows (except for the ages which I have inserted): "First is Arthur (10) with a trim, plump form, a fair skin with red cheeks, large laughing eyes and short thick brown-black hair, a manly little fellow ready to help Papa outside in numberless ways or Mama as the case may be, loving and true, ever ready to put a loving arm around Mama and give her a kiss of cheer. Then there is sturdy Fred (8) with thick white hair, blue eyes and strong but small hands and feet, who is forever in mischief but never knows it, and is so solemn about it when reproved, a real boy all over, but loving and kind when reminded about it.

"Then comes Clarence (almost 7), tall and very slender, skin olive, hair soft brown, eyes dark brown that sparkle and dance or suddenly grow serious and sad, a thoughtful and dignified boy who scorns anything little or mean, has noble thoughts and plans worthy of a man, is extremely loving and kind to all, especially to baby who is his to care for. He is a gentle judge. When the boys disagree and when he reasons out a matter and decides a case, the boys seem to be satisfied in doing about as he bids them, so we call him little judge.

"And Howard (5) I think, is like Grandpa Bradley, a neat trim little fellow, graceful in all his ways, has fair skin with blue eyes, thick light brown hair, is full of business, sees everything and attends to everything that seems to have been neglected, is also full of mischief and very sly about it—can't keep his hands off the boys. He loves so well to tease so that all the boys pick at him, but he stands his ground well. He can play with the big boys well and can do all sorts of chores and do them well, is capable and faithful.

"Then comes Hal (3) a great big, strong boy, looks like Fred and is nearly as large as Howard, a "happy-go-lucky" boy, takes care of himself and gets along comfortably no matter what happens, takes anything offered him at table, no matter how poor, as a matter of course and seldom grumbles; is a sweet songster. He can sing nearly everything I sing after hearing me sing it two or three times and also remembers all the lines he hears to the song. He could sing when he was a year old and long before he could talk. Nearly every morning he is the first to wake and always wakes with a song on his lips, a daily reminder to me of dear Grandmother and Aunt Irene who used to sing before she could talk." Mother did not mention it but Hal sang alto as well as soprano at this early age. He later developed a very deep bass voice so that he could sing an entire octave lower than the rest of us.

"Last of all is Ralph (1), a pretty boy with very pretty pink and white skin, dark gray eyes under long black lashes, has a sweet gentle face and a head of thick curly hair. His form is perfect, rather inclined to be slender; he is so patient, gentle, playful and loving that his grandma and papa think he is the finest baby we have had, but I think they were all just as sweet though perhaps not so pretty."

Since Father's election as justice of the peace the previous fall, he and Mother spent their evenings reading law together. "In this way," as Mother wrote, Father was "fitting himself to act his part in deciding differences between his fellow men, and possibly paving the way to something more desirable for the family and more congenial to his tastes than the life we now lead." Mother was surprised to find "law is so interesting, for it is interwoven with all the relations of life from the cradle to the grave." When in bed I often listened to the reading with a feeling of awe and respect, although the strange words and ideas had little meaning for me. Very soon, however, I would drop off asleep.

From Mother's hint regarding a more congenial way of life and from other considerations, I now believe that Father must have had reasons for the study of law besides wishing to be able to do his duty as justice of the peace. He may well have considered becoming a lawyer by reading law and passing the bar examinations which, at the time, were not too strenuous. He had been urged to do so by Lyman I. Henry, a Delta lawyer with whom he later formed a business connection. Henry said Father's speech and general handling of the Teachout controversy showed a remarkably clear legal mind.

Another motive for Father's study of the law was doubtless the constant strain caused by the uncertainties of farming. It began to appear that the shortage of water for irrigation was not due merely to one or two dry seasons, but might well be permanent. According to Mother's letters, Father began to be discouraged with the farm largely because of the water problem. The range was being overgrazed and the winter snow and spring rains ran off rapidly, early in the season for lack of vegetable humus to retain them. Further, our farm was toward the end of Grand Mesa which did not get as much snow or rain as other parts due to lack of elevation.

The following spring Father decided to go into the hog business in a more substantial way. He took me with him in the lumber wagon to one of the nearby mesas where he purchased a large boar, three or four sows and about a score of their little pigs. We brought these all home in the wagon box, well covered over so that they could not escape. There were many grunts of disapproval from the grown swine, and many squeals from the little ones as they were bounced over the rough stony roads.

Father planned to divide an alfalfa field into two plots fenced in with barbed wire, so that while one field was being eaten by the pigs, the other would be growing. When we first brought the animals home, however, the dividing fence had not been set up. Clarence and I had to keep the hogs within their allotted confines during the day time. At times it was very cold, so we dug a shallow pit and made a little brush shelter over it. Here we could watch the swine and still escape the cold for a few minutes if they did not stray beyond their bounds. Sometimes we built a small fire to keep us warm. We composed a little fire song at this time. It ran:

> *Blow, wind, blow, and make our fire start up;*
> *Blow, wind, blow, and make our fire start up.*
> *Then the wind started up with a terrible gale*
> *And blew up a blast of rain and hail.*
> *Blow, wind, blow, and make our fire start up.*

When we were herding the swine we would often take a ride on old Timothy, the big boar. We did not know that this was a dangerous thing to do. We had not been warned against it, doubtless because Mother and Father never imagined that we would do such a thing. Certainly, they never heard about it from us, as riding an animal seemed to us too commonplace for discussion.

That spring I made my third trip to town. When we reached the Gunnison River, we found that heavy, warm spring rains on the snow in the mountains had made it a wide, roaring flood, the water extending over its banks for several hundred yards into North Delta. The ferry had stopped running and the only way to get across was to go in a skiff. We unhitched our horses and tied them to the wagon so that they would stand while we were gone. Taking with us a basket of eggs for market, we started for the southern shore and Delta. The water was swift and muddy. Trees, brush, planks from bridges up stream that had been washed away, and even dead animals rushed by. The skiff operator had to dodge in and out to prevent the vessel from being struck and turned over. At last, we reached the shore in safety. After purchasing a few groceries which we could well carry, we went back across the raging river, hitched the horses to the wagon and started for home.

It began to drizzle. The roads grew slippery, and the adobe mud began to clog the wagon wheels. At times the road was so bad that the horses could hardly pull up the hills. Soon it became so dark that we could not see. I was afraid that when we crossed the little creeks and "branches" we would fall off the bridges—none of which had any side protection. Father assured me, however, that the horses could see well at night and would take us home safely. It was very late before we reached home. There was Mother with a kerosene lamp in her hand, standing in the doorway.

Mother always looked and listened for Father's return from any journey. As children do, we mirrored her attitude, and if Father happened to be late, we would lay our ears to the ground hoping that we might hear his wagon wheels in the distance.

Two bits of injustice were done to me this year that left a strong impression on my mind. One day Grandmother found her stove lid lifter, which she called a "snavy," broken in two. Clarence, as I found out many years later, had broken it, but being confronted with Grandmother's wrath, he had allowed her to think that I was the culprit. I protested my innocence, but was not believed. Grandmother said that I was "destructive." I did not like this; and furthermore, I did not like to be considered a liar. It seemed to me that the whole world was backward and that there was no justice in it.

The only whipping that Father gave me I also regarded as being absolutely unjust. Due to the fact that a visitor had left the bars down, our horses had strayed from their field. Father said he would round them up and bring them down the lane between our place and that of Henry Teachout; while I was to stay just below our gate and turn them in when they came along. The horses came running toward me and showed no sign of stopping. They looked as big as elephants. I feared that they would run over me. Instead of stopping them and turning them into the gate, I gave way to panic and ducked under the fence, while the horses ran by. Father was angry for the horses were going toward the main road, and he would have to borrow a neighbor's horse to turn them back. He cut a switch with his knife and gave me a sound whipping, saying that I had not only disobeyed him but had acted as a coward. From my viewpoint, I had saved my life.

That year we had about twenty acres under cultivation, mostly in alfalfa, corn and garden vegetables. Although we had a good early garden and raised some wheat and potatoes, the corn and all the late garden burned up. The hogs had done fairly well on the alfalfa pasture, but there was no corn for fattening them, and Father disposed of them as best he could. The young apple trees whose growth I had watched with eager anticipation did not seem to be badly bothered by the water shortage; they gave us three barrels of bright red apples.

Toward the end of the summer the creek began to fail. There was some water in holes, but it contained so much alkali that it was not fit to drink. We had to haul drinking water in barrels from Tongue Creek several miles away. Since the alkali in our own creek water made laundering difficult, one day we packed up a large bundle of dirty clothes, prepared an ample lunch, and went down to Tongue Creek to do the washing. We built a fire over which we hung a great kettle for boiling water; and after the clothes were washed, we hung them on trees and bushes to dry. For us boys this was a fine picnic. I can now imagine what it meant to Father, Mother and Grandmother.

These various troubles, and the impossibility of sending the boys to school, must have led my parents to discuss with relatives the advantages of a change of residence and occupation. Uncle Dan Bradley and other members of the family advised us to move to a farm near Yankton, Dakota, a small place where Uncle Dan was serving as minister of the Congregational church. However, Father had evidently had enough of farming; and he wisely decided against that plan. While he was still considering what action he would take, he and some of the neighbors talked of building a reservoir in the mountains to conserve water for the late summer, as had been done by the farmers on Surface Creek Mesa. Nothing was done in the matter since the topography of the country was not favorable and the project would have been costly.

As Father's health had greatly improved on the ranch, he decided that an outdoor life was no longer essential, and that he was now able to enter into a business connection in Delta. Toward the latter part of the year he found one. At the outset, I believe, he was an employee of the prominent attorney, Lyman I. Henry, who also operated a real estate business. But within a short time, he became a full business partner. Father had to live in Delta, coming home for weekends only once in a while at first, as he had no adequate means of transportation. We boys had to manage all the work of caring for the live-stock, milking the cows, and hauling and cutting wood for the ravenous wood stove.

The year 1890 brought great changes in our family circumstances. Father was now doing well in the insurance and loan business, had made several good real estate deals for himself, and was participating in the financing of two important irrigation ditches. The Bona Fide irrigation ditch, which was started in the northern entrance to the Black Canyon on the Gunnison, was being developed, and Father was instrumental not only in helping to work out the financial plans for the project, but also in lending money to the farmers who would be under it. I think that the money for these purposes came largely from Winstead, Connecticut, through the influence of Dan Baldwin. The North Delta Ditch was also developed at this time, bringing water from the Gunnison River to quite an expanse of land to the north and west of Delta. Real estate appeared to be booming.

Father now purchased a fine bay trotting horse and a light buggy, so that it was possible for him to spend every weekend at the farm. He engaged a man to plow and plant a rather large vegetable garden. The care of the garden, as well as the orchard, fell to us boys. The garden flourished, particularly the weeds. Many a day we spent trying to keep them from submerging the crops. The garden had to be kept clean at all costs, for such had been Father's instructions, and his instructions we never dared to disobey. Cutting stove wood was quite a chore, for the large cook stove was going all the time, both summer and winter. Luckily for us, some of the wood was pinon and was reduced to stove lengths quite easily. Although the logs were from four to six inches in diameter, a strong blow of the ax would break them straight across, much as one would break a peppermint candy stick. We had to milk the two cows morning and evening, and had to feed the calves. Clarence was delegated to look after the chickens. All of us, particularly Arthur and Howard, had quite a little house work to do; for Mother had not been strong since the birth of Louis the previous fall.

Another striking change in our circumstances was caused by the fact that in the spring of this year Grandmother Blachly bought and moved into a little house in Delta, where Father lived with her except on weekends. Her absence was a great relief to Mother, I am sure. Mother and Grandmother were of very different temperaments. Mother was highly artistic and sensitive. Grandmother was of a practical and matter-of-fact nature, although very religious. She was inclined to criticize other people's ways of doing things and to insist upon her own methods. Mother wrote, after Grandmother had left for Delta: "People respect and like her, until she begins to chide and tell them their duties." Mother felt that she was "watched," and that Grandmother "misconstrued everything I did for her, or said to her." We boys knew nothing of the difficult relations that had existed between the two ever since the removal to Monument. The only inkling of Mother's feeling that I ever had, came a short time before Grandmother moved, when Mother left the house and started up the road crying. I followed her, without her seeing me, and I heard her say, "I cannot live with Mother any longer." Grandmother was delighted with her new home and with the chance to go to church, do temperance work and meet people again. The time on Oak Creek must have been rather hard for her, with the many noisy boys and the mutually strained relations.

Father now wished to sell the Oak Creek place and move the family to Delta. I think that Mother had more or less fallen in love with the place and wished to stay if possible, at least until it could be sold. The little apple and peach trees were beginning to bear well for the first time and the vines that covered the grape arbor were full of grapes. There had been additions to livestock, chickens and bee colonies. Many years later, I heard Mother say that this was the happiest period of her life, especially since she felt that she was bringing up her boys to be "strong Christian men."

A memorable occasion was the visit of Uncle Cornelius about the middle of June. At that time he was a professor of English at the University of California. For days before his arrival Mother had warned us never under any circumstances to use any slang in his presence, for he not only taught English but also wrote articles and books! We were rather apprehensive. Our fears were soon overcome, however, for instead of standing on his dignity, as Mother had thought he would do, he immediately came down to the level of the little boys and used such a wide and brilliant vocabulary of slang as we had never heard or even dreamed of.

Uncle Cornelius, who was quite a naturalist, took us on long walks, telling us the names of all the flowers, birds and stones. As the winter and spring had been wet, wild flowers were blooming everywhere. The mesa just southwest of us was covered with brilliant cactus blossoms of many colors: red, yellow, buff, pink and some nearly white. Mariposa lilies bloomed in abundance. The Colorado columbine was in full bloom, and dainty blue flax could be found. Mallows were plentiful, as were many other flowers. Although our uncle was able to stay for only a few days, he opened to us a new understanding of the world in which we lived. Incidentally, he left with us some school books which had been used by his own children. Mother tried to squeeze out from her busy life two hours a day in which she could give is lessons.

Early in the fall (1890), without any previous intimation to us boys, it was announced one evening that we were going to leave the Oak Creek ranch and move to Delta. On the day of our removal, Father came up from town, and Mother and the two youngest boys rode with him in the buggy. The rest of the boys, with such furniture as was saved, went in the big lumber wagon to our new place on Garnet Mesa, about a mile from Delta proper. Thus ended our life on Melvale Farm.

From the viewpoint of an outsider, these years on the farm

in Oak Creek Valley would seem little short of tragic. Father was recovering from a long and dangerous illness, and was able to work only by sheer will power. As we had very little money, at times we almost faced starvation, and would have been destitute had it not been for our relatives. The land on the farm was not fertile except in a few spots near the creek. Even today it is not cultivated, and in the late summer great cracks appear in many places. Several dry seasons prevented good harvests. We were cut off from schools, except for a portion of two years, and also from church and social activities. There were no children of our own age in the valley.

On the other hand, the great improvement in Father's health which had taken place while we lived at Melvale Farm counterbalanced all hardships. There were many other compensations and rewards. We were a compact family, all working day-by-day as a unit, all having work to do that each one could see as a definite contribution to the family welfare. We were not scattered hither and yon as so many city families are today: the father away at business of which the children have no knowledge, the mother perhaps working in some other place, the children going to different schools. Instead, we all worked together. The work that we did was direct, rather than indirect, as is the work of most city people. We raised crops to feed cows, milked the cows to get our daily supply of milk, put the milk in pans to raise cream, churned the cream to make butter. We were engaged in the fundamental processes of living and we knew it. If the cow kicked over the bucket of milk, we could not go to the store for a quart or so. We had to do without. Without knowing it, we were learning the most basic principles of economics.

We were also learning responsibility for the care of animals, as well as other tasks. The animals had to be fed and watered regularly or they would suffer. Wood had to be hauled, cut and brought in or we would be cold. I often think that much juvenile delinquency today is caused by the lack of responsibility of city children, and the lack of opportunities to care for dogs, horses, cows, and calves—a duty which imperceptibly develops habits of trustworthiness and feelings of affection and tenderness.

At Melvale Farm the air was pure and filled with ozone, as the elevation was over a mile, so that we developed strong hearts and lungs. Since the soil was virgin and we nearly lived off the land, the food that we ate must have supplied most of the minerals essential for good growth and strength. The fact that we were almost isolated from other children, except for the few months when we were at school, prevented us from contracting many childhood diseases which, as has been discovered, may severely injure the system. Yet we were so numerous that we never lacked companionship.

We also had almost complete freedom. We were outdoors most of the time, instead of being shut up in a house. Even in the cabin we had a kind of freedom that is denied to children in city homes. There were no carpets to track with dirty feet, no bric-a-brac to break, no fine furniture to scratch, no delicate and irreplaceable china. Hence, we did not hear constant admonitions of "don't touch," "don't do that," "be careful." Because we were outdoors most of the time, there was no one to exercise a moment-by-moment and hour-by-hour supervision and control over us. We were free to work out our own salvation. Even in respect to things that might have been dangerous, such as whittling with sharp knives, chopping wood, or working with cattle and horses, we were not supervised in detail. There were only general instructions, such as: always whittle away from yourself, be sure that all the tugs are fastened before you begin to drive, be sure that the saddle is cinched before you start to ride, and so on. We learned a great deal by experience, although some of it might be painful.

The riding of a horse almost unconsciously, at least in us little boys, created a strong and beneficial reaction composed of several factors: the feeling of pride in a certain elevation from the ground, the possibility of danger and the overcoming of fear, an increase in the sense of one's own power, knowledge of the ability to control the horse's power for one's own purposes, the sensation of great mobility, and the development of a strong companionship between rider and horse.

Although we had no musical instruments except Father's flute, we did not lack for music. Father and Mother knew a great number of songs which they would sing to us. Mother, who had studied in the Oberlin Conservatory of Music for two years, had a fine voice and trained all of us to sing a bit. The whole family would be divided into sopranos and altos, with Father singing the bass; and we would sing together most of the contents of the Presbyterian Hymnal, which contained many compositions by the masters of music.

We did not have many books, and there was no public library in the county. But the few books that we did have were classics. We did not lack periodical literature, either, for our relatives in the east sent us *St. Nicholas* and *The Youth's Companion*. I have examined with interest recent collections of articles from these two magazines which helped to bring up four generations of American children, and in so doing "brought up the nation." These collections show that many famous authors, editors, and statesmen, such as Homes, Lord Bryce, Gladstone, Theodore Roosevelt, and a whole galaxy of young poets and novelists, wrote for these magazines.

We also took the *American Bee Journal* and *Farm and Fireside*. Above all, our family worship and the memorizing of Bible verses every day gave us a knowledge that is basic for the understanding of western religion, ethics, poetry and belles-lettres in general.

Finally, we boys were happy with what we had, for we knew of nothing else. We had no basis for comparison, since we saw almost no other people. Father and Mother never intimated to us that we were poor. It is true that few toys and games were given to us, but we were always able to devise games and to make any object needed for them, thus increasing our creative ability.

That this time on the farm was a period of great development for the boys was due to the immeasurable courage, faith and love of our parents. We never heard a word of complaint or discouragement. We knew nothing of the financial stress, the bitter disappointments, the injury to pride, and the fears that must have been theirs. Had they given way to such feelings, as many people would have under comparable circumstances, the lot of us boys might have been sorry indeed. But as it was, we were always happy and contented.

CHAPTER IV

School Boy

WHAT WAS THE NEW ENVIRONMENT in which we found ourselves? Things had moved rapidly in Delta since the Indians had been driven out in September, 1881. The Denver and Rio Grande Railway had run a narrow-gauge road over the Marshall Pass to Delta in 1882 and had expanded it the following year to Grand Junction. A railway station had been built about a half mile from the center of Delta and a water tank had been set up nearby to furnish water for the engines. A large stockyard had also been constructed for cattle that were to be shipped in, or shipped to market.

An act of the Colorado State Legislature in 1883 had created Delta County and named the town of Delta as the county seat. By the time we moved near town, a log structure, which had served as the first county courthouse, had been replaced with a substantial building. A bridge had recently been built across the Gunnison River to replace the ferry, and had been made high and strong enough so that spring floods would not take it out. A large, deep ditch had been dug, running parallel to the Garnet Mesa, as a means of preventing the mesa's alkali seepage water from flooding the town.

A two-story brick school house with twelve rooms had been completed in the fall of 1886. It housed all grades including the high school, whose first class graduated in 1889. The large school yard was divided in the center by a high wooden fence to separate the boys from the girls. The boys' side of the yard was adequate for all games but it had one drawback. The water running in the drainage ditch east of the school house had not drawn all the alkali out of the soil. Hence when we played marbles, as we did almost continuously if weather permitted, the remaining alkali chapped our hands badly.

A waterworks system had been set up. Water was pumped from the Gunnison River into a large tank on the brow of Garnet Mesa which stood high enough to provide pressure to put out fires in Delta or the nearby homes on the mesa. From this tank the inhabitants of Garnet Mesa could secure water for domestic use on payment of a dollar or so per month. The water was usually hauled in barrels or small tanks by the families that bought it.

Delta had a volunteer fire department with a hand-drawn cart. The members rejoiced in competing in fire drills with teams from the other towns on the Western Slope. A community band had been formed which played once or twice a week and gave special programs for festive occasions on a bandstand erected in the middle of Main street.

A cemetery had been established about a mile from the town on Garnet Mesa. From the viewpoint of scenery its location was magnificent for it looked toward the Grand Mesa, and below it lay the green valley of the Gunnison. However, it was rather dreary as it was overgrown with sage brush. The soil was very stony and there were no trees or grass.

There were at least three churches in the town, all competing for membership and for funds: the Methodist, the Baptist and the Presbyterian. The Presbyterian Church, with which we cast our lot, was the smallest, both in size of its building and in number of members. The building, which was regarded as temporary, was a frame structure about thirty feet long and twenty feet wide, with no steeple or belfry. It was lit by kerosene lamps attached to its walls. Since the congregation was small the church was partly financed by the Board of Home Missions.

Two newspapers had been established: the *Delta Independent*, a Republican weekly owned and operated by one of our neighbors, R. D. Blair: and a Democratic sheet called the *Delta County Tribune*, which was considered by many staunch Republicans as being somewhat radical, if not absolutely Socialistic.

There were new wooden sidewalks on the chief streets of Delta. A boardwalk had been built east of town over the alkali swamp to meet the road running up the side of Garnet Mesa.

The place Father had selected for our new home was a ranch about a mile and a quarter from town on Garnet Mesa. This mesa consisted of three elevations: the Lower Mesa, the Middle Mesa, and the so-called Upper Mesa. The last was about a hundred feet higher than the surrounding country and was, therefore, too high to be watered from a regular gravity flow ditch.

Most of the farm of 125 acres that Father had bought was on the lower part of the mesa. The place was under the Garnet Mesa Ditch and, as we understood at the time, had good priority rights in the Uncompahgre River. As this stream ran a large amount of water, except toward the end of the summer, it appeared that our irrigation water problem was solved. Father ran a pipe from our main irrigating ditch on the hillside of the Middle Mesa to the house so that we could have running water for domestic use. This did not work too well as the water contained alkali, which made it very hard and quite unfit to drink. Moreover, during the coldest months no water could run in the pipe because of the freezing. We soon found that our drinking water had to be brought in barrels from the town tank.

There was a large vineyard near the house as well as a small orchard protected by a windbreak of cottonwood trees. We imagined that the trees grew for the sole purpose of giving us opportunities to climb them and to enjoy their swinging motion when the wind was high. Much of our land was planted to alfalfa, which produced three cuttings of hay a season. We must have put up one hundred tons or more each year, as the land was very fertile.

We boys were greatly pleased with the farm building. There was the main house with four or five rooms. Standing beside the back room was a little separate building, or rather a detached room which Father occupied as his special territory. Back of the house were a granary and a wagon shed. Across a little gully was a small tenant house to work on the farm.

We had a good deal of livestock. Besides the horses we had brought from Oak Creek, there were many others, some of which I learned later had been taken by the bank on foreclosed mortgages or other debts. The majority of these were colts about two years old, but there were also a few work and riding horses. As we had moved to the farm after most of the crops were harvested, there was little for us to do at first except to milk the cows and feed the numerous horses after the pasture had been used up.

Father had rented a piano for Mother. Nearly every evening he would take out his flute and they would play together. I am sure that after Mother had been without a musical instrument for five years she felt particular joy in this music. She had a little more leisure now, as a young woman was soon engaged to do part of the housework.

Father bought for the living room a fine, new hard-coal base burner. The upper part was surrounded with isinglass so that we could see the beautiful red and blue flames shooting up from the burning coal. We enjoyed sitting before the stove in the evening, feeling sleepy and lazy as we watched the fire burn, or warming and drying wet socks on the fenders which seemed especially made for that purpose.

We found our neighbors congenial. Nearly all of them, like Father, were not only operating farms but were also engaged in some sort of business or official capacity in Delta.

There were now eight of us brothers, as Mother had recently given birth to Edward. A few days after our arrival on Garnet Mesa we older boys started school. Before doing so we had been fitted out with new clothes. At Oak Creek we had nearly always worn overalls. In moderately cold weather we often merely put on an extra pair or two, but for winter we had red woolen long underwear and woolen stockings. Now we were fitted out as became the sons of a banker, with nice shirts, woolen trousers and coats, and good woolen sweaters. We found on reaching school that we were rather overdressed.

I was filled with fear and trembling at the thought of school. My experience with school in Oak Creek had not been too happy. Now I realized that I was far behind other boys of my age. I did not know how to read very well, how to write, or how to do any work with numbers except "mental arithmetic" which Grandmother had taught me. Arthur, of course, was in much better shape than I was, for he was of a more studious nature and had learned from Grandmother how to read and write very well. I had rather balked at learning so far, largely because there were so many more interesting things to do. Clarence, who knew how to read a bit, did not suffer from being much too old for his grade. Grandmother led us to school the first morning. Arthur, I think, was put in the fifth grade. Grandmother persuaded the principal that since Clarence and I knew how to read we should be put in the second grade, and Howard was put in the first grade.

The first day of school was torture for me. The teacher asked me to go to the board to write and add some numbers. She said, "Write four plus four on the board with the answer." I knew well enough that four and four made eight, but I had never been taught, or had forgotten to make the figures and the mathematical signs. My heart beat fast. I was in a sweat. I would try to write something and then would rub it out with my small wet hands. The other children began to laugh at me. Here I was, a boy of ten and much older than they were, yet I could not write four plus four. The teacher then suggested that I write the sentence, "I see a cat." I found this equally impossible, for although I had certainly done copybook work at the Oak Creek school, in the two or three years intervening I had evidently forgotten how to write or else was too flustered to remember how it was done.

Mrs. Minton, the teacher, was very kind. She gave me special lessons in writing and in making the mathematical signs and within a month I was doing as well as the rest except that my handwriting was very poor, as it has always been. As Mrs. Minton talked to me gently about arithmetic, she found that I could do problems in my head well in advance of the work of the class. I knew the multiplication tables pretty well and could add and subtract and do very simple division. I worked at my studies as only a farm boy can do who is accustomed to take a heavy task like plowing and harrowing and keep at it hour by hour and day by day. My ambition was to catch up with my rightful age grade as soon as possible, for I felt shame and frustration at being in a class with boys and girls two or three years younger than I was. About Christmas time I was promoted to the third grade and shortly thereafter to the fourth grade. At the end of the school year, by the advice of Mrs. Minton, I took the fifth-grade examinations and passed them as well as those of my own grade. This was possible because the fourth and fifth grades were in the same room and I had listened very carefully to the recitations of the pupils in the grade above me.

The first days in school were not easy, however. There were several big boys in the upper grades who were looked upon by the little boys as bullies. They made the life of the little boys miserable by appropriating their marbles, hitting them, and trying to stir up fights among them. One day as we were walking home, Raleigh Pope persuaded his brother, Billy, to have a fight with Clarence in back of the blacksmith's shop, which was the standard place for fights. Billy easily got Clarence down and began punching his face. As I saw the blood run down Clarence's nose, I became suddenly furious. I picked up a wagon wheel spoke that was lying near and hit Billy over the head. Down he went and lay there, apparently almost dead. An awed hush fell upon the other boys. The bullies left me alone for a while after that.

On the farm at Oak Creek we had had little opportunity to learn much in the way of games and sports except for riding, hunting, playing marbles and skating. We found the boys at the Delta School playing a number of games entirely new to us: Bull-in the-ring, foot-and-half, a kind of rugby football, and many different games of marbles. These games, except for a few such as mumbly-peg and pegging-the-top, seemed to run in a sort of seasonal sequence, perhaps depending somewhat upon the weather. There was no adult supervision of any kind over our games. We followed the rules laid down or inherited by the older boys and never questioned whether they were good or bad, right or wrong. At first my brothers and I were at quite a disadvantage, partly because we had never played such games on Oak Creek, but more particularly because even now we did not have so much time to play as the "city kids." We walked more than a mile to school and were also burdened with several farm chores such as feeding the horses, milking the cows, driving the live-stock to water when the ditch was frozen, and cutting the wood.

When school started in the fall and the weather was quite warm, we would play marbles. This also seemed to be the standard game toward the middle of spring. We had several different kinds of marble games: "Purgatory," "Knuckle Boston," "Fate," and "Drops." In the game of "Purgatory" four holes were arranged in a square of about six feet, with another hole in the middle. The game was to shoot marbles in such a way as to go around the outer holes three times and then into the middle holes. With each completed round you were allowed to take the advantage of a "span" (the distance that you could stretch from tip of thumb to tip of middle finger) toward the hole you were shooting for or toward your opponent's marbles. Any shot that hit your competitor's marbles counted as a gained hole. As four boys usually played the game, there developed quite a science of hitting the marbles of opponents in order to gain a hole and to drive them as far as possible away from the holes where they should go, or of hitting the marble of your partner so that it was driven nearer the right hole. Scientific playing also demanded that the choice of the right marble for a given purpose be quite as careful as golfers think necessary in the selection of the proper clubs for different situations. Very large marbles were used to shoot from hole to hole.

Medium-sized ones were used to shoot your opponent's marbles. And very small marbles were used to "flue" or glance off your opponent's or partner's marble, to reach a nearby hole, or to move close to another marble.

Agate marbles were held in high esteem. They were not only far better made than the glass or china marbles, but were much heavier. The boy who could boast of a full complement of large and small agate marbles was considered lucky. The only difficulty was that from our viewpoint they were frightfully expensive. A very large agate marble of almost an inch in diameter cost a quarter, which in terms of the value of money as of this writing was equal to a whole silver dollar [the 2021 value would be over $7.00]. The medium sized ones cost ten cents, while the little "flue jays" could be had for a nickel. Four or five of the inferior "glassies" cost only about ten cents.

In "Knuckle Boston" we made a circle about five feet in diameter. The marbles would be placed in the center. The game was for each one to shoot from outside the ring and knock out as many marbles as possible. If your shooter stayed in the ring after knocking out one or more marbles, you could have another shot from inside the ring where your "taw" had "struck." The boy who shot the most marbles out of the ring won the game, or when the playing "keeps," secured the most loot.

In the game of "fats," a small ring about eighteen inches in diameter was made and all the marbles were placed in it. A larger ring about fifteen feet in diameter was made around the small ring. Standing on the large ring we would "plunk" at the marbles to try to knock them out. In the game of "drops" we would place the marbles in a small ring like a "fats" ring. We would stand over this ring and merely drop our marbles on those below in the ring. As in the game of "fats" the one who knocked out the most marbles won the game, or retained all that he knocked out in case the game was for keeps.

One of the big boys devised a game that was quite different. He had a cigar box with a hole in the center of one side, perhaps an inch in diameter. You bet one marble against two that you could shoot into the hole at about six feet away. It looked easy, but the owner of the box nearly always won. It proved to be such a losing proposition for the others that it was soon given up.

The boys usually acquired agates either through playing "keeps" or through selling empty whiskey bottles to the saloons for five cents each. At first, I was at a considerable disadvantage in respect to agates. My pious parents would have been shocked and horrified if they learned that any of their sons had gone to the door of a saloon to sell whiskey bottles, but I secured some extremely good agates in that way. I had to be very secretive, however, for fear Arthur or Clarence would tell our parents of my wickedness.

The prohibition against playing "keeps" placed me in an awkward situation. Since there were very few boys who did not play keeps and those few were by no means the best players, I was not able to compete in the class of players to which I thought my ability might entitle me. Moreover, since I was unable to acquire marbles except through purchase, I was not properly equipped. I never thought of asking Father or Mother for marble money. It is clear to me now that had they known how important it was in the boys' world to have many and good marbles, they would have given me the necessary money to buy them. Certainly, they would have done so at all costs if they had thought that their gift would keep me away from the dens of wickedness or prevent me from "gambling."

Finally, I yielded to temptation and began to play keeps. More secretiveness was needed since I was constantly afraid that Arthur or Clarence would find out what I was doing and tell about it at home. I even had to do a bit of lying to explain to them how it was I had so many marbles. This I attributed to my "trading" ability. But with Howard in school most of the possibility that I would be found out disappeared. Howard was a regular little devil in school and almost always had to stay overtime. I was assigned to stay at the school grounds until he was freed, and to escort him home. This gave me a chance to play keeps without brotherly intervention.

Whether selling whiskey bottles and the adoption of a course of conduct that necessitated sneaking and lying and the feeling of guilt due to disobedience in order to play keeps is more harmful to character than the development of an inferiority complex because of inability to compete with other children, I shall leave to the good Lord to decide. My parents would probably have said that the cardinal sin was yielding to temptation. At any rate, I became an expert at marbles.

As the fall became colder and the alkali in the soil made our hands severely chapped, we gave up marbles and played a kind of rugby football. We tried to send the ball over the opponent's goal line by kicking it, but were supposed never to touch it with our hands. The game was a bit hard on the shins, particularly when the big boys were playing with the little boys. Those big boys who enjoyed inflicting minor cruelties on smaller boys found plenty of opportunities when we played this type of football.

We little boys did not enjoy such petty persecution. Now and then we talked of ways in which we might stop it. On several occasions a group of us tried to "frame up" on the bullies, but as one of them could easily knock out eight or ten little boys at one time, we found that this did not pay. However, once when Archie McKinley kicked me in the seat of the pants very hard, I picked up a stick lying near and hit him across the shins with all my strength. He did not bother me after that.

During the winter, of course, when there was snow on the ground, we not only played football but also had snowball fights. Two sides would line up and make forts. The fighting between the sides was often fierce. Some of the boys would make "soaked balls"—snowballs soaked with water until they were just about like round lumps of ice. This, however, was generally considered unfair, as the "soaked balls" were really dangerous. Once, during a snow fight, Judge King came by wearing a stovepipe hat. We immediately, with one accord, began throwing snowballs at it and he soon retreated muttering words of prayer.

In the early spring we would play "foot-and-a-half." We would set a line against which each one had to place his heel and jump. The one who jumped farthest was to be the "pace setter" while the one whose jump was shortest had to kneel down as in leap-frog while the others placed their hands on his back and jumped over him. The pace setter went first and set a line where his heel landed. The first boy who could not reach this line as he jumped had to become the "frog" and a new pacesetter would start the jumping all over again. While this was a fine game, it was terribly tough on the legs for the first few days. Excessive jumping made the muscles of the legs so sore that a boy could hardly walk, much less climb the stairway to the second story of the school house. With the advance of spring, we played baseball, as every boy in the whole country does.

Besides the school work, we had our chores on the farm. Every morning before going to school I had to feed the stock and milk one cow. The hay stacks were by the corral and barn, and since it was prohibited to open up the whole long stack of hay, it was necessary to cut down a short strip with a hay knife. This consisted of a long blade with several sharp cutting projections on one side. This job I did not like, as on many wintry mornings the hay was covered with snow which got into my clothing. The same thing had to be done in the evening. As the winter grew very cold, the Garnet Mesa Ditch froze up and it was necessary to drive the cattle and horses for water down to a spring and little stream about a half mile away.

One evening I threw a rope over one of the new horses that Father was keeping on the place, threw a half-hitch around her nose instead of a bridle, and with Arthur, drove the cows and horses down to the water. Arthur and I waited until all the animals except the horses we were riding had finished drinking and had started home. Riding the mare, I started back a moment or two before Arthur. Arthur came up from behind on the lope. My mare, thinking that a race was under way, started to run. We neared the gate. To my horror, I saw that the wind had blown it nearly shut. I pulled on the rope to stop the mare. The rope slid off her nose and I had no control over her. Over the four-foot wooden gate she went. As I was riding bareback, I fell off, striking my left shoe in the barbed wire at the side of the gate and tearing a gash in the leather. However, I was not hurt, as the wire had partly broken the fall. Father told me that the mare had formerly been a race horse. I did not doubt it.

That same fall and winter Father again had a good many horses, most of which were two or three year old colts. Sometime during the winter, he gave each of us one. Mine was brown and weighed about 800 pounds. One day Howard and I drove the colts, which were wild range horses and had never been handled, into the corral. I roped my brown colt. Howard and I gradually worked near him and began to pat him. We then fed him some hay, which he ate without showing any fear of us. After we thought that we had "broken" him, I jumped on his back. Howard, with some hay in his hand and holding the rope, gradually led him up to the house where Father and Mother were sitting on the porch. They were dreadfully frightened. I was forced to get off the colt immediately and was made to promise never to ride a wild horse again. Howard and I were outraged. Had we not broken the colt and made him gentle for a riding horse?

The first spring that we were on Garnet Mesa, Arthur, Clarence and I were asked to join the Presbyterian Church of Delta. It was quite the ordeal. We had to know the short catechism, much of the Bible, and a modicum of Presbyterian doctrine. We spent a good deal of time in preparing for the examination given by the minister who was a Scot of the old school. "Who is God?" "What is the chief purpose of man?" These and many other questions we had to answer. Although we were quite well acquainted with the Bible from learning verses morning and night and hearing chapters read aloud, we were a bit weak on the Presbyterian tenets. Mother had become a Congregationalist while at Oberlin, and Father was never given to teaching us in terms of theology. Despite our lack of proper grounding in doctrine, we passed the examination and the following Sunday were duly admitted into the church.

At home we observed Sunday quite strictly. The boys were never permitted to read "secular" books or sing "secular" songs. We were not even allowed to whistle, which was one of my chief joys. I was always whistling—it was my proud boast that I could whistle soprano and alto at the same time. But not on the Sabbath! One thing pleasing about Sunday, however, was the fact that on this day Father usually took us for walks. As we always had family singing in the evening and went to Sunday school and church in the morning, Sunday was not unbearable.

Almost immediately after going to Delta, Father became superintendent of the Presbyterian Church Sunday school and leader of the choir. These positions he held until his death. Father was a strict disciplinarian with the choir. I have seen the organist in tears because Father spoke to her about missing "accidentals." The church was the center of all our religious, social and musical activity.

Much of the time during our first and second winters at Delta I stayed at Grandmother's house, as she had grown quite old and feeble. She was a very religious woman and was almost as passionately devoted to the "temperance" movement as was Frances E. Willard, whom she had known as a girl. Many a Wednesday evening I had to accompany her to prayer meetings, which seldom had an attendance of half a dozen persons. The good parson, however, was fond of reminding us that "Where two or three are gathered together, the Lord is in the midst of them." Grandmother and others had organized a "Loyal Temperance Legion" which I was required to attend. At its meeting we not only heard discourses on the evils of alcohol, but learned many temperance songs. How alcohol addles the brain was "demonstrated" by placing the white of an egg in pure alcohol and pointing out that it was almost cooked by the pernicious fluid. This was very convincing. None of us realized that few human brains, while still in living bodies, are soaked in 100 percent alcohol.

Some of the many temperance songs that we sang might appear ridiculous nowadays, but they were taken quite seriously.

Occasionally they were sung by adults, especially in homes, or as part of a "temperance program" at the church. Among them were "My Father is a Temperance Man," "Down with King Alcohol," "Where is my Wandering Boy Tonight," "The Drunkard's Grave," "Down in the Licensed Saloon," and the like. My favorite was "The Belle of the City." It ran as follows:

> *"It was ten years ago when the belle of the city*
> *Gave her hand to the young millionaire.*
> *Every bell in the steeple, every rose in the garden*
> *Whispered joy to the heaven blessed pair.*
>
> *She was fair as a rose that blooms in the garden*
> *He was manly and free and brave.*
> *Tell me where are they now? In the rag-robed*
>   *procession,*
> *Marching down, down, down to the grave.*
>
> *Hark, Hark, the pageant passes, tramp, tramp,*
> *tramp, tramp;*
> *I hear the tread of moving masses, tramp, tramp,*
>   *tramp, tramp;*
> *Oh, heaven save our young man! 'Tis King Bibber's*
>   *army*
> *Marching down, down, down to the grave."* [3]

Great emphasis was placed on the "Tramp, tramp, tramp" by all who sang. "Down, down, down to the grave" went in a descending scale that was very impressive, particularly when sung by big men with deep voices. Who or what the composer of this effusion meant by "King Bibber" is anybody's guess. My own thought is

---

3 https://home.lyon.edu/wolfcollection/songs/morrisking1257.mp3

that through a confusion of ideas "Bibber" is used to mean alcohol.

Temperance, which meant total abstinence from all alcoholic beverages, was a very real issue in Delta. Although the town at this time contained not more than 1,000 persons, there were half a dozen saloons, all apparently doing a thriving business. As we knew almost everyone in town and were in fairly close touch with everyone's family life, business, church and fraternal affiliations and so on, we had an intimate knowledge of the difficulties caused by excessive drinking. One of our neighbors had killed a man in a drunken brawl and was now serving time in the penitentiary at Canyon City. One of the best blacksmiths in Delta was losing his business because of drink. Several respectable women of our acquaintance were taking in washing to support their families while their husbands loafed around the saloons. At the funeral of a State Representative, so many of his fellow lodge members were drunk as to cause a scandal. "That was perfectly proper" said one of the pallbearers. "If he were alive, he would be leading the funeral procession, drunk as a lord."

Cowboys coming to town from the range would ride down the main street yelling and shooting as the result of indulgence in too much hard liquor. At times men could be seen lying senseless in the gutter after they had been kicked out of the saloons, or sprawled beside the road where they had fallen from their horses or wagons on the way home from town. There would have been many more accidents of this sort had it not been for the good sense and judgement of their horses. "A sober horse," I have heard Bill Lance say, "has a damned sight more sense than a drunken man."

I dreaded to go down the west side of the street, which meant that I had to pass the saloons. A group of half-intoxicated men always loafed in front of each bar door, telling dirty stories, leering at the women who went by and making rough remarks to the children passing on the street. Even at the age of ten or eleven I could see that the saloon in Delta was a prime source of evil. I suppose that my very limited viewpoint had been influenced strongly by Grandmother and my parents.

Another institution which seemed to me nearly equal to the saloons in viciousness was the livery stable. Almost the same kind of person would be loafing around these businesses as in front of the saloons. I think that at this time there were three livery stables in Delta. They did a thriving business in furnishing horses and carriages to traveling salesmen bound for the little towns throughout the county which had no railroad or other transportation facilities—Cory, Echart, Cedaredge, Reed, Hotchkiss, Paonia, and Crawford. They also rented out conveyances for funerals. And because a principal method of courtship in those days was driving, many a horse and buggy would be hired from the livery stables by young men who wished to please the ladies.

The barber shop was another place which seemed to me at the time a den of iniquity. The barbers vied with the traveling men in collecting off-color stories, which they delighted in retelling to their customers. Nothing seemed too lewd, coarse, or vulgar for these artists.

The blacksmith shops were a continual source of pleasure to me with the roaring bellows, the sight and sound of white-hot and red-hot iron being hammered on the anvils, the sizzling of the hot iron when it was dipped into water to be cooled off or tempered, the horses being shod, often against their will, the setting of iron tires on wagon wheels, and the multitude of other operations connected with a blacksmith shop of those days. All the blacksmiths in town were extremely strong men, as they had to be in order to hold up the legs of not too tame horses while shoeing them, to pump the bellows, and to hammer on the anvil all through a twelve-hour day.

I saw a good deal of the blacksmith shops, not only because the one owned by Mr. Cramer was just across the street from the back of Grandmother's lot, but also because it was necessary to get our horses shod, plow shares sharpened, wagon wheel tires set, picks sharpened, and so forth. On the Fourth of July all the blacksmiths in town would start the day's celebration very early by exploding powder between anvils.

Staying with Grandmother was the occasion of a frightening experience. Before dawn of Christmas morning in 1890, when the morning star was still shining, I started home from Grandmother's in order to be sure to share the festivity of opening the Christmas stockings. As I neared the cemetery two coyotes came out from it and began circling me. I knew that if I ran, they would immediately pursue me, so I simply walked as fast as I could but with a rapidly beating heart. I had not gone far when Mr. Wolbert's dog, evidently smelling the coyotes, came running toward me. The coyotes immediately slunk away into the cemetery, much to my relief. I arrived home early enough to be at hand for the opening of the stockings.

CHAPTER V

Family Tragedy

Sometime before the spring of 1891, Father had bought forty acres of the Blair place on middle Garnet Mesa which bordered on ours, largely I believe as a speculative venture, for land was selling rapidly at that time. As he had not yet been able to dispose of it, he wished to plant it to a mixture of oats and alfalfa. During the latter part of February, he told me that I was old enough to break the land, which had never been plowed. For this work Father allowed me to use a beautiful team of grey colts that had been broken only recently. On the first day he put the plow in the back of the wagon, and we drove up to the new plot of land. Father laid out five or six acres of the land that were to be plowed first, hitched the team to the plow, and watched me plow the first two or three furrows. He then left me alone. For the first hour or two I was so proud of being able to do the work of a man with my handsome team, that I could think of little else. The land was almost free from stones, and was just damp enough to turn over perfectly and scour the plow share smooth and gleaming. The only difficulty was in swinging the plow around the corners.

At noon I drove back to the house for dinner. I was tired, but when Mother suggested that I call it a day, I was indignant. No, I was man enough to do a day's work! Later in the afternoon, I wished that I had taken Mother's advice. My legs were barely dragging me along. Walking in the soft and newly plowed furrows, I found, was much harder than walking on bare ground. The glory of being a man gradually lessened with the declining of the sun.

By the end of the day I was so tired that I could hardly hitch the horses to the wagon and drive home. After a big supper, I immediately went to bed and slept the sleep of the just.

The next morning my legs were lame and sore, and my arms and chest muscles were in like condition from holding the plow and swinging it around the corners. After the first few hours of work, however, the lameness went away and I felt fine. The spring morning was cool and perfect. Meadow larks would fly up into the air, poise in some spot above the earth, and sing in absolute rapture. Farming was a great life, and at the age of eleven I was certainly large and strong enough to be a farmer! I must have spent all of the spring vacation and a good deal of time besides, in plowing, harrowing and leveling about ten acres. My school report shows that I was absent for 23 half days in February.

As a reward for my work, Father gave me "A Life of Washington," which I dutifully read without too much comprehension. When I returned to school, I was a bit behind, but seemingly soon caught up. I found out later, however, that I had missed two important subjects in arithmetic.

About the time school closed for the summer, haying began. It was the painful duty of the boys to turn the grindstone for sharpening the mowing machine sickles. At least two or three sickles had to be sharpened daily. Each large sickle had twenty or thirty little blades, every one of which must be ground to keep a cutting line along two edges. Turn, turn, turn the grindstone. No let-up. It seemed to me that the man holding the sickle blade to the stone continually kept bearing down harder and harder, thus making the turning more difficult. I had to take the major responsibility for the grindstone work, as Arthur was just recovering after being hit in the head by a baseball, and Clarence was hardly old enough to do much.

I was also considered large enough to run the hay rake, which gathered the hay into windrows. The only difficulty of this work was judging just when to put my foot on the dumping apparatus, so as to get the windrows in a straight line. One of my chief delights was to run the hay rake while men swinging great pitchforks tossed the hay on from both sides. One of the men taught me the science of loading the rack so that the hay would not slide off, after I had been embarrassed by seeing a load stacked by me do just that as we were going along a little hillside. Our hay racks were flat, about sixteen feet long and eight feet wide, with a ladder seven or eight feet tall fastened in front, so that it was easily possible to get on or off a full load of hay.

As we had no derrick on the lower Garnet Mesa place, the hay which had been pitched on the racks had to be pitched off again and built up into stacks, all by hand. I enjoyed helping one of the hired men do the stacking. When a big load of hay was driven up against the high stack, we would often dive down from the stack into it, turning a summersault as we went. I well remember how hot it seemed on the south side of the tall haystack right after noon, with the sun pouring down, until by working we had made ourselves sweat again.

One day when Howard and I were loading hay on the rack, we left a large hole in the center of the load, concealed by a slight covering of hay. When our hired man started to go from the front of the load toward the back in order to shape it up a bit before driving to the haystack, he was much surprised to find himself up to the neck in hay.

As we had fifty or sixty acres of alfalfa and raised three crops each year, haying was going on most of the time. In the intervals between the cuttings of alfalfa we cut and hauled grain or worked in the orchard. We raised a good crop of oats on the land that I had plowed in the spring, and left a stand of alfalfa that had grown along with the oats. The grain had to be hauled on the hay rack about half a mile from the field to the barn, over a very rough road that ran for some little distance along a hillside and slanted a bit. One day a whole load slid off the rack and down the hillside, carrying two of us boys who were sitting in the middle of the load. The hired man, who was driving the team and was sitting close to the hay rack ladder, saw what was happening and by grabbing the ladder was saved from the ignominy of taking the slide with us.

Along with the summer work there was much fun. We rode horseback, played marbles, practiced baseball in the evening, and when the wind was rather high, climbed the tall cottonwood trees and let them sway back and forth. We had a large garden, the chief joys of which, insofar as we boys were concerned, were the watermelon and musk melon patches—particularly the former. Very often we would take a large watermelon into the hay field and eat it in the middle of the morning or afternoon. We would often go into the patch, and after testing the melons very scientifically by thumping them and examining their little stem tendrils to see whether these looked dead, we would usually find one melon that was at the perfect point of ripeness. Splitting it wide open from end to end, we would cut out and eat only the bright red center. Melons were so plentiful that there was no market for them, and the patch was so large that we did not have to think about economy.

One night a neighbor boy, Johnny Barker, suggested to a group of town boys that it would be a good stunt to raid his father's watermelon patch. No sooner were the boys well located in the patch than Mr. Barker came out with a shotgun and began to bang away at them. The boys left the patch in a hurry. Johnny fell down with a cry of pain, for his father had hit him in the calves of his legs with a load of birdshot. The rest of the boys were too far away to receive such punishment. Luckily for Johnny, the shots did not go much deeper than his overalls.

Just before school opened in the fall, Father took Arthur, Clarence and me on a camping trip to the Uncompahgre Plateau country southwest of Delta. This plateau was very different from Grand Mesa. Instead of rising steeply and even perpendicularly toward the top, it went up with a gradual slope for more than thirty miles. Father had secured from cousin John some ideal equipment for such trips, consisting of a light buckboard wagon and two small mules weighing not more than five or six hundred pounds apiece. He had also procured a nice new tent and had obtained from the blacksmith a kind of camp stove, the top of which was shaped like a figure 8, with one of the circles to hold the coffee pot and one the frying pan. This stood upon three detachable legs. We pitched our tent near a grove of great pine trees and built a fire about eight or ten feet from the tent. All our equipment worked well. We had bacon and eggs cooked in the skillet and wonderful coffee made in a new coffeepot, rolls and doughnuts, as well as peaches brought from home.

We gathered pine boughs and overlapped them in such a way as to have a deep bed of small pine branches and needles over which we placed our blankets. The pine boughs and twigs acted as springs and the smaller twigs and the needles as a mattress, or at least that was the theory of a pine bough bed. Before going to bed we lay down near the fire and looked through the branches of the tall pine trees at the bright Colorado stars. The delicate odor of the pines, their graceful limbs and needles, with the stars shining through them, what could be more perfect?

About nine o'clock we went to bed. I was to sleep on the side of the tent near the fire. As I looked at the tent wall, I saw the shadow of a great beast against the white canvas, made quite plain by the fire light. Could it be a bear? I hardly knew what to do, whether to yell, arouse Father quietly, or lie perfectly still. The loud sound of the animal's breathing frightened me even more. When I could stand it no longer, I spoke to Father, who was awake. "Why", he said, "That is only the shadow of our dog Towser." In my fright over the "bear", I had entirely forgotten that we had brought along our large Newfoundland dog.

The next morning Father sent me to a nearby lumber camp to see about the possibility of getting a loaf of bread. After finding that bread could be purchased there, I asked in what I considered a very business-like way, "How much do you charge for your bread?" "It will be only twenty-five cents," replied the woman who was cooking for the camp. I remarked that this seemed pretty high. "Just you wait until you see it," she said. She went into the cook shack and brought it out. It had been baked in a very large dishpan, in a Dutch oven, and was perhaps a foot and one half in diameter and nearly a foot high. It was as good as it was large.

This was the first time I had ever been camping with Father. He was full of stories, songs and bright sayings. On this trip he was not, as he generally appeared to me, a sort of stern but loving god—he was much more a man. I really never knew my Father very well, partly because of his habitual sternness, partly because he and I were busy with our individual occupations, and partly because he was a man of few words. No one ever became familiar with him or called him by his first name. "Noli me tangere" (touch me not), Mother would say, was his motto. His looks, presence, and demeanor were all a part of his aloof nature. He was about six feet tall, and stood as straight as an arrow. He had heavy black hair, large piercing blue eyes, a stern mouth and a dark beard. He never lost his composure. Though I have seen his eyes almost flash blue lightning and his lips sternly compressed when he was angry at some wrong, never a hasty word would he say. But his aspect was quite enough to frighten the wrongdoer. He often quoted the proverb, "He that ruleth his spirit is greater than he that taketh a city." Men respected him and feared him when they were wrong. No one ever told a dirty story in his presence.

When we returned from the camping trip, it was nearly time to start school again. That winter in school was very interesting, and in the course of the academic year I completed the majority of the fifth and the sixth grades. By that time I was in my proper age group and no longer had the feeling of inferiority with respect to my school mates. The subject matter of our work was interesting. I had a passion for geography, in which I nearly always stood 100 per cent. Grammar had a special interest for me. The best part of it, I thought was diagramming sentences on the black board. To place the nouns, verbs, adverbs and adjectives where they belonged, and to arrange the subordinate phrases and clauses in a logical pattern, was not only an exercise in English, but also a form of construction. Arithmetic was not difficult for me. I rather liked the practical problems, such as those concerned with stone work, the measuring of carpets, the purchase and sale of materials, and so on. The fifth-grade course in hygiene and physiology included certain recitations, particularly those concerning human anatomy, that some inspired person had forced into doggerel verse:

How many bones has the human head?
Eight, my child, as I've often said.
How many bones has the human ear?
Three in each and a help to hear.
How many bones in the human spine?
Twenty four, like a climbing vine.

These rhymes dealt with the whole human skeleton, and ended by stating the sum total of the bones as follows:

So now altogether these many bones meet,
And form altogether two hundred and eight.

There was a slight awkwardness about the last rhyme, but we did not notice it too much. I still remember all the verses, except in some I have forgotten the exact number of bones!

For reading, we had McGuffy readers. We were required to learn by heart each and every poem in them, nearly all of which I still remember. The only things that bothered me in any way were spelling and writing. As the monthly school reports were issued, I usually had the highest general average of the class. One month the lead was taken by Nellie Ingersoll. Spelling had caused my downfall. I regarded it as a disgrace to be outstripped by a mere girl, for at that time I regarded girls as inferior beings.

There may have been several causes for my poor writing. It is true that on Oak Creek I had filled a number of copy books with my feeble attempts to make the letters look like those at the head of each page, but as the years without formal instructions intervened, I lost even the slight amount of proficiency that I had once acquired. Probably the greatest difficulty was the fact that I had had to do two years' work in one, and so did not have the usual amount of time to practice. Modern psychologists might attribute the difficulty to the fact that I was naturally left-handed, at least as to many operations. Be that as it may, my writing was not good, nor has it improved with age.

About this time the question of Women's Suffrage was quite an issue in Colorado. One of the most fervent advocates of the measure was Miss Bertha Brooks, the daughter of Bishop Brooks of the Methodist Episcopal Church, our sixth-grade teacher. She not only talked to us about it, but also taught us suffrage songs or ditties. The one that I remember best ran as follows:

> *They're good enough to make our beds, to bake our cakes and pies, sir.*
>
> *But then the ladies should not vote because they don't get tight sir.*
>
> *The reason why they should not vote is because they should not vote, sir.*
>
> *The reason why they should not vote is because they should not vote, sir.*

I do not know how much such propaganda helped, but only a year or two after we learned these remarkable songs, Colorado gave suffrage to women on equal terms with men.

Toward Christmas of 1892 an epidemic of scarlet fever began to rage in town, and it was decided to close the school. The teachers gathered us together and told us that several pupils had already died and that we should be very careful not to go where there were many people. As we sang, "God be with you till we meet again," I think all of us were rather scared. When we returned to school after some weeks, there were several vacant seats left by our classmates who had been taken by the scourge.

During the winter our hired man spent part of his time hauling coal from the Rollins coal mine. One day as he was driving down the steep grade that led from the mine, in some way or other his load of coal tipped over, breaking his leg, injuring the horses, and generally wrecking the wagon. Father seemed to think that the accident was that man's fault, and hired in his place a man by the name of Matlock, who was a very good worker and knew a great deal about farming. Toward that latter part of the spring, I had to stay out of school to assist him in planting the crops and irrigating the land. Father bought me a new pair of rubber boots. All day I would walk over the alfalfa fields seeing that the high places were covered with water. "If you see that all the high places are covered with water," said Matlock, "you may be sure that the low ones are."

Unlike the alfalfa fields, our grain fields were not flooded with water, but were soaked by means of irrigation furrows that ran about two feet apart. It was a hard job to see that each tiny furrow had the right amount of water, that the water did not break out of the furrows and wash the land, and that the water always reached the farther end of the field in each and every furrow. As our fields were somewhat irregular in contour, we had to work steadily all day to see that the water ran where it should. Starting new strips of furrows, wading through the mud all day, and repairing broken furrows was not exactly child's play. The rubber boots, covered with clinging mud, felt like lead before night.

That summer I helped Matlock almost as a man. I loaded the hay on the rack, and stacked much of the hay that Matlock pitched to me. Times were very hard, and Father could not afford much help. Clarence and even Howard came into the hay fields to work. Arthur, because of his baseball injury, was still unable to do much.

On an early August afternoon, Howard and I went out with

our ropes in our hands to bring in a couple of horses from the pasture. After catching them, we placed hackamores around their noses and started for the barn along a lane where many sunflowers were growing near the fence. As usual, we started to race. Howard's horse, which was faster than mine, in trying to pass me, brushed against the sunflowers. Howard was barefoot at the time, and a large sunflower somehow became wedged between his toes. The force with which the sunflower pulled him was so great as to throw him off the horse with a bang.

I soon managed to stop my horse so that I could go back to help. Howard lay on his back in the road. I thought for a few sickening moments that he was dead. In desperation, I turned him over on his side, and soon he began to breathe a little. Within ten or fifteen minutes he was breathing normally and seemed hardly worse for his fall, which had merely knocked all the wind out of him. I well knew the experience, for I had once fallen hard on my back when I made my first attempt to do the "big drop" on the horizontal bar on the school grounds.

Early in the summer, Father went to Oregon to look over the country with the intention, I think, of moving there—at least he talked of such a possibility after he returned. Just before he left, he called me to him and said: "I am going to take a long trip. If anything should happen to me I expect you to look after the family. Arthur is older than you are and knows more, but you are the stronger, and know much more about farming. I am depending on you."

During that spring we had often heard Father and the neighbors complain of very hard times. As the summer advanced, through the glaring headlines of the Denver paper, which Father took at this time, and the *Delta Independent*, we older boys could not possibly escape some little knowledge of what was happening. The situation, very briefly, was developing about as follows: The price of silver had been declining for some time. On June 26, a report that the mints of India had ceased to coin silver sent the price to new depths. In four days, the market value of silver dropped from 83 to 62 cents per ounce. This was a terrible blow to Colorado, since the economy of the state depended to a large extent upon the production of silver. Almost immediately the leading mine, mill and smelter owners felt compelled to close down their enterprises until a recovery in silver prices might again permit them to operate at a profit. Hence nearly 20,000 persons, according to Senator Teller, were out of employment.

A huge mass meeting convened at Denver on July 11th and 12th to discuss the situation. Speakers painted lurid pictures of the general hardships, and made irresponsible suggestions for dealing with them. Governor Waite, who had been elected on the Populist ticket—which among other things, advocated the free and unlimited coinage of silver—spoke energetically as the champion of the poor man. One of his sentences in particular received widespread notoriety. "It is better, infinitely better", he said, "that blood should flow up to the horses' bridles than that our liberties should be destroyed." As this and other immoderate utterances were widely circulated through the press of the country, the impression was given that a wholesale repudiation of debts and even revolution was threatened in Colorado. A panic in full fury broke out in mid-July. In every large city of Colorado, people crowded the streets, stormed the banks demanding their money, and participated in scenes of wild disorder. In three days, so the papers said, ten banks closed in Denver alone, while throughout the State many banks came down with a crash.

Sometime in August the Bank of Delta went under. Mr. Wolbert, the assistant cashier of the Farmers' and Merchants' Bank telegraphed Father to return immediately, which he did. In some way or another—I think due to Dan Baldwin's contacts with money in Connecticut—the Farmers' and Merchants' Bank stood the strain and did not fail. For the first time, as far as I can remember, Father shared with us some of his thoughts concerning public and private business. He talked about the panic, about politics, and about his plans to go farther west to live.

Father explained that the prices of farm products in the west had been falling, so that people were burning corn in Kansas for fuel, horses were selling as low as five or ten dollars per head, and the price of cattle was extremely low (I remember, when staying with Grandmother, purchasing good steak at ten cents per pound and having to pay nothing for calf liver). The price of silver, which was one of the great products of western Colorado, had dropped nearly fifty per cent. Father tried to explain to us the theory of bimetallism, and the reasons for the victory of the Populist Party in Colorado under Governor Waite, which seemed to threaten revolution. Father, who was a good Republican, took the view that notwithstanding the silver situation in Colorado, the gold monetary standard should be maintained. He was sure that the Populist Party would not bring us into the promised land. I listened respectfully, but understood little of the significance of the depression or of the bitter political struggle that was taking place, despite Father's explanation.

The latter part of the summer was dry and hot. The ditch going to Garnet Mesa had run dry. We had to drive the stock to water. There was no third cutting of alfalfa, and the garden was in poor shape. Perhaps the failure of the Uncompahgre River to irrigate all the land on the mesas surrounding it had been one of Father's reasons for wishing to go to Oregon.

Labor Day was celebrated a few days after Father's return. We all got into the buggy and the lumber wagon and went down to the Gunnison River for a picnic. Father was feeling particularly happy because the run on the bank had ended and there was confidence in its stability. We had a wonderful time, playing ball, wading and swimming, and climbing tall cottonwood trees. We were all very happy because of Father's homecoming, and excited about the possibility of going to Oregon. After we returned home that evening, Mr. Wolbert and Mr. Phillips of the bank visited us, singing songs while Mother played the piano and Father played the flute.

On September 7th, 1893, the morning after Labor Day, a strong wind began to blow. A reddish dust filled the sky and hid the sun, casting an unnatural and ghastly aspect over all the landscape. Howard and I were sitting beside the icehouse. I was thinking about having to return to school in a few days, and rather dreading it. Suddenly we saw a horse and buggy coming very fast. Dr. Brasted and Mrs. Worth stepped out of the buggy. "There has been a bank robbery," they said, "and your father has been injured." We ran to the house and called Mother. She had been in the orchard with one or two of the smaller boys, gathering peaches. As she saw Mrs. Worth's face she knew that she was overtaken by absolute disaster. "Is Trew dead"? she cried. Mrs. Worth was compelled to tell her the dreadful truth: Father was dead.

We learned from our kind and sympathetic friends that Father had been shot by bank robbers, and that a posse had been formed to follow one of the robbers who had escaped. I was stunned, but I soon made up my mind to saddle my horse and join the posse.

Mother and our friends dissuaded me by saying that I was too small, and also that by this time the posse would be miles ahead of me.

Gradually we learned the details of the robbery. The McCarty gang, a group of outlaws, had planned it systematically. They had stationed fast horses every twenty miles or so between Delta and the rugged canyon and mountain country in southeastern Utah, so that they would have a constant supply of fresh mounts while fleeing to their hideout.

Two of them had entered the front door of the bank just after it opened, while a third held three horses in the alley back of the bank. The two who came in the front door walked up to the cashier's window where Father was standing, and ordered him and the other members of the staff to hold up their hands. Instead of doing so, Father shouted for help and reached under the counter for his gun. One of the robbers immediately shot him through the head, and the other jumped over the railing and took about $3,000 in cash. The man who shot Father held a gun on H. H. Wolbert, the assistant cashier, and J. Ralph Phillips, the bookkeeper, to protect himself and his companion until they could escape through the back door to their horses in the alley.

Delta's leading hardware merchant, W. R. Simpson, was one of the "crack shots" of the town. He had just finished cleaning and loading his Sharp's rifle and was standing near his open back door, when he heard the shots, the bank staff calling for help, and the shouts of the crowd that began to form. As the robbers fled northward along the alley, spurring their horses on the run, Simpson instinctively understood what had happened and began to shoot at them. Bill McCarty fell off his horse dead, just behind Grandmother's place. Simpson's shot had entered the back of his

Members of the McCarty Gang who robbed the First Farmers and Merchants Bank on the morning of September 7, 1893. From left to right: Tom McCarty, his nephew Fred, and his brother Bill (both taken posthumously). Fred pulled the trigger that killed Andrew Trew Blachly, but he and his father, Bill, were subsequently shot and killed by Ray Simpson as they tried to make their escape. (Photographs by F. M. Laycook)

head, coming out above his left eye. As Fred McCarty, Bill's son, looked back for a second, Simpson sent a second bullet through his head. He fell about 345 feet beyond his father. Most of the stolen money was found on his body. A little later in the day, the bodies of the dead robbers were propped up against a building to be photographed by Mr. Laycook. Then both of them were placed in one large box, and buried in the Pauper's Field of the Delta cemetery. By the killing of these two outlaws the McCarty gang of robbers, who had robbed many banks and had terrorized half a dozen western towns, was largely broken up.

Tom McCarty, the other member of the gang, was evidently the first to reach his horse. He threw in his spurs and managed to escape. Charles Nutter, who was also well known as a dead shot, snatched up a rifle and attempted to fire at him, but unluckily the rifle was not loaded. If it had been, the McCarty gang would have lost all three men that day instead of two.

A posse immediately started after the fleeing robber. However, McCarty made good use of the relays of the fast horses along his escape route, and eventually took cover in the fastnesses of the La Salle mountains and the Moab Valley in southeastern Utah.

Mother and all of us boys were stunned. I kept thinking that the whole affair was a nightmare from which I might awaken. We were not allowed to see Father's body until the day of the funeral, which was held from the bank. Sawdust covered the wooden floor to hide the blood stains that washing had not been able to eradicate.

The funeral procession was the largest in Delta's history. An almost continuous line of carriages extended from the town to the cemetery. Mother was not able to go to the grave, as she was prostrated, but Arthur, Clarence and I went.

Over the grave the Presbyterian minister gave a little talk, telling of Father and his good works. The Masons performed their rites; the church choir sang, "Jesus, Savior, Pilot me," and "Lead, kindly light." Then, "Dust to dust and ashes to ashes." The red earth, gravel and small stones began to fall on the wooden box holding the casket, with a thud that seemed unbearable. The grave was filled, and the people started to leave. I had never noticed before what a bare and lonely place the Delta cemetery was, with no trees, no flowers, no grass, nothing but plain mesa land filled with gravel and rocks.

Poor Mother, I do not know how she stood it, with eight young fatherless boys. Not until many years later did I learn that at the time of the tragedy another little life was on the way, and that Mother had a miscarriage due to the shock of Father's death, with only Arthur present to help her. I remember hearing her tell Mr. Wolbert that she could not go on living. "But," he said, "you must." She not only went on living, but lived so bravely and magnificently that her life was an inspiration to the whole community. Once when I returned to Delta after an absence of many years, I met again many who had known her. With no exception they spoke of the nobility of her life. "Several women of the Presbyterian church went up to try to comfort our Mother shortly after the robbery," said one of her friends, "but instead of our consoling her, it was she who brought comfort to us."

Shortly after Father's death, some kind friends sent an appeal to the bankers of the State asking them to assist his family. I know that several of them responded and also sent beautiful letters of sympathy. But only a small amount of money was raised in this way, since most of the Colorado bankers were themselves hard pressed financially.

In order to obtain photographs of the family to send to relatives, it was decided to have a sitting for them on Thanksgiving Day. Mother told me long afterward that this engagement was made because she could not spend the holiday at home without Father. All the boys were dressed to their best. At first the photographer had much difficulty with the very large feet on which Arthur prided himself. The first photograph showed up the feet to such an extent that the photographer decided to cover them with a little mat before taking another picture, but his remedy did not make the situation much better. We still have these pictures. Despite the diversion of having them taken, this was a mournful Thanksgiving for us.

At first, the loss of Father was mainly an emotional blow, but we soon began to realize what an economic tragedy it was, as well. One day I went down to the store to buy a new pair of shoes. I put them on immediately because my old ones had holes in the soles and sides. "Please charge them," I said, as I had heard Father say

Family portrait, Thanksgiving Day, 1893, ten weeks after the murder of Andrew Trew. From left to right back row: Clarence Dan (b. Dec 20, 1881), Arthur Trew (b. Nov 11, 1878), Adelle ("Dellie" – she had just miscarried her 9th child), Edward Hugh on Dellie's lap (b. Aug 16, 1892), the author Frederick Frank (b Aug 20, 1880), William Howard (b. Aug 15, 1885). Seated in front: Ralph Reamer (b. Oct 5, 1887), Louis Bradley (b Nov 5, 1889), Howard Dwight (b. Dec, 1882) (photographer unknown)

when making purchases. "I cannot do it," said the store keeper, "for I do not believe you could pay me." I was forced to take the shoes off and leave them, and to wear my old disreputable ones again. Thus, I learned for the first time the bitter lesson that the more you need credit, the less you are able to get it.

From an economic viewpoint, Father's death took place at a most unfortunate time. The first shock of the panic was followed during the autumn by continued depression. There was mass unemployment, and business was at a standstill. Hundreds of people were losing their properties by foreclosure, and chattel attachments were very common. Following the general panic and the drop in the price of silver, another action by the Federal government further tended to cripple Colorado. On November 1st, 1893, Congress repealed the Silver Purchase Act. This was a body blow to Colorado, as the sale of silver to the Federal government had been a chief source of revenue for the mine owners of the State. Senator Teller of Colorado, in a final speech against the repeal of the Act, had said in the Senate: "We do not disguise the fact that we are to go through the valley of the shadow of death. We know what it means to turn out over 20,000 silver miners in the fall of the year." There was extreme unrest and much lawlessness in many portions of the State. Within a year several bitter strikes added to the economic unrest: the strike of gold miners at Cripple Creek, the strike of coal miners, and the Pullman strike, which began in Chicago but extended to the Colorado railways, almost paralyzing transportation for two weeks. Property values were rapidly falling. Many people were leaving the State, and capital was being withdrawn because of the confused and uncertain economic situation.

The panic brought a special type of disaster to us who lived on the Western slope. The silver and gold mines at Ouray, Telluride, Rico, and other places, had formed the chief market for all kinds of produce and livestock, such as fruit, butter, eggs, vegetables, poultry, hay, oats, beef, horses and mules. Now, with the shutting down of the mines, most of this market was cut off. Freight rates were so high that little or nothing could be made by shipping goods to Denver and the eastern markets.

Before the panic many farmers, after working their farms in the spring and summer, would haul ore or work in the mines in the fall and winter, thus bringing in money to improve their farms or assist their families. With the shutting of the mines, this source of income was cut off.

The town of Delta reflected the bad economic situation in many ways. Several businesses were forced into bankruptcy. Real estate values fell off in the town and in all the regions around it. Men who had lost their usual means of earning an income were looking for positions or jobs of any kind. But work could not be found.

These economic difficulties existed for several years. They were gradually lessened in part by the general recovery that always follows a panic as demand develops. A special factor leading to improvements in Colorado was the mining of valuable ores other than silver. As the rich deposits of gold at Cripple Creek were exploited, renewed employment for miners, markets for agricultural products, and many other favorable economic consequences were felt. Deep mining in the San Juan area produced lead, zinc, and copper as well as silver with similar beneficial results to the economy of Colorado. The discovery and exploitation of petroleum gave further impetus to recovery.

Meanwhile, our family had to face some hard years. During the period of extreme depression, it became necessary to review our whole financial situation. Mother had never had any business experience and knew almost nothing about the affairs of the family. Father had never told her of his business operations unless for some reason it became absolutely necessary to do so. He had always done the family purchasing, even buying all the groceries. However, at the suggestion of Father's former partner Lyman I. Henry, Mother was appointed administratrix of Father's estate. With the assistance of Dan Baldwin, Father's partner in the bank, and Mr. Wolbert, the assistant cashier, she finally worked out a financial statement of assets and liabilities. The statement showed that Father had left the following property:

- 300 acres of desert land, with a small mortgage on it.
- 160 acres of the old Oak Creek ranch, with a mortgage of $600.
- 115 acres on lower Garnet Mesa (the home place), nominally valued at $7,000, with a mortgage of $2,500.
- 35 acres on middle Garnet Mesa, with a $1,500 mortgage.
- The balance due of $500 for a ten-acre tract sold to Mr. Mays, to be paid by him in small annual installments.
- A very little cash.

There were several small bills to be paid, as well as the funeral expenses. What could be done in this situation? Upon the advice of Mr. Wolbert, Mother gave up the desert land and the old homestead in Oak Creek. The depression had devaluated these places until it seemed foolish to continue to hold them, paying interest and taxes.

The problem of basic importance was, what to do about the large farm on the lower Garnet Mesa and the thirty-five acres on the middle mesa. Mr. Wolbert advised Mother to hold the lower mesa farm and sell the upper thirty-five acres. However, she said that she preferred to sell the lower ranch. To this plan, I objected most strenuously. I felt that we boys were experienced enough in farming and could run the place. Its orchards, vineyards, alfalfa fields, and other long-time growths were already developed. There were plenty of buildings, livestock and equipment. Mother insisted that we owed too much to hold it, that the money obtained by selling it would help our financial situation, and that the boys were too small to work the large ranch. She also had a strong desire to escape from the constant reminder of her intolerable loss, which pressed upon her at every side in the house and on the land where she had lived with Father. Hence, we sold the large farm and retained only the land on middle Garnet Mesa. Because of the financial panic, Mother obtained only $4,500 for the farm or $2,000 above the mortgage.

I protested vigorously against moving to the middle mesa, for I had had some experience with this land. Since most of it was higher than the land immediately surrounding it, irrigation water could not be brought upon it in the ordinary way. To irrigate the ten acres that I had plowed and planted two years before, it had been necessary to build a dyke about three feet high, with an irrigation ditch through its center, running half-way across the south side of the place. This ditch, when extended, enabled us to water at most, only fifteen acres. There were five or six acres on the northeastern part of the place that could not be irrigated except by making another small dyke and running a part of our one-half acre foot of water[4] from the Garnet Mesa Ditch through the main ditch of one of our neighbors. Another five or six acres could be irrigated only if we graded off the tops of two knolls. In fact, we could irrigate only about five acres in the whole place simply by gravity flow of water from the main ditch.

I mention these details because they were a controlling factor in our economic situation and because for several years they profoundly affected my state of mind. With water as scarce as it was, I felt a constant rebellion against the waste from absorption by the soil and from evaporation as the water flowed slowly through the nearly level dykes. The work of keeping the water running through the dykes—dykes that were continually breaking, that had to be cleared of silt three or four times a season, and that

---

4 Water rights in the American Southwest are calculated by "acre feet." One-half acre foot is the amount of water it takes to cover an acre to a depth of 6 inches.

were always overgrown and clogged by yellow sweet clover which grew six or seven feet tall and must be cut back repeatedly—invariably seemed to come when we should have been planting, cultivating or harvesting.

When water was particularly scarce and we should have been supplying it directly to the land, it evaporated from the almost gradeless dykes and ditches. The grading down of the knolls, which with modern machinery would have been a simple process, was slow and expensive with ordinary slip scrapers. Also, where the top soil was taken off, the soil was of little value until heavily fertilized. The tract where we planted the orchard had to be irrigated on a bias, due to its steepness. This made for many short rows and small triangular spaces. Plowing and cultivating these numerous little triangles not only took extra work and time, but always made me furious because it was necessary to drag the plow around and around and to keep twisting and turning with the cultivator. As the garden land was subject to the difficulties connected with the dyke, the little water that we had toward the ends of dry summers could not be put to effective use to finish up our crops of vegetables needed for the winter.

Of course, I did not see all of these difficulties at the age of thirteen as clearly as I did later, but I saw enough of them to know that our move was a tragic mistake. During all my life on the middle mesa farm, I found no reason to think otherwise.

As I look back upon the move after many years of experience, my judgement is still against it. We left a completely workable and productive place, with its houses, outbuildings, barns, corrals, orchard, vineyard and large, well established alfalfa fields, for one in which we had to start with very little more than the soil itself. The configuration of the land made farming operations extremely difficult. The new place required a great deal of preparatory work before it could be operated. The orchard and vineyard on which Mother insisted, had to be planted and cultivated for several years before we could secure any return from them. Buildings and corrals had to be constructed. Even if the whole place had been planted to crops giving an immediate yield, it could not produce a good living for a family of nine, or give the boys sufficient work to do in the summer. This was shown by the fact that within two or three years, we had to rent a good deal of land.

Finally, if we moved at all, we should have gone to a college town such as Boulder or Colorado Springs, where the older boys could have found positions of various sorts, where all the children could have obtained a good education at the proper age, and where Mother could have made congenial friends and led a much more pleasant and less laborious life than on this inadequate farm.

CHAPTER VI

The Elms

As soon as Mother sold our farm on the lower Garnet Mesa, which was to be delivered, if I remember rightly, about the first of February 1894, we began to make plans for our new home. It was decided with the advice of Mr. Baldwin, who was a carpenter by trade, that we should erect a four-room house with two rooms downstairs, which were to be plastered, and two rooms upstairs which might be plastered when our circumstances improved. The house was to cost $700, thus using up nearly all our available capital.

Charlie Mundry agreed to help us haul stone from a quarry located some twelve or thirteen miles away on California Mesa. The weather was bitterly cold. Part of the time we had to walk to keep our hands and feet from freezing. We would quarry out a load of stone, deliver it at the new place, and go back for more. It took three or four days to get enough stone for the foundation, which was about twenty-four feet by sixteen, and two feet high. The frame house was soon completed and we moved in.

In the kitchen we had a large range which burned either wood or coal. A stove pipe running up through the ceiling had a "drum" in it, which was the only way of warming the boys' bedroom. We arranged the south room downstairs as a sitting room, with our trusty anthracite burner. For the first year or so we rarely used it in winter for lack of fuel. Above the sitting room was Mother's bedroom, with a large coal heating stove, which I remember she kept red hot during the coldest winter days.

In selling the large farm on the lower mesa, Mother had reserved far too little of the farm equipment and livestock necessary to do adequate farming. I think that perhaps she had to agree to throw in as much of the equipment with the place in order to make the sale. We retained a plow, a hay rack, and a cultivator. Mother also kept a rather decrepit lumber wagon with tires so thin that when brakes were applied to them for even a short time, they grew hot and expanded sufficiently to become loose from the wooden rim of the wheels. Often before taking a long trip we would soak the wheels in water so that the wood and the tires would not part company. Even then, at times, we would have to get out and drive the tires back into their right places. The old wagon was a continual source of annoyance, trouble, and even shame. One day when I was delivering a load of coal in Delta, I lost one of the tires. Some little boys in the main street of the town yelled: "Hey your tire's off!" I paid no attention to them for a moment, but then realizing that their statement might be true, I looked back, and there was my tire lying on the ground, while the wheel was running on the wooded rim. Luckily, we were within a few hundred feet of the blacksmith's shop where the tire could be reset.

Mother had reserved a nice part-Jersey cow called Juno, and her daughter Cleopatra, a young heifer who would have a calf in the fall. She also kept two horses. Old "Snoozer" was a large black horse weighing about 1,200 pounds, who was strong, kind, and absolutely trustworthy. Poor Snoozer had developed some sort of mange, which caused his skin to roughen until it resembled that of an elephant. This mange was a continual cause of mortification for me, for I felt disgraced whenever anyone saw me driving Snoozer. "Roebuck", a buckskin-colored Morgan horse weighing about 1,000 pounds, had once had a frostbitten ear, so that only about one half of it remained. This defect did not impair his usefulness, but in a minor way it also caused me a certain amount of shame. Roebuck was an extremely reliable workhorse, and could be used on occasion for riding or for pulling the buggy.

The first winter on the new place was relatively warm, and the ground was in shape for plowing by February. As there was little snow on the mountains, we feared a dry season. We decided to grade down a part of the knoll back of the house in order to plant a grain field there and a garden north of it. We had to clear a certain amount of sage brush from the knoll. Once again, the smell of the burning brush gave me pleasure.

When the land was cleared, we took a borrowed slip scraper and began to grade down the top of the knoll. This was slow work. At times, when the scraper would strike a large stone, I would be almost thrown over. The March winds began to blow and covered us with thick dust. I developed "pink eye" and felt miserable. To get away from so much dust I began to haul manure from the livery stables in Delta for the garden—the lesser of two evils.

About this time Mother fell sick with Bright's Disease. Uncle Frank, who had been staying with Grandmother after Father's death, took care of her. We had a dreadful time that spring. I think Mother had practically no money. Grandmother had no income except a small annuity, and was now very feeble and old. Uncle Frank, who had not been able to save much money from his small salary as doctor for the Ute Indians at Ignacio, was also having a hard time financially. This meant that we were in actual want for a time.

Mother was not expected to live. The wind was blowing gales each day and the sky was full of dust. Arthur spent most of his time taking care of her, while Clarence looked after the house as well as he was able, and with the help of Hal, did the cooking. Our meals consisted chiefly of a tough pan bread concocted by Clarence and Hal. It was about an inch thick and had the consistency of leather. The chickens were not laying well, and such few eggs as they did lay had to be sold in order to obtain the necessary groceries. The cow was far from "fresh," and milk was scarce. Howard and I had to spend all our time in the fields, grading off the miserable knoll, plowing, sowing grain and planting the garden.

About the first of April Mother grew better, the wind stopped blowing, and things looked brighter. I started back to school again, much behind, but I just managed to pass into the eighth grade by the time school closed.

Early in April several large boxes of fruit trees arrived. They had been sent by my Uncle John Blachly, who had a nursery in Kansas. Mother had decided that we should have a fruit and chicken farm. The papers were full of glowing accounts of the money that could be made from orchards. In print, the prospect appeared wonderful. You could plant about 100 apple trees to the acre. Each tree would soon produce more than a bushel of apples, at two or three dollars per bushel. After a short time, the trees would be producing eight or ten barrels apiece. Also, if you were smart, you could plant the apple trees about thirty feet apart each way, and in between them plant peach trees, which would start bearing within two years. The peach trees would then not only pay for the cost of getting the apple trees into bearing, but would make a profit in the meantime.

In support of this reasoning, it could be pointed out that several men in Paonia, on the North Fork of the Gunnison, had made a good deal of money by fruit growing. The county went wild with the idea of making fortunes, and thus, hundreds of acres on Garnet Mesa were planted to orchard. There seemed to be no thought of the fact that some parts of the county were subject to late killing frosts, that an orchard had to be constantly sprayed to keep down the insects, that the cost of selling in the eastern markets would be almost prohibitive due to the high freight rates over the mountains, that there might be a glut in the market, that the cost of picking and packing so as to conform with demand might be high; that commissions had to be paid, and finally, that the big money had been made when there was a strong market near home in the mining towns of Ouray, Telluride and Silverton.

The choice of apple trees for us, whether made by Mother or Uncle John, was not fortunate. A great majority of them were Ben Davis, which gave heavy crops of apples that were not much demanded in the eastern markets. We also had a good many Arkansas Blacks, which remained as hard as rocks until about April or May when they began to yield to the softening of old age.

The man who helped us to plant the orchard insisted that the rows of trees should run diagonally north east by southwest, instead of north and south. He was probably right from the viewpoint of getting the largest possible number of trees planted on ground watered from the irrigation ditch, and for preventing wash due to the steepness of the land, but this arrangement caused much difficulty later on. Altogether we planted some six or seven acres to orchard in this way.

I rebelled strongly at the thought of planting so much of our best land to orchard, as I felt that we needed it for hay and grain. I knew it would be several years before we could realize on fruit, but we could raise hay and grain immediately. I desperately wanted to get into the cattle business, as that appeared much more exciting than raising fruit.

Along with the fruit trees came eight little elm trees about the size of a man's thumb and six or seven feet tall. We planted them in a half square to the south and east of the house, and called the ranch after them: "The Elms." One of the elm trees was named for each boy. They grew very fast and soon became rather a landmark on the mesa, as most of the shade trees planted at that time were cottonwoods. These elms have been a source of pleasure not only to our family, but to those who followed us. The last time I saw them several years ago, they were fifty or sixty feet high and so large that it took two persons to reach around them. In the boxes from Kansas were also some roses, which we planted north of the house in a row parallel to the orchard.

Because of the winds, which for the best part of two or three years had been violent, we were advised to plant a windbreak west of the orchard. We secured many small poplar trees and planted them about three feet apart along the main ditch. They grew far more rapidly than the apple and peach trees, and soon gave the orchard real protection.

In order to have a pond of water for the livestock when the ditch was frozen in winter or when there was no water in the summertime, we built a dam across the little gully toward the north and center of the place. Thus, we had a reservoir some six or seven feet deep near the dam, which backed up water for seventy-five or eighty feet. We also used this pond for a swimming pool, as Mother would not often allow us to go down to the Gunnison River for fear we might be drowned. I suppose she was wise, as the river was swift and had many whirlpools. Howard was once caught in an eddy of the Gunnison and it was only by virtue of his great strength that he was able to swim out.

The summer, as had been predicted, was very dry. The wheat "made," and we had a good first cutting of alfalfa from the northwest plot of ground. We also had some early vegetables. As water became scarce, Mother insisted that it be applied to the orchard instead of to the alfalfa fields and the garden. Water grew scarcer and scarcer. The little that came into our ditch almost all evaporated, or was sucked into the earth as it ran through the dyke and the ditch. In addition to these difficulties, we had water only once in two weeks and then only for a day or so because use of water in the region was rotated among the large irrigation ditches drawing water directly from the Uncompahgre River. A water commissioner had the task of seeing that there were no violations. The alfalfa fields began to get brown, the garden withered, and the little trees looked as though they were going to die. In order to keep the new trees alive, we had to haul water from the Delta water tank that stood on the edge of Garnet Mesa overlooking town. Delta itself had plenty of water from the Gunnison River—water which only had to be pumped into the tank. The Gunnison was a large stream and there was little land under it that could be irrigated, so that it never ran dry. It seemed a tragedy that with this large stream of water so near, our crops should be burning up.

Toward the latter part of the summer, we convinced Mother that we should be allowed to go hunting on the Grand Mesa. We loaded our blankets into the wagon, filled the grub box, prepared our hunting equipment—consisting of a 40-92 rifle, a ten-gauge shotgun, and a 22 rifle—and started up the mountain from the head of Oak Creek valley. The old road had been washed out in places and was almost impassable. However, just before sunset we arrived at the old deserted Baldwin milk ranch, which was at the bottom of a rather large bare slope by the creek. "I wonder who that big man is at the top of the slope?" Arthur said. We looked up just in time to see a form resembling that of a tall man drop forward and slink down on forefeet. It was undoubtedly a bear. Though he disappeared at once over the crest of the slope, we slept none too well that night. We built our beds inside the broken-down walls of the old cabin. The roof had fallen in, and a large log lay over the top of the wall, projecting into the room. Suddenly in the middle of the night Arthur rose up and yelled, "There's that bear!" He pointed to the projecting log. I think he must have had a nightmare, as he often did.

As soon as we had eaten breakfast the next morning, we started after the bear. When we got to the top of the slope, we found his tracks along the cattle trail. They were over a foot long and eight or ten inches wide. A notable peculiarity of the tracks was the absence of the large toe of the left hind foot. We followed the tracks for a long time, hoping that we would find him. At one point we thought we saw him, as a dark form ran through the brush. It proved to be nothing more, however, than a large black cow. We finally lost the tracks in a large flow of slide rocks. God should be praised, that the little boys did not find that big bear! We spent two or three happy days hunting, although we did not get much game except a few grouse and rabbits. We also caught some trout. This expedition was one of the bright spots of that hard year.

When we returned from the hunting trip, it was decided that we must have a root cellar to store our potatoes, pumpkins, Hubbard squash, any fruit we had canned, and the apples or other fruit which we would surely have within a year or so. We dug a hole with perpendicular sides about ten feet wide, fifteen feet long, and six feet deep. We were able to take out some of the dirt with a slip scraper, but most of the work had to be done by hand. The days were broiling hot, the ground was hard and stony, the pick was large and the shovel grew heavier as we neared the bottom. We went down to the Gunnison River and secured some cottonwood logs for the sides, roof beams and timbers. We then thatched them over with willow wands, and later when the grain was thrashed, covered the whole thing with straw and then with dirt. It was not a thing of beauty, but it was efficient, and it still stands, or perhaps sits. Things never froze in it, although in the very coldest nights we kept a lantern burning to give a trifle of heat. We made bins for the different kinds of fruits and vegetables, which, while rather bare the first year, were afterward filled with supplies for the winter.

Led by the tireless and industrious Frederick Frank, the brothers teamed up to build several structures, including this root cellar. (photo by FF Blachly, c. 1934)

When we had harvested what little there was to harvest, our return for nearly a year's work consisted of an orchard that was still alive but not ready to bear, eight or ten tons of alfalfa hay from the land I had plowed up and planted to oats and alfalfa two years before, enough grain to feed the chickens, some potatoes that had matured before the drought, and some pumpkins and Hubbard squash. Most of the other vegetables, such as beets, turnips, and beans, had gone by the board.

In some way or other, we had also managed to build a combined ice house and granary. Now we had to consider the problem of protecting our horses and cows from the winter blasts. Before the threshers came, we set up some logs and poles with willow wands over them. Then, after the threshing we piled the straw over three sides and the top. This made a warm stable. The only difficulty was that by spring the animals had eaten much of the straw.

I started school in the fall of 1894 quite late. I had been compelled to stay out so much in the spring that I had finished the seventh grade only, I think, because of the mercy of the teachers. I had missed several important processes in arithmetic. When I arrived at school, I found myself in a new world of subject matter. The class was nearly a month ahead of me in algebra and Latin. I tried desperately to catch up, but did not seem to be able to do so.

One day Eddie Mays and I were playing at recess, pretending we were pugilists having a prize fight. We had made a ring and all the boys were standing around to see the big fight between Eddie and me. I hit Eddie square on the nose and it began to bleed profusely. Just then the principal, Mr. Harris, came out and immediately pounced on me. "A nice little Sunday School boy, a nice little Christian!" he said. I was as strong as a bull, or at least I thought I was, and as Mr. Harris was a slight man, I thought that he would be no match for me. My blood was hot from fighting. "If you talk like that," I said to him, "I will fix you as I did Eddie Mays." He walked away. That night I pondered the matter deeply. I knew that we were desperately hard up and felt that I should go to work. I did not see how I could catch up in school even if I attended regularly, much less if I had to stay out and work as the needs of the farm demanded while trying to carry such unfamiliar subjects as Latin and algebra. There might also be some slight difficulty with the principal! Mother tried her best to dissuade me from leaving school, but my mind was made up. I did not enter an institution of learning again for eleven years.

During the fall weather we prepared for winter by hauling several loads of wood, as well as coal from the Winton mine. The wood could be had without cost by going up into the cedar belt on Grand Mesa, and we could secure coal on shares by hauling an equal quantity to deliver to the mine's customers. One afternoon late in November, we drove up for a load of wood and camped on the banks of Dirty George Creek. As it turned very cold, we built a large fire by the south side of a great stone to act as a windbreak. We ran two poles from logs near the fire, on which we draped an old heavy quilt as a further shelter. After the fire began to get low, we went to bed, and soon fell asleep to the sound of the roaring mountain stream. Toward morning we were awakened by rain dripping onto our faces from the old quilt. We got up, rebuilt the fire, and cooked breakfast in the rain. Although the downpour continued, we cut a load of cedar and pinon wood and put it on the wagon. It was about one o'clock when we started for home.

The roads were very muddy and slippery. Wet to the skin, we drearily plodded down Dirty George Creek and Tongue Creek. As it was growing late when we reached the junction where we would either have to continue down Tongue Creek or turn into the road across the adobes, we decided to take the former route as it was shorter and would probably be less slippery. This road ran along the creek for a few miles, and then through some rather swampy land drained by several small runs or drainage ditches.

By the time we reached the low part of the road it was pitch dark. We could not see a thing except some sort of phosphorescent glow, known as St. Elmo's fire, on the harness hames. We trusted implicitly in our horses, who it was claimed could see very well in the dark. Suddenly, however, we felt the wagonload of wood going over. We jumped, and just missed being thrown under the side of the load as it went off a little bridge into one of the drainage ditches. It was so dark and was raining so hard, that we could do nothing but unhitch the horses and ride them home bareback for five or six miles. It was about twelve o'clock at night when we reached home, soaked, hungry, tired, and discouraged. We went back after the wood the next day. We had to unload the wood, drag the wagon out of the mud, right it, and reload it, all covered over with mud as it was. But we had our wood.

I began hunting for a job, but there was no work to be had. Everyone on the Mesa had been hit by the dry season. The town was still in the grip of the panic and was hurt by the general failure of crops.

On Thanksgiving Day we had no meat in the house, much less a turkey. Arthur and I went out hunting in the morning and killed a large jackrabbit, which Mother cooked for dinner. It did not taste too bad, at least not as bad as the proverbial crow.

Finally, one day early in December, Mr. Pike, who lived about a mile from us, said that he had a contract to ship some baled hay to the mining camps and that he would like Arthur and me to help him at wages of a dollar a day apiece. We agreed to do this. Arthur, who was not very strong, was to tie the bales, that is, adjust the wires and fasten them. I was given the job of carrying the bales away from the baler and stacking them in piles six or eight bales high. As the bales weighted from 90 to 100 pounds this was no easy task. I felt very strong, however, and was able to keep up the work, which lasted about a month. After this there was no work to be had.

One of our great joys about this time was skating. North of town was an old slough shaped rather like an "L" that would freeze completely solid. The boys from town and from the mesa would build a large fire on the bank, where we would put on our skates or rest after the strenuous exercise on the ice playing "popping the whip," racing one another, playing tag, jumping or trying to cut fancy figures. One night when I was skating around the elbow of the "L" very fast, I ran into Eva Sanders head on. Down she sank, entirely "knocked out." The crowd of boys and girls gathered around cut up flakes of ice with their sharp skates and applied it to her head. In a few moments she revived and went on skating again. I was mightily relieved, as I had almost feared that I had killed her.

We often skated for miles up the deep ice on the Gunnison River, despite the fact that this was dangerous, as in some places where the river was swift there would be great holes in the ice. Good skaters liked to go there, however, because of the long stretches where the ice was as smooth as glass and few skaters to cut it up. One day while I was gliding over a long smooth place, I suddenly saw within a few yards of me was not, as I had supposed, beautiful clear ice, but rather a stretch of water about thirty feet wide where men had been cutting ice for storage. I jumped sideways, threw my sharp skates at an angle into the ice, and stopped just in time to avoid going into the water. If I had gone in, I should not be living to tell the tale, since the water was deep and my companions were quite a distance behind me. I could not possibly have crawled out or even held on to the absolutely smooth ice on either side.

The same day I was skating backward and failed to notice that I was going toward the bank of the stream where the ice sharply slanted upward. Backward I went to the top of the slope, then like a flash my skates started down again. The back of my head hit the ice with such a bang that I thought the stars were falling.

By the spring of 1895, our circumstances were becoming more and more difficult. We had used up our very little money. No work of any sort could be found. Our cow, Juno, had dried up and would not be fresh again until late spring. The heifer, Cleopatra, should have had a calf in the previous fall, but unfortunately, she became bloated from eating green alfalfa. Following the usual custom, I stuck her with a knife about six inches in front of the hip line between this bone and the ribs, to let the gas out. Something went wrong. She lost her calf and became thin as a rail so that we thought she would die. The chickens were not laying half enough eggs to buy groceries. Mother was too proud to ask for help.

We lived for several days on boiled grains of wheat. Even our grain supply was becoming exhausted. Finally, as I learned later, Mother spent the whole night in prayer. The next morning, she had nothing left in the house to cook, no money, and no credit. Things looked desperate. At family worship Mother read the verse from the Bible: "I have been young, and now am old, yet have I not seen the righteous forsaken, nor his seed begging bread." Just after worship there was a knock at the door. Mr. Obert, the milkman, who I believe was also County Commissioner, drove up to bring us several sacks of flour and a big basket of groceries. He told us that he would be glad to give us two quarts of milk a day if we would come after it. Mother believed that this was a direct answer to her payers. I am inclined to think that some of the good neighbors had suspected our plight, and had asked the county commissioners to help us.

About this time Aunt Sarah came to visit us. I think she must have helped Mother a little financially or secured help for us from some other relatives, since after this we were able to buy groceries and to get enough seed for the spring planting. Clarence was asked by Aunt Sarah to go to California to live with her at her home in Oakland, which he did.

As the winter had been very snowy and cold, we felt assured that there would be a good supply of irrigating water. We therefore planted as much of the place as was subject to irrigation. We had fertilized the orchard with "alfalfa manure" partly made from alfalfa that had been allowed to go to seed, with the result that alfalfa began to grow there luxuriantly between the trees, although we wanted the ground clean for cultivation. The alfalfa had a very good start before we quite realized what had happened. As it did not yield to cultivation, during the latter part of the summer we had to dig it up with a heavy mattock. I hated the orchard and saw no future in it.

The dyke filled up with silt very rapidly, as the melting of the heavy snow, plus rain, had caused the river to assume freshet proportions and carry great quantities of silt. Sweet clover grew up over the dyke faster than we could cut it. We found that the northeastern knoll had not been graded enough in spots to permit the water to flow through the furrows without digging down each individual furrow some three inches to get over a little hump.

Mr. May's chickens began to scratch up the wheat that we had planted. I was too busy to do anything about it, but the smaller boys made slings, just like the one used by David in his fight with Goliath, as we thought. Filling the slings with small stones, which were plentiful, the boys "whammed away" at the chickens. The chickens would make a half-flying departure, but almost immediately return. They ruined about half an acre, despite the sling shots. I do not remember that the boys ever hit a chicken. Altogether I began to feel tired and discouraged.

Toward summer, however, things began to brighten up a bit. W. O. Stephens asked if we would want to put up some of his hay on shares. He said also that he had a colt which we could use if we could break it. As we thought we knew enough about horses to break any colt, we gladly agreed to this proposition. The colt proved gentle and was not difficult to break. All the boys, little and big, worked in the hay field. Presently we traded quite a few loads of the hay which constituted our share, for groceries, clothing, or meeting our bills. We hauled it directly downtown, which meant a trip of not much more than half a mile from the hayfield.

Due to the heavy snow in the mountains, there was plenty of irrigation water even in the late summer, and as a consequence we had good crops: plenty of hay for the horses and cows, many bushels of wheat for the chickens, and quantities of potatoes, cabbage, squash, pumpkins, beets and turnips. We had also gathered several barrels of apples from Mr. Stephens' orchard on shares. Old Juno had birthed a calf in the spring and was giving plenty of milk, and Cleopatra had recovered. Mother was able to can quite a few quarts of fruit and had dried several bushels of apples and peaches over a little dehydrator she kept on the back of the kitchen stove. The cellar was full and there was no danger of starving that winter!

Once, toward the latter part of the summer, when I was bringing a load of coal down a steep road near the Winton mine, the back tires of our old wagon became so hot due to constant use of the brakes that they expanded and started to fall off. I had to stop every half mile or so to bang them on again. The road was so narrow that the teamsters back of me could not get by. They swore that no one should be allowed on the road with such a "damned old rattletrap." Sadly, my vehicle was all that they said it was. Although our team could easily pull a load of two tons, the wagon would not hold up under a load of more than one ton, so that we lost much time and effort in making extra trips. Something had to be done. In some way or another, we persuaded the hardware man to sell us a wagon "on time." We promised to pay for it by hauling coal. This wagon was a new "three-and-a-quarter" Studebaker that cost $100. I was never prouder in my life than I felt as I sat in the spring seat and started to drive. It had a bright green wagon box and red wheels, and appeared more beautiful to me than would a new Cadillac now. But the thing which impressed me most was the fact that the tires were three-quarters of an inch thick. No danger that these tires would ever grow too hot and fall off!

We became ambitious to build a new stable for the horses and a good barn for the cows. I decided that we could do this by going up on the Grand Mesa for logs, and hauling the lumber on shares from the Uncompahgre lumber camps. To bring the logs we took off the wagon box and put a very long coupling pole in its place so that we could extend the distance between the front and back wheels sufficiently to hold logs twenty-five feet in length. We placed as much hay as we could on the arms connecting the back axle to the coupling pole, added a sack of oats for the horses, a "grub box" filled with provisions and cooking utensils, and a big roll of blankets. Thus equipped, we started up the mesa, taking turns between riding on the front bolster of the wagon to drive the horses, and sitting on the pile of hay and blankets.

At sunset we were a mile or so from the top of the mountain. We decided to camp in the quaking aspens instead of going on to the top, where we knew it was much colder. We blanketed the horses, made our bed on some of the hay we had brought for them, and went to sleep. What was our surprise to wake in the morning with five or six inches of snow all over us. We made an early start that morning. When we reached the top of the mesa, we saw across a large open space a beautiful grove of standing dead spruce trees that had no bark. These were just what we wanted. We worked very hard all day, cutting and loading fine logs about eight inches in diameter and twenty-five feet long. Although dried spruce is not very heavy, because of the size and the length of the logs, we had a hard time getting the last ones on the wagon. We fastened them all together with a log chain, so that they would not slip.

The sun was just beginning to set when we started across the large open space for the rim of the mountain. After we had gone not more than a quarter mile, the back wheels of the wagon sank down so that the horses could not pull the load. We got off to examine the situation. Evidently the open space was marshy land which had frozen up enough to sustain the empty wagon in the early morning, but could not hold the heavy load of logs.

We decided we could camp where we were, drag the logs over the edge of the mountain the next morning, and reload them. The snow was now nearly two feet deep and the air was beginning to feel cold. The first thing we did was to take off the log chain and to use it in dragging firewood from the forest. Then we dug down into the snow to make a place for a fire and for our bed. The poor horses had nothing to eat except some oats, as we needed the little remaining hay to serve as our bed. They had no water and had to lick the snow. We melted some snow over the camp fire for our coffee and drinking water. It tasted of the smoke from the spruce logs, but anything hot was appreciated. We were not cold down in the snow, and we slept well.

The next morning, we got up at the break of day and cooked breakfast. We then unloaded about one half of the logs; and by hitching the log chain around three or four at a time we "snaked" them over the snow below the rim of the mountain. This process took most of the day. Next, we drove the wagon with its lightened load over the rim, and reloaded the logs that we had snaked down. It was about four o'clock when we finally got all the logs back on the wagon and the chain set around them. We started down the mountain. After two or three miles we came to a part of the road that slanted to one side a great deal, so that in some spots one wheel-track was considerably higher than the other. Suddenly, in one of these places, the back end of the wagon hit a large stone, the wagon skidded, the left hind wheel struck a great rock with a frightful smash, and something seemed to give way. We got off to see what had happened, and found that the left wheel had caved in and would not carry the heavy load of logs farther. We unloaded the logs, left them on the high side of the road, and started home. Fortunately, the broken wheel would still carry the weight of the wagon—our new wagon.

We arrived home long after midnight. As we did not dare leave the logs long for fear someone would take them, early in the morning we went down to the hardware man and demanded a new wheel. It was our plea that if the wheel had been any good, a little skid would not have caved it in. We were honest enough about it, for we had no appreciation for the momentum that would result from the skid of a heavy load twenty-five feet long. The hardware man finally gave us a new wheel free of charge, and that same day we started up again for the abandoned logs. But we decided to camp there for the night as this location was much warmer than the higher land. There was a bit of snow on the ground here, but not nearly so much as farther up on the mountain. We used the hay which would be given to the horses the next day, as bedding. About the middle of the night, I was awakened by heavy breathing over my head. I looked up and there in the moonlight I could see a long-horned cow standing at the end of the improvised mattress, eating hay almost from under my head. I gave a yell. The cow snorted and disappeared into the cedars.

We rose before daylight, cooked breakfast, and started up after the logs. No one had taken them, so we painfully loaded them on and started home, at last arriving safely with most of the makings of a horse stable.

We still had to get lumber for the stable roof and for the cow barn. Mr. Skinner, who was a neighbor of ours on Garnet Mesa, managed a sawmill on the Uncompahgre Plateau southwest of Delta. We arranged to haul a load of lumber for him in return for a load ourselves. The mill was located near the top of the plateau toward the head of the Escalante canyon country, where we had gone camping with Father a few years before. To get the two loads of lumber meant almost a three days' trip. We rigged out the wagon as for the logging trip, started very early, and were able to make the camp near the lumber mill and loaded on about 1,500 board feet of lumber. The load was very high, and I began to notice that the road had a different appearance from the top of the load of lumber, going downhill, than it had displayed as we came up the mountain on the empty wagon.

About six miles from the mill was a very steep bluff along whose side the narrow road led down into the Cottonwood Canyon. Just about the time we were arriving at this part of the road, we met a lumber hauler coming up to the lumber mill. He told us that a few hours before another hauler had had a runaway down this bluff, and that he and his horse had gone over the steep mountain side and had been killed. The news did not make us too happy. We got down safely, however, and then started up the narrow road leading out of the canyon. It must have been five or six miles long, with hardly a place wide enough for two wagons to pass. We arrived safely and delivered the lumber, and after making another trip for our own lumber, we started to build the stable for the horses and the barn for the cows.

The stable was to be about twenty feet long and twelve feet wide. We had enough logs to build it up eight feet before we put on the roof. Since we had seen log cabins built, we had no trouble in making it. We thought nothing of using tools, for we had used them almost from babyhood. Father had secured a good tool chest when we first went to Oak Creek, and had encouraged us to learn the use of the various implements. Arthur was particularly handy with tools, and did brilliant work on the stable. This little building still stands, but is now used as a tenant house.

When the stable was finished, we built a barn for the cows about seventy feet north of the stable and parallel to it. The space between the two buildings was used for stacking hay. The next summer, we got another load of logs and built a large corral north of the cow barn. The horses and cows were now well provided for, even in the cold of winter.

Horse stable, constructed of logs by the Blachly boys, later converted for use as a tenant house. (photo by FF Blachly, c. 1934)

CHAPTER VII

Hauling Coal

As soon as the stables and barn were finished, Arthur started back at school, where the other boys had been going quite regularly since Father's death. I did not go with them. It was my plan to haul coal, partly in exchange for necessities, and partly for cash. Hence, I made arrangements with several men downtown, to supply them with coal in exchange for clothing, groceries and blacksmith work. I also hauled coal for several neighbors in order to get enough cash to pay for the new wagon.

Judging from various outcroppings, a thick vein of coal extended almost the entire length of Grand Mesa at a uniform level of about 8,000 feet. At the western end of the mesa, which was only 10,000 feet high, the coal was of a rather soft bituminous variety. As the mesa increased in height the coal became harder and of much better quality. Toward the eastern end of the mesa, where it joined the main range, its elevation was 13,000 feet and the coal was of a hard black anthracite type. Evidently the quality of the coal depended almost altogether upon the pressure of the rocks and soil above it.

There were two mines from which I hauled coal: the Rollins mine toward the western end of the mesa, and the Winton mine toward its center.

The Rollins mine was about nine miles from Delta, but according to the teamsters who hauled from it, the latter end of the road leading to it ran "three miles straight up." This road was in fact, so steep that despite its zigzag course, about all a team could do was to draw an empty wagon to the mine. Going down the steepest part of the road presented other difficulties. In winter when ice and snow made the descent especially dangerous, it was necessary to "rough-lock" the wheels. That is, great heavy chains two or more feet long with square steel links were fastened around the felly (rim) and tires of one rear wheel, then connected with a log chain to the front bolster of the wagon. This not only effectively locked the wheel, but also cut into the ice sufficiently to prevent the heavy loaded wagon from pushing the horses down the hill.

When the road was covered with ice and snow it was necessary to have the horses sharp shod to keep them from falling. Once when I was driving my four-horse team with a trailer down this road, some years after our move to the Elms, my rough-lock chain broke. As the wagon rolled forward on the horses I knew instantly what had happened. Taking my long four-horse whip, I cracked it over the leaders. The team leaped forward, and down the mountain we went on the run until we came to more level ground. Luckily the break had occurred just below the zigzag on a rather straight stretch. I had done a very risky thing, but it probably was not so dangerous as having the wagon strike the horses, throwing them down with a load of coal on top of them and hurling me into the very center of the grand mash-up.

The Rollins coal burned well, but did not give off as much heat or last as long as the harder coal farther east at the Minton mine, which I preferred. Although hauling from the Rollins mine was dangerous, there were several reasons why we patronized it, in part because Howard preferred it. In the first place, the coal was cheap: $1.50 per ton at the mine. The vein lay horizontally, so that the coal could be mined easily without great expense. We could also make the round trip in one day, instead of the two required if we went to the Winton mine for better quality coal. Moreover, since the road from the Rollins mine ran downhill all the way to town, there was no hard pulling up long grades as from the Minton mine, and we could haul heavier loads.

The Winton mine, with its high grade of bituminous coal, was about twelve miles northeast of the Rollins mine, on the north bank of Dirty George Creek. The road from the Winton mine was not nearly so steep or dangerous as the other, but it was nearly twice as long. It went down from the mine along the creek for five or six miles at a gentle slant. After this, one could either continue down Tongue Creek for another five or six miles and then go over the adobes to Delta, or pull up a long grade to the top of Surface Creek Mesa, and thence go downhill all the way to town. Although the grade was not very steep, a team of horses had about as much as they could do to pull two tons of coal up it. When the roads were hard and well packed, we usually chose the route over the inexpressibly dreary adobes. In rainy weather, or when the adobe roads were badly cut up, full of rut holes, and deep with dust, we chose the mesa road, which was gravel most of the way.

Since the Winton mine was about eighteen or nineteen miles away from home, we would usually start to it in the morning, and get our coal loaded the same day. The bunkhouse and stables about a half mile from the mine gave us and our horses shelter for the night. The next day we would go our weary way to Delta to unload the coal.

The Winton mine went into the mountain at a slight slant. Here the vein of coal was eight or ten feet thick, so that mining was rather easy. Mules drew the coal out of the mine in little cars which held about a ton, and hauled it across the creek to a tipple, where it was dumped into the wagons that backed up to take it. The coal, as I remember it, sold at the mouth of the mine for $2.00 per ton and at Delta for $5.00 per ton, so that if a person hauled two tons, which was the ordinary load for a two-horse team, he made $3.00 for each of the two days spent at the work with his team and wagon.

The stables of the mine were large enough to hold several teams and were used largely by professional coal haulers. The bunk house was about twenty feet long and about fifteen feet wide. Rough wooden bunks were placed all around the walls. A stove in the center served for both heating and cooking. The place smelled to high heaven of horses, tobacco, burning candles, perspiration and coal dust. Each person who stayed in the bunk house had to furnish his own blankets, and almost always had to share his bed, since there were seldom enough bunks to go around.

The coal miners would come into the bunk house with their hands and faces so covered with coal dust that about all that you could see was the whites of their eyes. They would wash up a bit and cook a hasty supper. After supper they always played cards with a deck so grimy that in the dim of the candle light it was hard to tell one card from another. The coal haulers often joined in the card playing. I never did, however, first because I had been taught that card playing was a game of the Devil, and second because I did not know the jack of diamonds from the ace of spades.

There were two kinds of persons hauling coal—farmers like us who hauled just enough coal for themselves, or who hauled loads once in a while to earn a little cash, and professional haulers. The latter were a rather sorry lot. Many of them were virtually financial slaves of Mr. Winton. Some of them had gone into the coal hauling business on credit furnished them by Mr. Winton to buy their team and wagon. They also bought the hay and grain for their horses from him. Somehow, they never seemed to get out of debt enough to quit. Among them was "Old Man Marsh," whose age was thought to be seventy or more. He had a little team of mules weighing only about 700 pounds each that could pull as much as a team of horses nearly twice as heavy. Mr. Marsh swore that someday he would be able to get out of debt and find easier work. Whether that happy day ever arrived, I do not know. I have seen Mr. Marsh hitch his little team of mules to a load of coal belonging to some farmer with a great "slick" team, and pull it up the grade when the farmer's team deemed the exertion just a little too much. Another character was Burton, who probably was never able to leave coal hauling because of drink as well as debt. I have seen him start driving from a steep grade of the Rollins mine highly "shot," singing merrily, "I don't care if I do die, do die, do die."

My first day hauling coal was an exciting one for me. I had started to the mine very early and was the first hauler there. As no one was in sight when I arrived, I decided to take a little miner's lamp I saw hanging at the mouth of the mine and find the miners. I had no idea that there was more than one shaft in the mine. Soon I found out that there were at least two. I took the one to the left. I walked a little farther and there was another branch. Again, I turned left. Suddenly my miner's lamp began to flicker and then went out. It must be confessed that I was rather in a panic. I tried to think how I had come in and how I must move in order to get out. Finally, I decided that if I should turn and then walk forward while feeling the side of the wall with my hand, I should get out. I fumbled around for half-an-hour in this way. Suddenly I heard a mighty swearing which seemed to be coming from my left. I turned and saw the flickering of a light in the darkness. I started toward the light and within fifty or sixty feet found a miner with a load of coal that had gone off the track. Evidently, I had taken an old shaft in going in, but in some way or another had come back out the main shaft. The miner "cussed me out" for coming into the mine at all, particularly with an almost empty lantern, since I knew nothing about mining. The cussing made no deep impression on me, as I was thinking only of my good luck in finding a way out of that maze of impenetrable darkness.

When we were out of the mine, the miner tipped two cars of coal into my wagon. It made a full load. After driving to the stable and feeding the horses, I went to the bunkhouse. I found that in addition to the central stove there was a little cookstove in the corner where I could cook bacon and eggs and make coffee. After most of the men had eaten supper, they sat around and told stories until about ten o'clock. Most of the haulers had had experiences all over the Rocky Mountains, teaming in the mining camps of Telluride and Ouray and Silverton, working in construction camps, or building railroads. Some of them had taken part in prospecting, hunting, or even fighting the Indian wars which had ended only a short time before in New Mexico. I found their stories very interesting, despite the fact that some of them shocked me. The person who could tell the tallest tales was old man Marsh.

On this particular evening Marsh was at his best. He told of a time when he was a young man in the Michigan woods and got into a dispute with a huge bully. The bully started toward him to beat him up. Marsh said that he had just had his boots hobnailed. As the bully came within striking distance, Marsh jumped high in the air and struck him square in the face with those wicked boots, knocking him out cold. The old man then told the story of a rabid skunk. Once, he said, when he was teaming near Telluride, all the men from the mine there were asleep in the bunkhouse. In the middle of the night, they were awakened by screams from one man after another lying on the floor bunks. There was a frightful smell of skunk. When the candles were lighted, a skunk was seen running wildly around the room and foaming at the mouth. He had bitten several men who had been sleeping on the floor bunks who were now crawling in terror to the upper bunks. Old man Marsh pulled out his pistol and shot the skunk dead. The next morning, so he said, all the men who had been bitten were frothing at the mouth and were running around trying to bite their companions. The latter had to throw ropes over these wild men and tie them down until doctors could arrive and take them away. As this tale was ending, we seemed to detect a faint odor of skunk, and I noticed that no man slept on the floor bunks that night.

Hauling coal was a tiresome task. The roads were usually either very dusty and filled with chuck holes, or muddy, or snowy and icy. Sitting for about five or six hours on the seat of the heavy wagon, in heat and dust, cold and rain, or snow and sleet, was a monotonous and dreary kind of work. When we reached town the 4,000 pounds of coal in the wagon had to be shoveled into Mr. Winton's coal bins, or delivered to individual families as he directed. In shoveling the coal, we would get very much overheated; then we had to drive home, risking a chill in extremely cold weather. I think I disliked this part of coal hauling more than any other. My face, already covered with road dust, would be completely black with coal dust by the time the coal was unloaded. Friends and acquaintances would not recognize me.

A year or so later we hauled coal in the winter with a four-horse team and a trail wagon. In this way we could bring three or four tons from the mine at one trip. This was heavy work, as it was necessary to grease and care for two wagons, take care of four horses, and shovel away all the coal at the end of a tiresome day with hands that were stiff from long hours of holding the reins.

The monotony of hauling coal from the Winton mine was broken at times by such incidents as horses getting colic, balking, slipping off the road or being "stuck" on the long Surface Creek grade. Several times when horses had colic, I prescribed a remedy that I had seen used by Mr. Johnson, Mr. Obert's hired man, who professed to be something of a veterinarian. The first step was to burn some wood until it became charcoal, which was powdered into fine dust. Then the horse's tongue must be pulled out of the side of its mouth and the powdered charcoal poured on the back of its tongue. The horse, in putting its tongue back into place and taking a breath, would swallow the charcoal and would soon be cured of colic.

"Balky" horses were quite common, particularly among farmers who came up to the coal mine to get coal for their own use. Perhaps the horses felt degraded by hauling dirty coal, but more probably they balked at the idea of pulling a very heavy load up hill. Each farmer had his own particular formula for making balky horses pull. Some men would lash them. Others would try to coax them. Others would simply let their horses rest a bit until the spirit moved them to pull. The last method was frowned upon by the regular haulers because it might greatly delay them, since they could not pass with a heavy load of coal on the grades where the balking usually took place. Often to save time, a regular coal hauler would simply ask the farmer to unhitch his team, and would put his own in its place as far as the top of the grade—or else the hauler would hitch his team in front of the farmer's horses to give added power. One farmer who had tried and tried in vain to get his horses to move when no help was near, finally built a small fire under them. They moved, but only far enough to leave the fire under the wagon. As we came to his rescue, he was putting out the fire and swearing something awful. But, like the proverbial Army mule, his horses did not seem to respond to swearing.

I found out a year or so later, when driving a four-horse team, that the best way to cure a balky horse was to hitch it as a wheel horse in a good four horse team. If it did not wish to cooperate, it made little difference, for it would be dragged along by the others. If in case of extreme obstreperousness, it lay down and was dragged along on its side, this was on its own account. After its hair began to wear off, the horse usually conformed to reason and went along with the rest of the team. If it jumped over the traces, as sometimes happened, wearing the traces on the inside of its legs for a while seemed to make it willing to conform with more conventional methods. Howard and I, after some years of experience, loved to trade adventurously with farmers for balky or otherwise mean horses and break them into good working horses this way.

One very cold snowy day, I was bringing a load of coal down Tongue Creek. Near Doughspoon Creek, which crossed the road, stood a rather tumble-down cabin that had long been abandoned. Some very poor people were living there for the winter. As I came toward the house a man came out and hailed me. His little baby had just died, he said, and he needed help to bury her. He had made a coffin of rough boards for his little girl, but he had been sick and was too weak to dig the grave in the hard frozen ground. We went a hundred yards back of the house and dug the grave. "Please make it deep," he said, "for I do not wish the coyotes to dig her up." After the grave was dug, we carried out the little coffin.

The man and his wife were crying. "I wish we had a service for her," he said. All I could do was to repeat slowly and in a choked voice the Lord's Prayer. Even this seemed to comfort them, for they thanked me over and over again. We filled the grave, and with my own heart heavy I had to leave them to their sorrow.

That winter I nearly broke my neck while hauling a load of wood. Usually, we took the two-day trip to a place near the Winton mine for wood, but on this occasion, as we did not wish to lose too much time from coal hauling, we had decided to go up near the Rollins mine. We put on a very large load of cedar and pinon wood and started down the steep grade, braking the wagon. The way we put the brake on when hauling wood, lumber or logs was to have a five- or six-foot brake stick attached for additional leverage to the ordinary brake bar near the rear end of the wagon. At the top of this bar, we placed a pulley through which we ran a rope, one end of which was fastened to the wagon's front axle. At the other end we made a small loop in which one could place his foot, and by pushing, easily put on the brake. On this trip, I had left six or seven feet of rope with a knot tied in its end, hanging beyond the place where I had tied the foot loop. Somehow the dangling rope caught in the spokes of the wheel. In no time it had wrapped around and around the wheel and pulled me down to the ground head first. Luckily the extra braking caused by the tightening rope, combined with the extra pull on the reins as I went down, stopped the horses and wagon just before the back wheel went over my head.

During the coldest part of the winter, when ice froze deep on the Gunnison River, ice cutting would begin. The ice was marked off in the river by ice plows, which made squares nearly two feet across, cut along the edges to a depth of two or three inches.

By sawing along the marks, great blocks of ice were cut. These would be dragged from the river up an incline, and either placed in the nearby ice house or loaded into the waiting farm wagons. As the river often froze two or three feet deep, the cakes of ice weighed two hundred pounds or more. Loading these was heavy and dangerous work and involved a risk of illness, as men would become overheated during the loading, and freezing cold while driving.

We would pack blocks of ice in rows in our own ice house with sawdust in small places between them, and six-inches of sawdust around the entire pack. This packing was efficacious, and we had plenty of ice to last all summer. A bucket filled with ice in the morning and at noon gave us ice water which, when we worked in the hot hay or grain fields, was quite as refreshing as the Biblical "snow in the time of harvest."

The spring and summer of 1896 were particularly discouraging for us. There was not much snow on the mountains, and it looked in the spring as if a dry summer were ahead. Alfalfa seemed to grow in an extraordinary way in the orchard. Much of it had withstood our attempts at grubbing it up the year before, and its long roots (nearly half an inch in diameter by this time) were as tough as shoe leather and valiantly resisted us. The heavy grub hoe did about as much injury to the back as it did to those tough roots. Sweet clover grew in profusion over the dykes and ditches and had to be cut. Cockle burrs began to start up everywhere. We had planted the northeast plot to oats and alfalfa, but our neighbor May's one thousand chickens decided it belonged to them. It was almost impossible to irrigate the southern end of the plot, due to the fact that the ground had not been graded sufficiently. When we divided up our one-half acre foot of water so as to irrigate this plot, it made such a small stream that we could irrigate only a few furrows at a time. The orchard demanded more and more of the little water we had. Altogether, I experienced a deep sense of frustration.

The early garden was pretty good, and we had raised a first cutting of alfalfa. At last, our little peach trees began to bear. Mother picked the first basket of the few we were to have that season, and sent it down by Hal to Mr. Wolbert in appreciation of what he had done for us. I was furious. Here was Mother placing sentiment ahead of our needs and desires! Mr. Wolbert sent the peaches back with a beautiful note saying that although he appreciated the spirit of the gift, he could not accept them, for he felt as did David who refused to drink the water from the well at Bethlehem which his three mighty men had secured at the risk of their lives.

Toward the end of summer there was no water for irrigation. Again, to keep the orchard alive and to water the stock we hauled water in barrels from the Delta tank on the edge of Garnet Mesa. I longed to buy a place on Surface Creek Mesa or in the Gunnison River Valley where there was plenty of water. One who has not lived in an irrigated country can have no conception of the difference that abundance or scarcity of water can make. With water: large beautiful crops. Without water: nothing. Without water all plowing, sowing and care are wasted in the end.

I grew more and more bitter toward the orchard. A great deal of time was needed to plow, cultivate, and irrigate it, to say nothing about grubbing out the alfalfa. Yet so far, it had only produced a few baskets of peaches.

In September all the boys, except me and Arthur, started to school again. That fall, the silver question was the main subject of conversation. William Jennings Bryan was running on the Democratic ticket for the Presidency of the United States. The major issue for which he contended was that there would be free coinage of silver at the ratio of sixteen to one. In other words, the United States should buy silver and should coin it at a ratio of sixteen ounces of silver to one ounce of gold. This idea was very popular in the silver producing states, where most people were able to see its direct benefit to them, and few were able to understand the disadvantages of bimetallism as a basis for currency. Many of Colorado's Populists and Republicans alike forsook their parties and joined the Democrats in the demand for this measure, which sounded like an unmixed blessing to the state. So popular was the cause, that W. O. Stevens, the Postmaster who was the wheelhorse for the Republican Party in Delta County, came up to our place and asked Mother to run for the office of County Superintendent of Schools. There were hardly enough Republicans left in the county, he said, to form a county slate! Mother allowed her name to be used, but this was only a brave gesture, as the Republican candidates knew themselves foredoomed to defeat. The Democrats were victorious in Colorado, as in the west generally, but Bryan was defeated for the Presidency by William McKinley.

About the middle of November, Father's cousin, John M. Trew, Arthur, and I arranged to go deer hunting toward the west end of Grand Mesa on Point Creek. Mr. Angel, one of cousin John's friends, had taken up a claim on a little creek bottom running southwestward from the end of Grand Mesa between Delta and Grand Junction, and had established a half-way house there. This was a primitive place where food, water, and shelter for the night could be supplied for "man and beast." The small creek bottom was the only oasis in the bleak adobe country that ran nearly all the way between these two places. Mr. Angel had told cousin John that it was easy to get up toward the western end of the Mesa through this creek bottom, and that many deer crossed over in the fall and early winter after the snow was deep on their way from Grand Mesa to the Escalante country south of the Gunnison River.

We loaded the wagon with supplies for ourselves and the horses, and started out. By the end of the first day, we reached Mr. Angel's place. He was happy to see us and entertained us as well as possible. The only drawback to his entertainment was the fact that the place was absolutely black with flies. The sugar in the open bowl could not be seen for the flies. I tried my best to eat, but could not. Mother had always been a great hater of flies, and I shared her feelings. Before going to bed that night, I sneaked over to our grub box and got something to eat.

I have never seen a more desolate setting for a building than that of the half-way house. There was nothing around it but the bleakest of adobes: no trees, no grass, not even brush. We were glad to leave in the morning, when we proceeded over the adobe flats up the creek. Mr. Angel came with us. As we went further up the little creek, sage brush, cottonwood trees, and rabbit brush began to appear. We saw a good many rabbits, particularly in the rabbit brush zone, and killed several for supper that night. After we had gone as far as we could in the wagon, we camped at about six thousand feet in the cedar belt, which as I have explained before, ran all the way across the Grand Mesa. Our camp was by a small ditch that during the spring and early summer carried water from the creek to Mr. Angel's land. It was always good to camp in the cedar and sage brush country with its clear perfumed air.

The next afternoon Arthur and I started up the mountain, going toward a trail that Mr. Angel said the deer frequently took on their pilgrimage to the Escalante country. It was snowing lightly as we started out, and the fall grew denser as we climbed the mountain. The snow on the ground became deeper and deeper until it was almost up to our knees. But as we had not reached the place where the trail was supposed to be, we kept on. Suddenly it became very foggy. We could hardly see fifty feet through the fog and snow. We finally realized that we were lost. About this time, I began to suffer with diarrhea, which greatly weakened me. We trudged on and on, probably going in circles. At last, I became so exhausted that I lay down in the snow and told Arthur I could go no further and that I did not care if I should die. Arthur let me rest a few minutes, and I began to feel better.

We started to tramp again, but now downhill in order to come out below the snow. Before long we saw Mr. Angel's irrigation ditch running along the mountain side. We breathed a sigh of relief, for we knew that by following the ditch we would reach camp. Soon it began to grow dark, but we were able to hold our course because the snow falling in the water had melted and left the ditch standing out, black against white. Suddenly as we came over a little hill, we caught the flicker of a light, and in a moment we saw a campfire where Cousin John and Mr. Angel sat anxiously looking for us. Never have I seen a more welcome sight. We took off our wet outer clothes to be dried by the fire, and were soon eating a great repast prepared by Cousin John, who had a reputation far and wide as a cook. We had hot biscuits with syrup, rabbit backs and hind legs browned to a queen's taste, stewed dried fruit, and potatoes baked in the coals. Not much of a meal, one might say, for a person ill with my trouble. Perhaps not, but it tasted like a feast to me, and did me no harm.

The next morning, as it was snowing in the mountains, I

decided to take the twenty-two rifle and go down the creek rabbit hunting. I soon reached the edge of the cedars, and came to an open place half a mile wide, toward the middle of which was a large herd of cattle. I started across, thinking that the cattle would get out of my way. As I came within 200 yards of them, a great red bull started running toward me, followed by the whole herd. I was in a tight spot.

Down on my knees I went, and kept the rifle aimed at the head of the bull as well as I was able. My plan was to drop him near me and then let the herd break on either side of him, thinking his carcass would serve as a protection. (I did not know at the time, that a bull's skull will withstand and far larger bullet that a twenty-two). When he was within about fifty feet of me, I lost my nerve, and suddenly standing up, fired my rifle towards him. I missed him, but my sudden motion, plus the rifle shot, frightened the herd out of their senses. They turned tail and bolted down the creek. I retired rapidly into the cedars, where I knew I could climb a tree if they started after me again. On the way back up the creek I found two or three rabbits, which came in handy for supper.

The next morning Arthur and I arose before daylight, and without waiting for breakfast, we started up the mountain alone. We had not gone far when we saw the tracks of a mountain lion. Soon we heard a heavy breathing or a kind of snoring on the other side of a little hill. Thinking that we might be hearing the mountain lion, we did not go farther, but returned to camp. Immediately after breakfast, we climbed the same trail again, this time well loaded for lion or bear. We finally came to the place where we thought the mountain lion was. Here, much to our chagrin, we found that a large bunch of deer had been sleeping or resting. We had missed the chance of getting a deer or two! We had not gone much farther when we saw a doe and her little fawn about two hundred yards away standing in a clearing. The moment they saw us, off they started, the little fellow following his mother almost track for track, leaping over rocks and dead trees. It was a pretty sight, and we did not destroy its beauty by shooting at either the mother or the fawn. Although we hunted for one or two more days, we never saw any more deer. As Cousin John and Mr. Angel were no luckier than we were, we returned home without a supply of venison.

That fall we added a kitchen to the north end of the house. Our new room had a curious history. A man named Schmidt, who lived in the northeastern portion of Poverty Flat on a most bleak and unproductive piece of land, had committed suicide. Arthur secured the little shack that was on the place, I never asked how: whether simply by preemption, since he knew that the owner would have no more use for it, or by some arrangement with the county commissioners, who, I believe, had been responsible for the man's burial in the pauper's end of the Delta cemetery. We took the shack apart in sections, loaded it on the flat hay rack and brought it over to our place. From its sections we made a lean-to kitchen. As the walls had only the thickness of the boards, it was far too cold to use in winter except as a storage room for such things as crocks of hominy, dried fruit, and quarters of beef. Any meat placed there froze so hard that the only way to cut it was with a large saw. In the spring, summer and fall, however, the lean-to served as a working kitchen, and left the former kitchen free to be used as a dining room.

That winter was a hard one for us, as the shortage of water in the late summer meant that we did not have the usual quantities of winter vegetables, hay and oats. Arthur obtained a position in a general store in Paonia kept by the Royces, who were related to my Grandfather Bradley's first wife. The change seemed to do him much good, and he gained a great deal in strength. I hauled many loads of coal throughout the winter and early spring, and also worked at odd jobs.

The heavy snows in the mountains during the winter promised better crops for the summer of 1897. Again, we made arrangements with W. O. Stevens for handling his hay and part of his orchard on shares.

Toward the middle of the summer one of our cousins and a companion of his came from Manhattan, Kansas, to visit us and remained two or three weeks. They had a gramophone with small cylindrical records, and hearing attachments that were placed in the ears. Their records included only about a dozen popular favorites, such as the "Sidewalks of New York," the "Election Picnic," and "Sweet Marie." They had toured from Kansas, making their way by giving recitals with this contraption. As this was the first time that a talking machine had come to the mesa, so far as I know, it caused quite the sensation. When the boys finally left, they gave us their old white horse, named Almont. This animal was shaped rather like a race horse, but had no other racing characteristics.

That summer a man named Bob Wright rented the Blair place just south of us. He was not at all the usual hardworking farmer. Instead, he hired help for nearly all of his undertakings. Often, when he considered it too hot to work by day, he would put up his hay by moonlight, singing and yelling most of the time. The neighbors always suspected that he diverted more of his share of water from the Garnet Mesa Ditch, but as that also was done at night (if done), it was a bit hard to prove. The flourishing condition of his crops, however, gave some slight indication of the validity of the suspicion. We boys did a good deal of work for him this summer, supposedly receiving as pay $1.00 per day, without board. He had agreed to pay us weekly but kept putting us off, promising that as soon as he sold some crops he would settle up. But that time never came, and one day in the early fall we found that he had skipped the country, leaving many persons "holding the bag."

After laying by or crops, which were good, the younger boys started to school again. Once more I started the monotonous job of hauling coal, hauling ice, and doing whatever odd jobs turned up.

Early in 1898, the United States Battleship Maine was blown up in Havana Harbor. The country went wild. I remember that soon after the disaster, while I was working on the dyke and feeling rather low, one of our neighbors stopped by and announced that Teddy Roosevelt was forming cowboys into a body of Rough Riders to participate in the war. I was eager to go, and considered for some few days whether it would not be advisable to leave the damned old farm and join the Rough Riders. Finally, without consulting anyone, I made up my mind that it was my duty to stay. As I was not quite 18, I was also uncertain whether I would be allowed to join the company, anyway.

In the summer of 1898 a nephew of Mr. Blair rented his place, but hired a man to do most of the work. I was impressed by the way in which this man trained the Blair horses: a process he called "whip breaking". He got the horses so that they would run out of the barn, move to the proper sides of the wagon tongue, and stand perfectly still until he arrived to hitch them up. After work, when unhitched, they would run to the barn and go into their proper stalls.

Once more, although there had been a good deal of snow on the mountains, the Uncompahgre River nearly dried up toward the latter end of the season. The chief reason for its failure was the fact that as more and more land had been placed under cultivation, ditches much higher up the stream had been constructed. Despite priorities, these ditches seemed to be able by hook or by crook, chiefly the latter, to take the water that rightfully belonged to those lower down with prior rights. There was some talk of the possibility of digging a tunnel through the Vernal Mesa to bring water from the Gunnison River into the Uncompahgre Valley.

Mr. Blair's nephew had two little boys who were regarded by the good neighbors as being filled with more than their share of original sin. They were always doing something that went contrary to the mores of the grown folk. Early in the fall after all the hay and grain were stacked in the farm yard, one Sunday afternoon while playing with matches, the boys set fire to the chicken coop. The flames spread rapidly to the barn, and to the hay stacks which contained nearly one hundred tons of hay. Not too far away from the hay stacks were three or four large stacks of wheat and oats. Neighbors rapidly assembled, but it soon became evident that nothing could be done to save the hay and the barn.

Someone suggested, however, that we could save the grain by hauling it a reasonable distance away. Several farmers, including ourselves, rushed to our barns, harnessed horses, hitched them to wagons on which were flat hay racks, and drove hell bent for election to the fire. Men without teams pitched the grain upon the hay racks as rapidly as possible. Then when the racks were loaded, we drove our teams on the dead run to a field nearby. We made very sudden turns with the teams still on the run, while we held fast to the hay rack ladders to keep from being thrown off. The jerk of the turns would cause all the bundles of grain to slide off. Then we were ready for another trip. Due to the flames and roaring of the fire, the people yelling, and the general commotion, the horses became so excited that they snorted and were almost out of control. I was glad enough that I had a steady team in old Roebuck and Snoozer. Within a short time, we had the grain out of danger but scattered over quite a wide area. The fire in the haystacks burned for several days, making a great glow at night.

It was that fall, I believe, that the Van Tyle brothers, knowing Mother's fondness for music, loaned us their grand piano. We placed it in the living room and began to enjoy group singing. Mr. Finney had hired a young man named Elmer Weiser who had a good voice and loved to sing. He and Ed Tucker, a young man from a farm on the Gunnison River who also sang very well, joined us. Now we had the material for not only a quartet but a double quartet. Howard and I together with the two other young men sang the bass and tenor parts, while the younger boys sang soprano. Hal, who had a powerful voice for a boy of thirteen, joined Mother in singing alto. In some way or another Mother had acquired four copies of a book called "Arion" which contained beautiful quartets, including many by famous composers. Mother trained us in our different parts, and we learned nearly every number in the book. The thoroughness of our work was shown a few years ago when some of us were together, and found that we were still able to sing these songs.

The composition of the quartet varied from time to time, as well as the boys who sang the different parts. As Hal became older, he developed a very strong bass voice and was able to sing a whole octave lower than I. When Clarence came back from California after some years there, he was able to contribute greatly, as he had had training on the violin while staying with Aunt Sarah. In some way or another Howard had learned to play on Father's old flute.

About this time Howard and I began to sing bass and tenor

respectively in the choir of the Presbyterian church. The choir had lately been strengthened by two members from the "east." Miss Botsford, who had been a leading soprano in a well-known New York Presbyterian church, led the singing. Miss Johnson, a graduate of Oberlin College and a teacher at Carleton College, had come to Delta for her health. She had sung in the famous Second Church choir in Oberlin, and was able to lead the alto section. I had begun to take a renewed interest in music even though previously my association with rough coal haulers and several uneducated farmers had made me wonder whether it might not be rather "sissy." In the evenings I would often steal into the living room, despite the fact that in winter it was very cold, and would try to pick out pieces on the piano. Mother told me many years later, just a few days before she died, that she had longed to help me but feared that if she did, I would stop playing altogether. Such is the perversity of youth! I did succeed in learning to read music a little bit; but as I had a good musical memory and a keen sense of harmony, I preferred to play by ear—something which I still do.

About this time, I began to take an interest in affairs outside the narrow confines of the Western Slope. Uncle Dan sent us regularly the *Review of Reviews*, which contained summary descriptions of the most important political and economic activities, both in the United States and in the world at large. He also sent us every week, the *Congregationalist*, a church paper of a rather liberal nature. For state and local affairs, particularly those regarding agriculture and livestock, we subscribed to the *Colorado Stock Farmer*, and for local news we took the *Delta Independent*. We received the *Ladies Home Journal*, from which in a rather furtive way (since I professed to have no interest in the inferior sex) I gained a very idealistic conception of girls by reading Ruth Ashmore's column,

"Side-talks with Girls." Since I had no sisters and knew no girls on an informal friendly basis, I was unable to obtain any realistic view of this branch of the human race. A few years ago, my wife gave me as a birthday present a little book containing many of the Ruth Ashmore articles. They would make the modern girl howl.

As I look back to these years, I see that although our home was small and poor, it was basically cultivated. We enjoyed a strong, true religious atmosphere, music in which all of us participated, a limited knowledge of some of the world's best literature, and a slight acquaintance with national and world affairs. Our small library was sufficient for the brief periods which we could devote to reading. At the end of a week spent in hauling coal, bunking with rough miners and coal haulers, and wrestling with nature for economic survival, the Sunday hours at the church or home were like oases in a dreary wilderness.

CHAPTER VIII

Poverty Flat

IN THE SUMMER OF 1898 when I was almost 18, old man Finney, who had bought the chicken ranch from Mr. Mays just north of our place, suggested that I go into partnership with him raising a crop of winter wheat on Poverty Flat. I suppose that this name had been given to the region because several families who had made an attempt to farm it had been driven out by bad crops.

Poverty Flat was about three miles southeast of our place just beyond the upper Garnet Mesa. It was more or less an oasis in the adobe country immediately surrounding it. The place which we thought of farming was one that has just been abandoned by a family names Rogers after several bad crop years. Mr. Finney persuaded me that there could not possibly be many such dry years in succession, and that even in a bad season, a crop of winter wheat would be ripe before the drought came in late summer. The ranch contained 160 acres, about ten of which were planted to alfalfa. Most of the rest of the place, except some twenty acres in the northeast part, had grown four or five crops on grain. I have never known whether or not Mr. Finney paid any rent for the place, for he never mentioned this matter to me.

The ranch was under a small ditch running from the Uncompahgre River, on which there were only a few farmers. On paper, it had a fair priority for water rights. Since the place had quite a comfortable log cabin of three or four rooms, and a good stable and corral, we decided to camp there while doing the work, rather than to go back and forth from home.

Mr. Finney agreed to provide a man, a sulky plow and two teams to help plow the fields, if I would furnish similar equipment. He was to supply the "grub stake" and the seed, and I was to care for the grain in the spring and summer— that is, do the irrigation. We were to do the sowing and harvesting on a cooperative basis. I bought a second-hand sulky or riding plow, and with my four-horse team, was ready for work.

Luckily for me, Mr. Finney employed Elmer Weiser to help plow the land. Elmer, whom I knew already as a member of our singing group, had recently come from Iowa. He was a year or two older than I, and was a fine companion, loving music and poetry. In fact, he often composed little poems while riding on the sulky plow. We "batched" in the log house. It was our system to make hot biscuits every morning, eating the left-over ones for lunch and supper. Our meals consisted largely of biscuits, bacon, eggs, and coffee. Since Mr. Finney had 1,000 chickens, eggs were about as cheap an item of food as he could provide under our agreements. Saturday afternoons and Sundays, which we spent at home, brought us a welcome change in diet.

The job of plowing this particular land was unusually difficult. As no rain had fallen for months, the ground was hard and there was much dust. In places, the dry earth would turn up in clods a foot or more in diameter. The horses developed sores on their shoulders because of the hardness of the ground, the steady pulling in extremely hot weather, and the continuous dust. We had to use powdered alum on the sores, to keep the horses in condition for work. When we first started to plow in the morning the poor animals would wince as the collars tightened on their shoulders. We were sorry for them, but the plowing had to be done in time for fall seeding.

Sitting on the sulky plow day after day was very monotonous; but Elmer and I had good times in the evening, singing and reading. It was in the log cabin at Poverty Flat that he and I first met Browning. One of the Rogers girls, a member of the family which had left the Flat discouraged and broke, had evidently been in high school and had been required to read a small volume containing twenty-five or thirty of Browning's poems. This book had been left in the rubbish when the family moved. The selection, as I now see it, was terrible; but the book was there and we read it. Most of the poems did not make sense to us; for example: "Mesmerism " "Popularity" (Hobbs hints blue—straight he turtle eats), "Memorabilia." and "Waring." A few of them we loved and immediately memorized—notably "Pippa's Song," "Meeting at Night," "Home Thoughts from Abroad," and "My Star." I began here for the first time, I think, the practice of reading poetry for pleasure and then trying to memorize it, while doing work that required no thought —such as plowing, or sitting on the wagon hauling coal.

The Sunday after we had discovered Browning, we went home. Mother had a guest, Miss Cornelia Johnson, who had recently been teaching English at Carleton College. I told her about reading Browning and insisted that most of what I had read was not poetry, for up to that time, I thought all poetry had to have very definite patterns. She laughed at me and then read aloud a good many of Browning's other poems that were certainly more comprehensible than some of those in the Rogers girl's collection. One that I loved most was "Rabbi Ben Ezra." She gave Elmer and me several books of poetry to read, and a few novels.

One Sunday morning, instead of going home, Elmer and I decided to take a trip to the Black Canyon of the Gunnison, which we had never seen. After riding some ten or twelve miles through the adobes and climbing the Vernal Mesa, suddenly we found ourselves on the top of an almost perpendicular canyon which was very narrow and seemed to be half a mile deep. The river below appeared as merely a bright ribbon. To get a better view, Elmer leaned over a larger projecting ledge that sloped downward toward the canyon. I stood by not wishing to trust myself in such a position. "Help me, Fred!" said Elmer, "I'm dizzy." I seized his feet and pulled him back. Both of us were a bit unnerved for a few moments.

In September all the other boys—except Arthur, who was working for the Royces in Paonia, and Clarence, who was still in California with Aunt Sarah—started to school. Several of my former friends and schoolmates left for college that fall. I felt much disturbed because I was not going, too, and worse because I had been away from school so long that I was already four years behind them. It seemed impossible for me to stop working to go to school, and even if it had been possible, I doubt very much that I could have faced the prospect of going back into the Delta schools with my younger brothers and their friends in the same grade as I. In any case we were still very "hard up," and I could not leave the ranch.

Although we finished plowing the Poverty Flat land toward the latter part of September, our hopes of sowing it to winter wheat were dashed by the fact that there was neither rain in the valleys nor snow on the mountains early enough to provide irrigation water to bring the wheat up. We kept hoping against hope that the rain would come in time, but it did not start until November, too late for planting winter wheat. Since the uncertainty of water in the spring meant that planting of spring wheat was a gamble, we had to face the unpleasant possibility of having no wheat crop the following summer.

I now had four horses, and by hauling another wagon could drive a four-horse team pulling the new wagon with the old one as a trailer. There appeared to be special advantages in this combination. By hauling nearly four tons of coal instead of two, I could hope to make more money than before. With this outfit I started hauling coal again from the Winton mine.

A break in the coal hauling business took place toward the latter part of November. Miss Johnson had conceived the idea of going into the cattle business. She said that her uncle, who was a wealthy Chicago banker, would back her up in the enterprise. According to her plans, she would purchase a ranch and a herd of cattle, and I would be responsible for both. We heard of a place near Crawford that was for sale because the rancher's wife found it unbearably lonely to live so far away from relatives and neighbors. We drove up to see the ranch and it appeared to be just such a one as I had always dreamed about. It was at the edge of the Black Mesa cedar country, only eight or ten miles from the eastern rim of the Black Canyon. The cultivated land was largely planted to alfalfa. A small mountain stream running through the place furnished pure water for irrigation and for stock. Many white-faced cattle were standing near large hay stacks fenced with spruce logs. What a place, in comparison to Poverty Flat!

When we went to the house, we found no one at home except the wife of the owner and her little girl of about three. The mother invited us in and insisted that we stay overnight, since her husband had left on some business the day before, and would not be back until the following day. In the meantime, she said, their mountain lion had not been fed and watered since her husband had left.

The howls that we were hearing came from the famished beast. She was afraid to feed and water it and asked if would I be good enough to do so? I very nobly volunteered to try.

The mountain lion was quartered in a little shack made of cedar logs that had not been chinked. As I approached his quarters he lunged at the side of the shack, snarling and showing his teeth in a ferocious way. I feared that in his hunger, thirst and general rage, he would break out of his not-too-strong prison. Perhaps I had made a mistake in offering to feed and water him! However, when I gave him some meat and a pan of water, he more or less calmed down. How in the world, I asked the good woman when I returned to the house, had she come by such a creature? She said that her husband and some cowboys had located the mountain lion in a rather large and bare dead pinon tree. They determined to catch it and sell it to a zoo. From the opposite directions they threw their ropes over the beast. He sprang just before the ropes became taut, and almost took the tail off one of the horses. Since he was caught by the ropes, however, they were able to stretch him out, "hog tie" his feet together; lay him in a neighbor's wagon and bring him into the little shack, preparatory to selling him.

As we looked over the place further the next morning, it appeared to be an ideal site for the cattle ranch. It had plenty of alfalfa hay, good pure water, and a location not too far from the mountain ranges where the cattle would be driven to pasture in the spring.

Miss Johnson wrote to her uncle about the place and her plans, asking him to back the venture. He replied that he was opposed to the plan at the moment, both because I was a bit too young to manage such an enterprise, and also because he thought it unwise to buy cattle at the prevailing high prices, which were almost sure to fall. This reply made me feel disappointed and chagrined, for I certainly thought that I could handle hay and raise cattle. And what, after all, did a banker in far-off Chicago know about cattle, in comparison to what I knew? Little did I realize at the time how much a Chicago banker must know about the finances of the cattle business. From his viewpoint, experience in feeding cattle, branding them, roping them, and driving them up to the range was of little importance in comparison to financing them.

I went back to hauling coal. That winter I managed to do a good deal of general reading under the direction of Miss Johnson, and to memorize many poems. I also read Green's *History of the English People,* Macaulay's *History of England,* a history of the United States and Irving's *Life of Washington* to such good advantage that later in college I was able to pass satisfactory examinations in English history and United States history without taking courses in these subjects.

The coal hauling dragged drearily on until about the end of February 1899, when we decided to prepare for sowing the spring wheat. Sometime during this winter Miss Johnson had bought a grey horse much like one of mine, which she said I could use while she was away on a trip. This gave me a beautiful team of greys, beside old Snoozer, Roebuck and Almont. I had a sense of real pride when I drove this fine team to town, instead of the feeling of shame because of Snoozer's mange.

One night a drainage ditch up in the adobes broke and allowed alkali seepage water to flow into the Garnet Mesa ditch. Miss Johnson's grey, who was running in the pasture, drank the seepage water and became very sick. I called on Mr. Obert's hired man for help. We gave the horse aconite and did everything that we could to cure him, but he died. It took nearly half a day to dig a hole large enough to bury him. We dragged him with a team over to the hole and covered him up. I was much distressed especially because the tragedy occurred while the horse was entrusted to me.

As Almont was not a work horse, it was now necessary to find another horse to complete my two pairs. I inquired around the neighborhood whether someone did not own a colt that he wished to have broken. Mr. Long, who lived about a mile from us and who hauled lumber for a living, said that he had one. I could come and get him the next day. Mr. Long would not be there himself but would leave the colt tied to the log corral. I rode old Roebuck down after the colt, which Mr. Long said had been taught to lead. I came up to the corral and began to untie the colt. He struck at me. I got him untied, however, and jumped on my horse. The colt reared high up on his hind legs and struck at me as I sat on the horse. I threw the spurs into old Roebuck and away we went, so fast that the colt had no further time for striking.

When I reached home, I ran the colt into the open corral, snubbed his rope around the center pole and shut the gate. This colt, I thought, had been mistreated. Accordingly, I got a wisp of hay and started toward him. He immediately came at me striking with his front feet. I had to climb over the side of the log corral to escape his attack. I tried for several days to win over his confidence by treating him gently, but got no response from his hard heart.

Finally, I asked Mr. Finney to help me. We roped him by the neck and the front feet, threw him down, put on the collar and as much of the harness as we could, and then ran a rope through a pulley on one of his forefeet and through another pulley on the collar. We let him get up. Whenever he would start to strike, we would pull up his front foot toward his chest. I worked with him a day or so in this way, and then hitched him up with old Snoozer without a wagon and tried to drive him around. Every once in a while, he would kick viciously or try to strike. I would then pull one of his feet from under him. Howard, Mr. Finney and I at last hitched him to the wagon, with double pulleys on his forefeet. Before we could get the pulleys in operation, he kicked the front end out of the wagon box.

We worked him for several days and seemed to be making a little progress, when I came down with measles. All the other members of the family except Mother and myself had had it over a period of a month. Uncle Frank had taken care of them. Though I had sworn that I was too strong and husky to get the fever, it came on me suddenly. I did not give up until I was almost delirious. Before the disease left me, I had a bad time of it. After nursing all the family through this sickness, Mother herself, came down with the cursed malady and was very ill for a while.

In the meantime, Finney had left the colt in the barn at Poverty Flat, feeding him only once in two days, and carrying him a minimum allowance of water. He was afraid to take the colt out of the stable, and afraid to have much contact with him even there.

I was so anxious to go back to work that I got out of bed when I was still very weak. I told Finney that I could not do much at first, but that I would at least look after the colt. I rode up to Poverty Flat on horseback, although I was so weak that I felt several times as if I were about to fall off.

I crawled through the manger to unfasten the colt so that I could lead him to water. He struck at me, but I dodged. At last, I got the long rope loose and threw the end of it back toward the stable door, which was closed. I then went around, opened the door, grabbed the rope, and started for my horse. Like a flash the colt was after me with blood in his eye, snorting furiously. I was barely able to snub the rope around the post in the center of the corral, and to jump on my horse. The gate was open. With a sudden lunge the colt loosened the rope, ran through the corral gate, darted across to the outside gate which, likewise, was open, and disappeared up the road. As far as I know, he was never seen again. When I told the story to Mr. Long he merely laughed and remarked that it was "damned good riddance of bad rubbish." Then he added: "By the way, that colt's name was Swamp Angel, I've found out that he had a mighty bad record before I got him."

The next day Howard and I went up to Poverty Flat to harrow the ground and sow the grain. Miss Johnson went with us to help us with the cooking and also to assist us in our English studies. She felt that she was beginning to recover from her lung ailment, and believed that the dry, hot atmosphere in Poverty Flat would do her good.

The first day of harrowing was torture for me. My legs were so weak from fever that I could hardly stand. I stuck it out, however, until evening. When Howard and I arrived at the cabin a good meal awaited us. I think I never appreciated one more. Within a few days my old strength seemed to come back. After harrowing the fields thoroughly, we sowed them all to spring wheat. Mr. Finney had rented a seeding machine that would sow about twenty-five acres per day. After the sowing was done, we spent several days harrowing the grain in and running a float over the ground to make it smooth. It was then necessary to make irrigation furrows, which took a good many more days.

When going over the large ditch from the Uncompahgre River, which brought water to the farm, we discovered that in places it was pretty well filled with silt. As there were one or two neighbors who also depended upon the ditch, we got them together and with slip scrapers and shovels cleaned out the worst places. This delayed our usual farming operations for about ten days. The water was now turned into the large ditch. When it came to a place where the ditch crossed an arroyo, it broke through. There was nothing for us to do but to go up farther on the ditch were the ground was more level, and cut the water off into the flat land lying below. As the gully or arroyo was some twenty feet wide and eight or ten feet deep, Howard and I made up our minds that we would ask help from the water users of the ditch. They came with their teams and scrapers, but did not seem to know just what to do. "First," I suggested, "let us plant a few fence posts in the outer edge of the dam, then go over to that old straw stack and get a load of straw to fill in, and gradually dump dirt over the straw until the horses can go across. We can then build the dam rather easily with our slip scrapers." This appealed to them. I was rather proud that these old, experienced farmers were following my advice.

We finished the dam and turned in the water. It backed up the arroyo and formed quite a little lake. As it came toward the top, I stood on the middle of the dam to see if it would stand the strain. Almost in front of me a little column of dust, like a small whirlwind, started upward. I knew that something was wrong, and ran as fast as I could to the solid bank. With almost incredible speed, the whole dam slid out and was soon disappearing into muddy water. Had I been on the dam when this happened, I would certainly have been drowned.

We rebuilt the dam, making it much thicker and stronger than before. This time, it held. There was plenty of water after this and we could irrigate ten or twelve acres a day. It took hard work to get several hundred little furrows started each day and to be sure that the water ran through every one of them and soaked all the land. Our legs would be fairly aching at the end of the day from tramping with heavy boots through the muddy fields and repairing breaks.

A very heavy shower struck the northeastern twenty acres of wheat on the virgin soil before we had a chance to irrigate it, and baked a hard crust all over the field. I thought that the grain could never get through, but I irrigated the field anyway. Only about one-fourth of the grain appeared. I never saw a sorrier stand. We gave the field up. Within a week or so, however, the grain began to "stool" or spread out, until it covered the ground. We put on the water again, and the field looked splendid. It appeared that the new soil had great potency.

But another difficulty came. There were many prairie dog mounds near one corner of the field. The hungry little animals ate, almost down to the roots, a large section of the growing wheat. We ran water into their holes to drown them out. When they came out to avoid being drowned, we would hit them over the head with our irrigation shovels to kill them. As we would hit them, the poor little fellows would dodge back, sometimes wounded, so that the water was bloody. They put up a brave fight between us and the water for their lives, but always lost.

After we had killed ten or twelve in this way, I was sick of the business. I went downtown and asked the druggist if there were not some poison that would kill the animals humanely. He sold me liquid carbon disulphide. This volatile poison forms a gas heavier than air, which consequently moves downward. We placed the liquid on dry horse manure and threw the soggy masses into the holes. Howard was overcome by the gas one day, and I had to pour water on his head to revive him. The prairie dogs evidently succumbed to the poison, for we had no more trouble with them.

The grain now began to grow better where it had been eaten off than in any other place. Strange to relate, the twenty acres which we had at one time given up, produced as much grain as all the other eighty acres, yielding a thousand bushels.

That spring, at my urging, Clarence returned from California. He could play the violin and rattle off bits of Latin, and seemed to have developed a certain polish that Howard and I lacked. Something had taken place to make him different than us in an enviable way. Early in the summer he secured the job of "ditch walker" on the ditch that ran from the Uncompahgre River to Poverty Flat. He, therefore, came to live with us in the Poverty Flat cabin. His job was to make sure that no one was stealing water, to see that any minor breaks in the ditch were repaired, and to take out the algae that grew profusely in several places where the ditch had almost no fall. At one place the ditch became so filled with this growth that he asked Howard and me to help him take it out. We stripped off our clothes and waded into the ditch to work. The sun was shining in all of its Colorado glory. By night, Howard and I were covered with blisters and sunburn, but we had cleaned the ditch so that the precious water could flow through it freely. Since Clarence's skin was naturally dark and he had been walking through the hot adobes for some time, he had a deep tan and did not sunburn.

As the summer advanced, Howard and I took great pride in the green fields of grain that billowed in the wind and formed such a pleasant contrast with the bare adobe land surrounding them. Then, just about the time the wheat had headed out, the water failed. The snow in the mountains, as we could easily see, had all melted except for deposits in a few deep crevasses. The sky was like brass day after day. The sun poured down its heat. Unless we had water in a few days, all the grain would be lost. All the work and cost of caring for these great grain fields would amount to nothing, and we would lose nearly a year of our time, and would also be several hundred dollars in debt.

One day when we were out in the fields trying to irrigate with the petty stream that came to us as the result of prorating the water in the river, a strong wind came up. Almost before we knew it the sky was filled with clouds. Lighting began to play and the thunder was crashing. We headed toward the cabin. A great flash of lighting struck the barbed wire fence near us and almost knocked us over. We dropped our irrigating shovels and ran. The rain poured down. Thank God, our crop was saved! The rain was widespread and filled the large ditches with water for several days, so that we could continue to irrigate all the fields. The grain filled out beautifully.

Miss Johnson read a great deal of literature and poetry to us this summer and encouraged us to read more. Much that I know of literature I gained in this way. She arranged the reading so that by the end of the summer, we had covered most of the great works by English and American writers that were usually taught in secondary schools and were required for entrance to college. I shall always be profoundly thankful for the help she gave to Howard and me, and grateful for her friendship.

We farmed the home place this summer too, but did not raise a large crop. There were two good cuttings of alfalfa hay and some grain. The peaches began to bear pretty well and we had some apples.

About the first of September, or a little earlier, the grain was ripe on the Poverty Flat place. We hired it cut at a dollar per acre. Instead of stacking the grain, as was usually done, we decided to thresh it in the field. We got together some four or five teams with hay racks and took the sheaves directly to the threshing machine. It was customary to sack grain, but we simply omitted this process and kept several wagons hauling my share of the grain to town for sale, and Mr. Finney's share to his place, to feed his one thousand chickens. By loading the loose grain directly into the wagons, we saved not only the cost of sacks, but also the cost of extra handling. When the threshing was done, we found that we had raised 2,000 bushels of wheat. We got 90 cents per hundred for our share, or somewhat more than five hundred dollars. After all expenses were paid, I had a check for $250. That check looked extremely insignificant to me in comparison with the great billowing grain fields and the wagonloads of wheat. It represented the work of at least five or six months by Howard and me. However, to have any money at all was much better than being in debt, as we had feared we might be before the rain came.

After a month or two of ditch walking, Clarence went to work in the Farmers' and Merchants' Bank as a bookkeeper. Arthur was still at Paonia. The other boys continued with their school work.

Mr. Crabill, who owned the mill and to whom we had sold our grain, asked me if I would sell him the straw stacks and the use of the pasture at Poverty Flat for his cattle. He also asked me to drive the cattle to water every day about one mile to the Garnet Mesa Ditch, as the ditch going to Poverty Flat was dry. I agreed to do all this for $100. It seemed to me that the work of watering the cattle would last about two months. As in that time it would take me only an hour or two each day to do the work, most of my time could be used in working around the home place. There I could put a final coating of ice over the orchard by very late irrigation so the trees would not bloom too early in the spring and be blasted by the late frosts. Mr. Crabill's $100 looked like easy money.

About this time, we bought ten head of range cows with money we had made from the wheat. We had a chance to choose them from a herd of perhaps two or three hundred. I selected those that I was sure would have calves very early in the spring. Incidentally, I picked cattle that were all roan shorthorns. We had enough hay and straw on the home place, plus some hay from Poverty Flat, to last them through the winter. This was the start in the cattle business that I had so ardently desired. We registered our brand, of which we were quite proud. It was "M="—read as "M lazy eleven". This was considered a very good brand because it was made wholly of straight lines.

In caring for the Crabill cattle I learned quite a little about range cattle and how to handle them. While driving them back and forth to water I continually had my rope down and would practice roping the hind feet of the cows and calves at the back of the herd. This, I knew, was a very valuable accomplishment on the range, where I hoped to be within a few years, as soon as I had obtained enough cattle to warrant caring for them rather than farming. Of course, I did not pull the rope tight, so the cattle would easily step out of it and leave it free for more practice.

The care of the Crabill cattle marked my first fall from grace in respect to swearing since that day at the Oak Creek school house when I was six years old. It happened this way. The weather was cold in early December. I had to cut holes in the ice for the cattle to drink. Immediately after drinking, as a rule, they would saunter slowly back to pasture. One day a warm south wind blew, the sun shone brightly and it became very warm. Above the ditch was a gently rolling slope, facing south. After drinking, all the cattle wished to lie down on the slope and enjoy themselves in the warm sunshine. As I had an appointment downtown, I did not sympathize with their desire for relaxation and warmth, and tried to drive them back to pasture. I would get one end of the bunch up and started, and then try to get the other end going. By the time I got the second group started the others would be lying down again. I ran my horse back and forth in this way vainly for half an hour. Then suddenly my temper became entirely exhausted and before I knew it, I was using much of the choice vocabulary common to coal haulers, cowboys and mule skinners that had almost unconsciously been accumulating in my mind. Soon the cattle, of their own volition, arose from their siesta and started to wander back to the pasture.

I was much ashamed, not merely because I had blasphemed, but also because I had lost my temper. To me, keeping one's temper was a chief requisite of a person who handles horses and cattle. I am not so sure about mules! Old man Marsh, who might be classified as an expert on the subject, maintained that cussing is the only language that a mule really understands. Although this does not apply to cattle, I must confess that there are times when a "cow brute" can try one's patience more than anything else can. It may switch its tail in your face while you are milking, kick over the milk bucket, place its foot in the milk pail, or refuse to be led. Range cattle may stampede. Sometime later, when we were delivering to farmers their cattle which we had kept on the range in the summer, an ornery critter would often refuse to go into its owner's gate and would run back and forth as if no gate were within miles. You might ride toward it, heading it off from the way it was going and trying to start it toward the gate again. Once more it would pass the gate. After some ten or fifteen by-passes, not even a saint could refrain from expressing his feelings.

The story of Brother Duvall offers another illustration of the cussedness of cattle. Brother Duvall was a "holiness" convert and was noted for his piety. He bought a bunch of rather wild cattle that had to be given his brand before they were turned on the range. With some other men, I was helping him brand his cattle after they had been placed in a rather large corral. We would maneuver one into a small side corral, throw it down and brand it, then open a gate to let it go into the field. After we had branded a particularly large and wild steer, instead of going through the opened gate as protocol required, he took after us. All of us ran and climbed the log sides of the corral, except Brother Duvall. In some way or another the snaps on the bottom of his chaps caught together, so that he could move only a few inches at a time. Immediately the enraged steer attacked him, knocked him down into the mud and slush, and would have trampled him to death had not one of the cowboys roped it and pulled it away. Brother Duvall arose on his knees and instead of praying, he swore a blue streak. We were highly amused at this display of inverted piety. Clarence Mower, who professed to be a good Presbyterian "by marriage only," put on the face of a sanctimonious parson and in a solemn manner remarked: "May the good Lord forgive you for swearing like that, Brother Duvall." I imagine that He did.

One frosty morning, I started to hitch Snoozer and Roebuck to the wagon. As I stooped to pick up the neck yoke, with no warning and for no cause whatsoever, Roebuck opened wide his mouth and bit me in the large muscles of my back just a few inches below the shoulder blade. Luckily for me I had on a sheepskin vest which prevented his teeth from going into my flesh, although I heard them bang together as they slipped off the sheepskin. The bite, however, caused a tremendous bruise and gave me excruciating pain. In a frenzy of pain and anger I raised the neck yoke I had in my hand and tried to kill old Roebuck by hitting him over the head. He dodged the blow, and by the time I was able to strike another I was too weak from pain to do anything.

As we had run our home farm well, and had made a success of Poverty Flat, our neighbors seemed to recognize that we were responsible farmers, so when I asked Mr. R. D. Blair if he would rent his place to us on halves, he readily consented. Probably he must have thought that he could not do very much worse with us than with his previous tenants, the man who skipped the country without paying his numerous debts, or his nephew whose little boys had burned the chicken coops, the barn and the haystacks. Finney and I decided that we would not trust our luck again with Poverty Flat.

CHAPTER IX

Farmer

THE BLAIR PLACE, which we had rented for the season of 1900, lay south and east of ours. In fact, our home place had been the northwest quarter of the original Blair 160 acres. The western part of the Blair farm, containing about 50 acres, was planted to alfalfa. The land had an even slope toward our place, so that it had just the right fall for irrigation. East of the alfalfa field, and separated by our own main ditch, which had washed out rather deep and wide, lay a field that could be planted to anything we wished. Beyond it lay a little strip of five or six acres of orchard, mostly apples just starting to bear. There were also two hundred or more apricot trees in full bearing. To the east of our home lay two strips of land, including about twelve acres each, that we planted to oats. Just north of these lay a small strip of very fertile land that we used as a garden. Practically all the land on the Blair place was easily irrigated, as it lay lower than the Garnet Mesa Ditch. It had rather large water rights as measured in cubic feet per second.

We were to farm the place on shares, Blair furnishing the seed, machinery and horses, while we supplied the labor. The crop was to be divided equally between Blair and us.

Along with the place went three work horses, Sandy, Lucy and Stub, as well as a little mare called Nettles, the mother of Sandy and Stub. Each of these horses had characteristics of its own, all of which entered into our life picture.

Sandy was a beautiful bay horse weighing nearly 1,300 pounds.

He had a rather large body but legs like a race horse. His spirit was that of a thoroughbred. However, he was very treacherous, and would run away at the drop of a hat. Stub, whose sire had evidently been a Clydesdale, was as different from Sandy as could be. He weighed only about 800 pounds, but was built just like a Clydesdale, with heavy legs covered with long hair. He was a calm, even-natured horse, with nothing of the fiery spirit of his half-brother Sandy.

Lucy caused me much embarrassment. She was a black mare as big as Sandy and almost as wild by nature. She had cut her leg just above the hoof on a barbed wire fence a short time before, and it had swelled up with "proud flesh" or something of that sort. I "doctored" her with four different prescriptions given me by a quasi-veterinarian, but to no avail. The outer surface healed over in the course of time in a rather rough scab, but she always retained the large swelling that made her appear to have a club foot.

Little Nettles had had numerous colts, each of which assumed much of the form and characteristics of its respective sire—a different one each time. She was well named, for although she was about twenty years old, she was still wild. Nettles thought nothing of trying to buck a person off, or of attempting to run away at the least provocation. She did not believe in mechanical transportation, for she was deathly afraid of bicycles and cars. I was driving her together with a larger horse when the first automobile in the county appeared. She started to run away, but when held in check by a hard pull on the reins and by the weight and size of the other horse, she lay down in the harness, scared almost to death. She never reconciled to such contraptions.

By this time, we had a very good labor force. I was nearly twenty, Clarence eighteen, Howard nearly seventeen and amazingly strong, Hal fourteen, Ralph twelve and Louis Ten. We could readily handle the situation. Although Clarence was now working in the bank, he could help us with the regular morning and evening chores and look after our account books. Everything was ready for scientific farming.

I was the boss of the whole force, and would get them up at a little after four o'clock in the morning. When talking about those days with some of my brothers in recent years, I have been assured by them that I was a terrible taskmaster. Howard and I usually looked after the horses and did the irrigation for the day before breakfast, while the other boys helped Mother get the breakfast, milked the cows and fed the chickens. We were at work in the fields by seven. But I am running ahead of my story, for this was in the summertime and the spring work had first to be done. Most of this I did myself, as Arthur was still at Paonia, Clarence was working in the bank, Howard was hauling coal, and the little boys were in school.

The spring broke rather early, so that it was possible to plow in February. Other farmers made fun of me for attempting to plow while there was still a little frost in the ground in the early morning and the air was chilly. "He that will not plow by reason of the cold, shall beg in harvest and have nothing," I replied, quoting the Scriptures with some bravado. At any rate, I had the two grain fields east of us, and our home fields, all plowed before others thought of starting spring work. I also sowed the east fields to oats nearly a month before the standard time. As, by luck, we did not have a late frost, the early planting was a great success. The oats filled out in a magnificent manner in the cool weather of early summer, and were therefore much heavier than ordinary oats. Because we were the first to cut our crop, we secured the threshing machine ahead of others. As hold-over oats were scarce, we were able to sell our new heavy oats immediately at a high price. Thus, we avoided the expense of storing them, the interest charges for holding them, and the inevitable shrinkage due to the drying out process, handling, and the possible inroads of mice and rats.

In marking out irrigation ditches for the oats, I remembered a saying of one of our former hired men: "If you make the furrows straight, you can stand at the head of the field and see the water clear to the end of each furrow, thus saving the time of going down to the end of the field to make sure that it runs through." I took great pride in making the furrows perfectly straight. To do so it was necessary to stand on the marker and sight through the ring in the center of the reins which connected the horses, to a distant object, and then drive toward that object. I held a very tight rein on the horses so that they could not get an inch out of place. All the neighbors commented on the straightness of the furrows. However, one of them remarked "more crops grow on crooked furrows than on straight."

That spring every cow we had purchased the previous fall had a calf. It always gave me a thrill of pleasure to go out in the early morning and see these little new arrivals standing on their shaky legs by their mothers. To the simple joy of seeing each small white-faced fellow was added the satisfaction of knowing that our herd was doubling.

About the first of May we turned our cattle over to Charles Mundry, to be taken by him to the Grand Mesa range for the summer at $2.00 per head. Most of our neighbors with only a few "critters" did likewise. The cattle would be driven up the various little creeks of the region, to a level where they found sufficient salt weed and new grass to sustain them. Then as the snow receded and the grass became green and abundant, they would gradually climb the mountain into the cedar, oak, quaking aspen and spruce belts. Cattle that were so thin after a winter of inadequate feeding that, according to Bill Lance each one would need "two blankets over it in order to cast a shadow," would be as fat as corn-fed porkers toward the middle of summer.

Just before the time for cutting the first crop of alfalfa hay, the apricots became ripe. There were three varieties: a very large juicy fruit that was delicious but rather soft when ripe, a California variety with a beautiful reddish tinge on the side that was extremely good for shipping or canning, and a small kind. We debated for a few days whether to pack and ship the crop, or to sell it wholesale to the canning factory that had recently been established. Some of our neighbors advised the first method. We finally decided that since our hay was ready for cutting and we had no time to spare, we would accept the canning factory's offer of $20.00 per ton. The cannery agreed to furnish the crates for picking and hauling. To save our very limited money, we secured several North Delta girls to pick the large apricots in exchange for the smaller ones. We then loaded the filled crates on our big hay rack and hauled them to town. There were three or four tons, besides the very ripe ones which all pickers automatically ate. The money received for them appeared to be almost pure velvet, and came at just the right time to pay for a little extra help that we needed in putting up the hay and grain. Some of the neighbors picked and packed their apricots, wrapping each one in paper, placing them in small crates, and shipping them east. Many did not receive sufficient returns to pay for the crates and wrapping paper, not to mention the costs of labor. As was quite common, the commission men blamed a glutted market and spoilage for this sorry outcome.

Immediately after the apricots were harvested, the haying season began. The period when the alfalfa fields were in bloom was just the right time to secure the honey sweetness that added so much to feeding value. From our farm we could look up across the blue carpeted fields and see in the distance the San Juan Range still covered with snow. Following the advice of one progressive farmer, we put up the hay somewhat differently than most others did. Just before we cut the hay, we gave the alfalfa field a thorough irrigating. In this way, the ground would be in fine shape to start the second growth the minute the hay was cut. In the second place, instead of letting the hay dry for a day before raking and shocking it, we raked it absolutely green and shocked it immediately. Due to the almost complete lack of humidity in the air and the hot sun, instead of rotting, as it most certainly would have done in the east, the alfalfa simply packed down and cured perfectly.

Two other favorable results arose from these methods. First, none of the leaves and sugar-filled blossoms fell off to be wasted, as was the case when hay was allowed to dry before the raking and shocking. Again, since the green hay settled down into a rather compact mass, the whole shock could be picked up at one forkful (provided the pitcher were strong), whereas, when hay was shocked dry it was so loose that several attempts with the pitchfork might be needed in order to gather up the sprawling pile. Some of our neighbors said that we were "damned fools" to use such a system. They would have been right, of course, in the east or in case of rain; but in our area during June and July rain was almost unheard of.

For hauling the hay to the stacks, we put together eight or ten boards a foot wide and about fourteen feet long, making a rough sled. On these we placed rope slings, which were arranged in two parts connected by a snap in the center. One small boy drove the team between the rows of shocks, while a man on either side of the sled pitched the hay on the sling. Howard and I bragged that we never swung the pitchfork more than once to lift any shock of hay, no matter how heavy it might be, and that we could pitch more hay in a day than any two men in the county! Be that as it may, we could easily pitch twice as much hay upon these sleds as upon the high wagon racks.

Mr. Blair had a large derrick that could be moved from place to place. It was tall enough to make a haystack thirty feet high. When the sled was driven to the side of a stack, we attached the derrick rope to the sling filled with hay, and lifted it by horse power to the place where the hay was to go. The hay stacker manipulated the load until it was exactly where he wanted it, and then pulled the cord holding the snap. The hay fell upon the stack. Thus, we were able to throw half a ton or more of hay into place in half a minute, instead of pitching it by hand. This system made it possible for one man to stack the hay. We usually made stacks about thirty feet high and thirty feet wide. As one foot of the length of such a stack would weigh a ton, it was easy to figure just how much hay we had put up. By using these new methods, we could cut and stack the hay from nearly sixty acres in about two weeks, thus saving a good deal of labor.

Two rather exciting events occurred during the haying season. One day the mowing machine cut into a hornets' nest. The hornets immediately attacked me and the horses. Sandy and Lucy started to run away with the mowing machine. It was impossible to hold them. We soon ran into a minor irrigation ditch, with a jolt so great that I was thrown off the seat. The jerking of the reins blistered my hands. The team tore over to our large irrigating ditch

Use of a derrick like this one made the work of piling hay much easier and faster. (photographer unknown)

running through the Blair place, which was some five or six feet in depth and about the same in width. Into this ditch fell a tangled mass of horses, harnesses and mowing machine. The horses could not get out, although we unhitched them from the machine and removed a part of their harness. Here was a mess. Suddenly a bright idea struck us. Why not lift the horses out with the derrick? We brought the derrick to the ditch, fastened ropes around the bellies of the horses, tied these to the derrick ropes, to which we fastened another team to do the pulling, and out came the horses, one at a time, covered with mud and considerably subdued.

Old Man Marsh came up one day with his little team of mules to buy a load of hay. We pitched the hay on his rack while he loaded it. After he had piled up a very large load, he got off the hay rack to have a drink of water and to pay us. He told us goodbye, and started to climb the ladder in front of the hay rack. No sooner had he reached the first rung than his little mules began to kick at him, following him up the ladder with their heels. In trying to kick him down from the ladder, one mule kicked over the outside trace. I started to get its leg back in place. "Get away, get away!" yelled Old Man Marsh; "those damned little fiends might kill you. You are a young man. If they kill me it makes no difference." Down he crawled and straightened out the mules. As he started up the ladder they began kicking again. But luckily this time they did not kick over the traces. He finally brought them under control, and drove off with his load of hay.

In the spring we planted several acres of potatoes. During the previous winter potatoes had sold for so little that some growers had not felt it worthwhile to take them out of storage cellars and ship them to market. Early in the spring Mr. Hutchinson, who had a large potato farm a few miles west of Delta on the Gunnison River, put an advertisement in the paper offering people all the potatoes they could use if they would haul them out of his cellars. As it seemed to us unlikely that there would be two years of low prices in succession, we went down to his place and secured several tons of potatoes with which to plant ten acres.

Between the first cutting of hay and the harvesting of the oats, Mother suggested that I should go to the grand and glorious Fourth of July Celebration to be held at Ouray about sixty miles south of us. The railroad was offering an excursion for the occasion. This was my first experience of going more than twenty-five miles from the town of Delta, since we had moved there—and my first train ride since we had come by train to the Western Slope. During all the intervening years, I had had no occasion to go outside our home territory, which I could quickly and easily cover on horseback.

I was much interested by Ouray and also by the celebration. When we arrived in the morning it was snowing, with two or

The town of Ouray, about 60 miles south of Delta, was a thriving mining town in 1900. (photographer unknown)

three inches of snow already on the ground. About eleven o'clock the sun came out, and the day was cool and sparkling. Ouray, which was a mining camp, was located in a sort of pocket in the mountains. High and often precipitous mountains surrounded it everywhere except on the north. The sides of the mountains were covered with mines and prospect holes. In many places heavy cables ran from the mines down to the stamping mills in the town. Toward the southwestern part of the town was a high perpendicular cliff, at the top of which the Uncompahgre River suddenly plunged underground, and dropped into a narrow, box canyon as a waterfall perhaps 150 feet high. Nearby were two springs, one hot and the other cold, which Father Escalante had noted in his diary when trying to find a trail from Santa Fe to the California Missions in 1776.

Two kinds of contests at Ouray were particularly interesting to me: the mule packing contest and the rock drilling contests. In the mule packing contest, each contestant was supposed to pack three sacks of ore on each side of about fifty mules, and tie them in place with a diamond hitch. Some of the mules objected to the packing process and would snort, kick, or buck. If I remember rightly, none of them brayed, for that expression of emotion, I was told, was reserved for moments just before lunch and quitting time, when a whole string of mules would simultaneously lift up their voices in prayer. I have forgotten the time taken for packing the winning string of mules, but it was remarkably short.

There were two different drilling contests, one for a man working alone, and one for two men. The second type of contest was quite exciting. Two men stood upon a solid block of granite about eight feet square. Near them was a man with a bucketful of water to pour into the drill holes or over the men, if they became too hot. One man held the drill while the other wielded the hammer. They started with very short drills and increased them in length as the hole grew deeper. It was amazing to me that the man holding the drill could change it and put another in its place while the hammer was in the air. A single false stroke of the hammer might split the hand of the drill holder wide open. But there were no slips! Every two minutes the men changed places. Unless my memory fails me, the "Terrible Swedes" who won the contest, drilled thirty-seven inches into hard granite in fifteen minutes. This was considered to be a normal day's work.

Between the different cuttings of hay and the harvesting of the grain, we tried to make things around the house a little more convenient than they had been. Ever since we moved to The Elms, we had hauled water for domestic use in barrels from the town water tank on Garnet Mesa, using an old wagon for the purpose.

This was very unsatisfactory because our supply would always seem to run out just when we were busiest. It was also hard for Mother to dip and carry the water that she needed for cooking and dish washing from barrels outside the house, particularly if, as sometimes happened, we had left the barrels standing in the water wagon. To do away with these difficulties we build a large stone cistern by the house. In order to fill the cistern, we constructed a wooden tank that we left on the water wagon. We filled our tank from the town tank and emptied it into the cistern. This arrangement worked satisfactorily for a year or so, until seepage water with a tinge of alkali permeated the stones of the cistern and made the water unfit to use. From that time on, we simply used the wooden tank, which was provided with a faucet so that Mother could obtain the water easily.

Later in the summer, Arthur came back from Paonia—where he had been working in Mr. Royce's general store—to visit us for a few days. He was soon to leave for Boulder, Colorado, to enter the State Medical School. He and I went up toward Cottonwood Canyon on the Uncompahgre Plateau for a load of wood. After camping that night in the cedars, we cut our trees and made them ready to be put on the wagon. Then we drove the wagon from place to place and loaded it with the small cedar logs. I held the reins in my hands or else kept them close to my feet for I did not trust Sandy and Stub, the horses. About the time we were completing the load while the reins were lying at my feet, Arthur swung the ax to cut a binding pole, a small pole used to twist the log chain tight. A twig hit Sandy. With no warning whatsoever, the team started to run, just as I was in the position of lifting the last log. I snatched up the lines but they slipped through my fingers, burning the skin as they went; Away tore the horses through the cedars.

It was only a moment until Stub went on one side of a cedar tree and Sandy on the other, breaking the neck yoke. The wagon came dead up against the tree and the horses could go no further.

We ran to see what damage had been done. Stub had cut a long gash in his left front leg, which appeared to be over an inch wide and nearly an inch deep. Luckily it ran the length of the leg and had not severed any important muscles. We unhitched the horses and tied them to trees. Then by using the brake rope, we fastened Stub so that we could sew up the wound. Arthur, who had become the cobbler of the family and had learned to sole shoes and mend them, took out the sewing outfit he usually carried with him for repairing shoes and harnesses, and sewed up Stub's wound with a waxed end. We cut a piece of cedar and with our axe and jackknives, made it into a new neck yoke, to which we attached the old hardware. Arthur then sewed up the lines hitching the horses together, which had been broken in the escapade, and away we started. Although Stub limped, we were able to reach home very late at night with a load of wood. Within a week or so, after being kept in the barn, and having his wound treated daily with carbolic acid and water, Stub was well again.

Quite a large part of the hay that we had raised on the Blair place was hauled to town and sold to individuals. One day when Hal and I were taking a large load to town, at the top of the grade leading off the mesa we locked one of the back wheels with a chain, as we usually did, to keep the load from pushing too heavily on the team. We started down, but had not gone far when the chain came loose, and the weight suddenly shifted and pressed on the horses. They started to run. Near the bottom of the mesa was a fork in the road, one branch going down to town and the other turning back up the mesa again. Very foolishly, I tried to make the team turn up the latter road. At the junction the road bed slanted and was partly circular. The slanting curve, combined with the momentum caused by the running team, suddenly overturned the whole load of hay, with the hay rack upside down on top of it. I felt what was going to happen, and yelling to Hal, "Jump!" we both jumped as far as we could, landing just beyond the load of hay. The horses, pulling nothing but the running gear, raced up the road, crashed through a picket fence surrounding a Catholic monastery, and were stopped by some of the inmates. We drove the team back to where the load of had tipped off, fastened the chain to the hay rack, dragged the rack to a place where we could put it on the running gear, and with heavy hearts pitched up most of the hay again.

Toward the early part of the fall, I made up my mind that I wanted a large, good looking bay horse to match with Blair's horse, Sandy, instead of the club-footed Lucy. I had seen a large bay horse in Obert's field—one that I thought would make a good match, although he was larger than Sandy. I found out that he was considered tame, was halter broken but had never been harnessed, and that I could purchase him for $100. I bought him.

He was a beautiful colt weighing nearly 1,400 pounds. As he had been running all his life in the open fields and all summer in a rather damp alfalfa pasture, his hoofs had grown to a great size. The first thing to do, I thought, was to get those huge hoofs trimmed down and have the colt shod. He seemed so gentle that I anticipated no trouble in the world of breaking him. Howard and I took him down behind the lumber wagon to Mr. Cramer's blacksmith shop. Mr. Cramer, who was a rather slight man with a bald head, evidently shared our assumption that the colt was gentle, and started to pick up his left front foot preparatory to trimming it. Like a flash the colt lifted both of his front feet high in the air, and struck. One foot came down on poor Cramer's head, cutting a gash three inches long. We called a doctor, who took several stiches in the scalp. Mr. Cramer's helper, who was a large and powerful man, swore that there was never a horse in the world he could not shoe. He picked up the colt's front foot. With a mighty lunge, the colt reared, struck, and threw the man half way across the shop. "We will fix him yet," said the blacksmith, as he arranged a twitch to put on the colt's nose as a method of holding him down. The twitch consisted of a strong thick leather cord tied firmly to a stick about two feet long. A noose of the cord was placed over the soft part of the nose, and so arranged that when one gave a pull on the stick, it would tighten. The twitch would give the horse considerable pain if drawn tight. This was usually an effective method of preventing a horse from rearing. I held the twitch while the blacksmith tried to get the horse shod. By the time he had put on the two front shoes, both of us were tired out. "Come back for the hind shoes when the devil is broken," said the blacksmith.

The colt seemed to be in a fury at being mastered. I started to tie him to the back of the wagon in order to lead him home. He struck at me but I dodged. Both of his front feet went in between the spokes of the wagon wheel, and I feared that he would break his legs. He soon freed himself, however. Howard and I were mighty blue. How could it be that a colt which seemed so gentle when being led could be such and imp of Satan when being handled? We put him in the stable. The next morning when Hal went into the stall beside the colt to curry him, he suddenly lunged sideways against Hal and nearly crushed the boy to death against the wall.

The next day I harnessed the colt and drove him around the

corral with Sandy, without hitching him to anything. He seemed tame enough, and would accompany Sandy and go and stop without trouble. The next afternoon, Howard and I took another team and pulled the large 3 ½ inch wagon[5] out to the main road in front of our place, to be sure we had some maneuvering room, just in case! We took the team back, hitched Sandy and the colt together, and drove them up to the wagon, bringing one on either side of the tongue. Howard held a hackamore around the colt's nose, while I held the lines and hitched up. I got in the wagon seat and Howard was just getting ready to jump in, when like a flash, both horses started to run. The hackamore was jerked out of Howard's hands and he was thrown to the ground. In a moment, one of the horses had stepped on the hackamore and it was broken in two. Up the road we flew, to the upper part of Garnet Mesa, which was entirely barren except for a little salt weed and low sage brush. Here was a level open place of several hundred acres. I ran the horses around and around this mesa until they were white with foam. Even after they had their fill of running, I urged them with the whip, hoping to teach them not to try such antics again. Then I went back and picked up Howard. As we drove around for another hour or so, both horses were quiet and tractable.

The next afternoon we again hitched the team to the wagon. They started out as though they were perfectly gentle. I drove up to the ten-acre potato field, where a sulky plow had been left for use in harvesting the crop. Thinking that the colt was all right, I hitched the team to the plow. Something startled them and away they went! With the long lever on the right side of the plow, I sent the blade down deep into the ground. This did not stop them. Around and around this ten-acre field they ran. I have never seen potatoes turn

---

5   This refers to the size of the axel hub, or "skein"

out so well and so rapidly, being thrown in every direction.

Soon the foaming horses were tired. After they wished to stop, I struck them with the end of the lines and urged them on. I would show them a thing or two! By this time, I was so angry with both horses that I decided to subdue them thoroughly by driving them up to Winton's mine for a load of coal, leaving Howard and the boys to pick up the potatoes. Though it was now rather late in the afternoon, I carried out this plan. Before I reached the mine, night had fallen, and I could not see more than a few steps ahead. I was afraid that at any moment the team would go off the road and cause a wreck; but they finally brought me up to the lighted bunk house safe and sound.

The next morning, after loading on two tons of coal, I started home. As soon as I got into the wagon seat, the team broke into a run. Luckily the road was slightly upgrade for the first two or three hundred yards from the mine, so that by putting on the brakes and pulling hard on the reins, I could prevent them from dashing toward their home stable too rapidly. After they had lost this round, I was able to control them well enough for some miles. At the grade up Surface Creek Mesa, I found a man with a load of coal just in front of me stuck on a curve. Stopping the team just before the steep grade began, and tying the lines slightly around the brake, I went ahead to assist him. A sound made me look back; and there was my team coming up the grade on the run. I rushed down and stopped them. Half a dozen times that day the team started to run, but could not make too much progress with the heavy load of coal.

Although we drove the new colt for over a month, we never succeeded in taming him. I began to have a suspicion that he had been roughly handled before I bought him, and by bad management had become spoiled and vicious. With the coming of the snow and ice it was not safe to use him for hauling coal from the Rollin's mine, which Howard was doing. We named him Satan, and I began to make plans to trade him off or sell him.

Rather late in the fall, the cattle began coming off the range and into the winter pastures and feeding places. The ten cows that we had sent out on the range came in, bringing their calves, which had grown large and fat.

That winter, in order to keep the teams busy and lay up a little cash, we hauled coal from the Rollins mine. Although hauling from this mine was rather dangerous, we believed that it would yield more money than we could make in the two-day journey to and from the Winton mine. Howard and I took turns at hauling coal, looking after the cattle, and doing the winter farm work. In order to be among the first ones loaded at the mine, the boy whose turn it was to haul would rise at four, have breakfast eaten and the team harnessed by five, and start out in the dark. Once all the side connecting points had been passed, and the road ahead led only to the Rollins mine, Howard would often put a lighted lantern under a blanket for warmth, lie down in the hay we carried for the horses' noon-time bite, and go to sleep, trusting the team to follow the road up to the mine, as they always did. One morning when Howard was going to the mine under those circumstances, he was suddenly awakened by a bump, bump, bump. He stopped the team and went back to see what had happened. The floor of the bridge over a deep ravine was made of heavy planks, some of which projected a foot or so beyond the others. The bumps had been caused by the wagon wheels running over the edges of the longest planks, and sinking down in the spaces between them. From the places where he could see the wheel marks, it appeared that if the wagon had gone two or three inches further to the right, it would have tipped over into the ravine. I do not know whether Howard mended his ways, but I forever after that stayed awake on my trips to the mine, even at the expense of a little sleep and warmth.

That fall we did not suffer for lack of farm produce. We had planted our large garden on the Blair place very near the Garnet Mesa Ditch so that we could use the water, however little, to good advantage. As the garden did well, we had many vegetables to store. Although the home place had suffered from a shortage of water in the late summer and fall, it had, nonetheless, yielded more peaches than we could use, and several barrels of apples that we stored in the cellar. We shipped some of the peaches to market, with the usual unsatisfactory results. However, farming the home place had become a rather secondary consideration to us, since our labor force now made it possible to expand our activities in several directions.

That fall Delta began to receive more entertainment than had previously been furnished by the local churches. Some years before this, Frank Sanders, who had "struck it rich," built a brick hardware store, the second story of which he dubbed the "Anna-Dora Opera House." Sanders devised this name in honor of Ray Simpson's daughter, Anna, and his own daughter, Dora. The story told around town as to the source of Sanders' wealth was that he had been prospecting for gold in the San Juan region, and after working a long time and finding nothing, became discouraged and decided to quit. "Try just one more day, Frank," said his wife, "and then if nothing turns up, stop digging." The next day he struck a rich vein of ore.

Several road shows played in the opera house, but I was never able to attend. About this time, Thomas Kearns, who according to local newspaper accounts was a star of Gilbert and Sullivan operas in New York City, came to Delta for his health. With the aid of Miss Johnson and others he staged several musical comedies. The only one that I could manage to hear was The Mikado. Unfortunately, Kearns died within the next few years, as did also Miss Johnson, his alto star.

Delta in my time, almost always had a sprinkling of teachers, actors, singers, and artists from the east, most of whom, like many other newcomers, had moved there because of lung trouble. Many of these persons came to our home, where they found in Mother an intellectual companion. I felt rather ignorant and uncouth beside them. Among them I remember well a young Polish pianist named Poffsky, who was kind enough to make our old piano ring. He was very lonely and longed for city life again. He went down to the station almost every day to see the train pull in, as it seemed to be his only contact with the outside world.

In 1899 a new minister, Dr. Frothingham, a member of the famous Frothingham family of Massachusetts, came to the Presbyterian church. He was an extremely well-educated man and had far greater general ability than might have been expected in a town the size of Delta. The reason we were so fortunate to secure him was that he had been ordered to Colorado for his health. He was a rather small man, with keen eyes that often betrayed an equally keen sense of humor. As he was very friendly, I enjoyed talking to him. Almost immediately after his arrival he began to make plans for a brick church, which was completed within a year or so and still stands.

One day, I asked Dr. Frothingham to give me some topics and problems to think about when I was hauling coal, plowing or riding for cattle. "In order to do much thinking," he said, "you must have a large store of information in your mind. The mind cannot think without information any more than a mill can grind without grain." He followed up this advice by lending me several books to read. His viewpoint was a surprise to me, as I had supposed that a person could take a large subject and by pure thought regarding it could arrive at some lofty conclusion. I began to consider Dr. Frothingham's suggestion. Perhaps my limited knowledge was the reason why I did not seem to be able to talk with well-educated people as I should have liked to do. Would I have to obtain a formal education before I could really associate with Dr. Frothingham, Uncle Cornelius, missionaries or educated people from the east who stopped off to see us, or even my friends who were going to college?

Meanwhile, we were still wrestling with the problem of what to do with the wild colt we called Satan. One day in the early part of February, I was riding down by Mr. Barker's place on the Gunnison River. As I passed a field where several horses were standing near the fence, I saw a horse that appeared to be almost a duplicate of Satan. Mr. Barker was standing by his corral as I rode in and greeted him. Then I said, "What will you take for that colt? I have one that just matches him. The two should go together." "I will not sell him, replied Barker; "but if your colt is what you say he is, I might give you a trade. Bring him down." The next day, I led Satan down behind my saddlehorse.

Old man Barker looked over the colt with an experienced eye, for he was a good horse trader. Finally, he said, "They surely would make a fine span of horses and should go together." "Well," I suggested, "sell your colt to me and I will match them up, and sell them for fire horses." "No," he said, "I need a team of large horses; I'd rather trade you for your colt." This was just what I wanted.

"What have you got to trade?" He took me to the corral in which there were eight or ten horses, saying: "You see those two little brown mares? I will give you those for your colt. They are three and four years old and are full sisters. They have never had a halter on, but seem no wilder than most range horses."

The young mares did not look any too prepossessing. They weighed about 1,000 pounds each, their hair was long and shaggy from the winter, and their manes and tails were filled with cockle burrs. It seemed to me, however, that when broken properly, they might make a fine team, especially since they were young enough to grow, if well fed. We made the trade. "I reckon you will have some trouble getting those mares home," old man barker grinned. "They are full sister of Swamp Angel," he announced—that devil of a horse that I traded to Long and that you let get away."

I looked at the mares again. Sure enough, they were of the same build as Swamp Angel, and if their long hair were off would probably be about the same color. "That's alright with me," I said. "The colt I have just traded to you is not too tame. His name is Satan. He might make a good fire horse at that, for he surely can run. I tried two months to break him and had to give it up. He was too much for me—and a horse that is too much for me, is too much for any man." Despite this bluffing, I felt a bit sick.

Mounting Roebuck, I managed to separate the mares from Barker's other horses and to drive them along, though with some difficulty, until at last I had them in our corral. There I found some nice long wisps of alfalfa hay and offered it to them. The older one stood in the corner trembling, and would not approach me. I put a box of oats out for them and brought them a tub of water and some hay. In this way, I fed and watered them for several days.

For the next few days, I worked to win their confidence. In only a day or so, I could pat the older one, whom I called, "Topsy." One day I took a rope and put it around her neck. I held a little hay in front of me and gradually backed off, holding the rope tight. She followed without protest. The other mare, which I had named "Jess," was much harder to tame; but gradually she learned to eat hay from my hand and to let me pat her neck. Finally, I was able to put a rope on her and lead her around. She did not seem to be vicious, but was terribly frightened and nervous. I had to move slowly as a burglar, for at any quick move she would tremble. At last, one day, after harnessing Topsy quite easily, I tried to put the harness on Jess. After several unsuccessful tries, I finally got the collar on. It took me the greater part of a day to add the rest of the harness: the hames, one part of the breeching, one part of the bridle at a time. After I finally got the harness on Jess, I did not take it off for nearly a week. In the meantime, I hitched the horses together and drove them around and around the corral, teaching them to go and to stop.

After a few days of this kind of training, Howard and I hitched the mares to a wagon and started out with them on a walk. After going about a mile or so, we let them trot. We drove them this way for a day or so and then tried them on the harrow, which required an easy but steady pull. At last, I started to plow an alfalfa field with them; a sure test of pulling ability, for alfalfa roots are almost as tough as leather and it takes both strength and steadiness to cut them off.

During all this time, I spent hours in currying and feeding the pair. Within a week or so, their old rough winter hair had all come off and they were as sleek as a seal just out of water. In order to make their coats even more shiny, I purloined eggs that the chickens had laid in the mangers and fed them to the mares.

In a few months they weighed nearly 1,300 pounds. They had so lost their wildness and fear that very soon the smaller boys were riding them when cultivating the garden. They became the most satisfactory team I ever had, very good looking, perfectly steady, and completely gentle.

One day for devilry, I drove the team into old man Barker's yard. "My," he said, "that is a swell team. Where did you get it?" "These mares are the full sisters of Swamp Angel," I answered. "How is your colt?" Barker would not believe me at first. "Well," he admitted, "you skinned me. I have never been able to do a damned thing with that colt. I guess you told me the truth when you said he would make a good fire horse, for he surely likes to run." I found out much later from the blacksmith who had first tried to shoe him, that Satan was finally conquered and became a good work horse.

The real test of my brown team came when it was time to do the country "road work." It was the custom for many of the farmers to work out their road taxes by furnishing teams and drivers. The road overseer had a very large plow for tearing up the ground preparatory to using the slip scrapers. To pull it through hard, packed roadway, or through stones and brush beside the roadway, required really powerful and steady teams. Many a good farm team, that never made any objection to dragging a harrow or even hauling a light load of coal, balked when confronted with such a stiff pulling. This was particularly true in the early spring when horses had not been worked much for months past.

On the first day of road work in front of our place, I drove up my brown mares. A neighbor's team, hitched ahead of the overseer's, was jerking, balking and getting nowhere with the plowing. "Well, young man," said the overseer, "do you think your hand-polished little team is good enough to put on the plow in front, along with my big steady horses?" "You bet," I answered; "they are as steady as yours." He laughed and told me to hook on. I did so, while the neighbors watched to see what would happen. I pulled the reins very tight, spoke gently to the team, and away we went, all four horses pulling as one. Roots, stones, hard packed roads and other obstructions made no difference. The neighbors were generous in praising my handsome, steady, obedient mares, and although I tried to conceal the pleasure such remarks gave me, inwardly I was proud and happy.

CHAPTER X

Peach Valley

THE YEAR 1900 had seemed to demonstrate several things: first, that we could manage the two places so that most of the boys could go to school in the winter. Second, that the boys constituted a summer force large enough to handle more alfalfa and grain than we could grow on our place and the Blair's place combined. Third, that the continual shortage of water under Garnet Mesa Ditch made highly uncertain a good crop of spring wheat and late cuttings of alfalfa. Fourth, that it was unlikely we would be able to make much money from our orchard. Finally, that we would need a place to winter our numerous cattle.

The last factor was probably the most compelling. Aunt Sarah had just received from the King of Siam a large amount to settle her late husband's claims upon a teak business in which I believe he and the King were jointly interested, and she had made Mother a gift of $1,500. Howard and I persuaded Mother to invest the bulk of this money in cattle, and had contracted for 50 head of "springers"—heifers that would drop their first calves in the early spring. For these we were to pay $28.00 per head when the train load of cattle purchased by several Delta men arrived from Oregon. I think that Mother consented to this largely because our orchard had yielded a minimum of fruit, although it was about seven years old. Season after season late frosts had killed the blossoms, despite our efforts to protect them by using "smudge pots."

We began to look around for more fields to conquer. Toward

the middle of February, 1901, we learned that a Denver company which still had some 600 acres of land in Peach Valley had finally given up the idea that the valley was an orchard paradise, and was willing to rent it to someone who would gradually plant all of the good land to alfalfa, and pay the almost negligible taxes. The entire valley had originally been laid out by these Denver real estate promoters in small tracts of from ten to twenty acres, which were planted to orchards and called "fruit farms." The tracts were sold to innocents who were led to believe that within a few years they could make a living as independent fruit raisers. I never knew whether the whole proposition was merely a fake, or whether the promoters were themselves, innocents. At any rate, we decided to rent the acreage still owned by the company as a place where we could handle our cattle.

Peach valley consisted of two parts. The region to the west was covered by very thin adobe soil, under which lay, at varying depths, nothing but shale. It was here that the land had been planted to orchards. The fruit trees on most of these flats were nothing but dead wand-like sticks. On others, where the soil was a bit deeper, were pathetic struggling little trees with a few yellow leaves, slowly dying as their roots reached shale. Several small houses which had been built in this section were now deserted. Some of this land, however, was apparently good enough to produce a few crops of grain.

Between the western and the eastern parts of the valley was a little ridge, on which stood a small shack or farm house and a barn belonging to the development company. By the barn was a good-sized pond made for watering stock. Our rented land included a good deal of almost useless land on the west side, the land on the ridge, and some good land to the east.

On the east side of the ridge lay by far the best part of the valley. Here were perhaps a hundred acres of rather deep rich soil. A little stream ran through the center of this land—at least, it was a stream in the early part of the year, after heavy snows or rains, or when irrigation water flowed into it. In places the stream bed was twenty or thirty feet wide, and much of it was covered with tall grass which the cattle loved. It was in this part of the valley that some forty or fifty acres had already been planted to alfalfa. We figured that by planting fifty or sixty acres of additional land we would have an alfalfa field large enough to feed our cattle, and would have hay to sell, besides.

The lower end of the valley had become seepage land, with a coat of white alkali. In spots it was like a mire. Evidently, the seepage water from the irrigated fields above had struck the underlying shale, and had come out in all the low places.

Peach Valley lay about eight miles east of Delta, beyond Garnet Mesa. Between Garnet Mesa and the valley lay barren undulating adobes, except for a few little grain farms in places where the soil was not too thin. In the early spring time, these adobes would show streaks of green, where great tumbleweeds blown from irrigated country had scattered their seeds. Within a week or so, however, the green streaks of young tumbleweed shoots, which never grew over and inch or so high, would wither away. Nothing remained but the dreary grey adobes, which in the hottest of days of midsummer radiated a quivering glare.

East of Peach Valley, beyond a few miles of adobes, was the Vernal Mesa. This was a high ridge covered with sage brush and scrub cedar. From the top of this ridge, going down precipitously in places, fell the walls of the Black Canyon of the Gunnison. A very rough wagon road, or rather trail, led up from the valley, and a different route that passed for a trail, went into the canyon.

Nature had played strange tricks in this country. The adobe land had evidently been the bottom of the ocean. When anyone dug a few feet into adobe ridges, great streaks of white alkali crystals were found. As water came into contact with them, they made a reddish alkali solution. The base of the mesa was filled with shale, shale oil, and in places a very low grade of iron ore. The upper part of the ridge, however, was a sandy, gravelly loam. South of the valley for many miles the adobe country continued. It would be hard to imagine a more desolate and uninviting place than Peach Valley. The only thing pleasant about it was its name.

Peach Valley was poorly named. A more infertile and desolate piece of land would be hard to find. (photo by FF Blachly, c. 1934)

There were, however, as we saw it then, several reasons why we should rent the valley land. In the first place, the Peach Valley ranch was under the Loutsenheiser Ditch, which ran from the Uncompahgre River above Montrose, about twenty-five or thirty miles from the valley. This fact seemed to assure us a better chance at water than we had under the Garnet Mesa Ditch, which started much lower down the river. We believed, mistakenly, that the Loutsenheiser Ditch had very good priority rights to the water of the Uncompahgre River, and we knew that the ranch was entitled to three acre feet of water, which was a large amount. In the second place, the prospects for feeding cattle were good. We could raise a great deal of hay and could arrange very cheaply with a few grain ranchers scattered through the little valleys in the nearby adobe country to obtain fall pasturage and straw stacks. On the eastern side of the ranch, toward the Vernal Mesa, there was salt weed the cattle liked. Third, there was practically no rent to pay for the place. The company furnished alfalfa seed, which we could sow together with oats in the spring. We could count upon raising a good crop of oats. The oat straw would contain some alfalfa hay, making an excellent mixture to feed cattle. After one season in our hands, the fertile eastern area would contain a well-established alfalfa planting of nearly 100 acres, which would give us several cuttings of hay each year. Although the Peach Valley ranch furnished no horses or other livestock, it had good farming implements, including plows, mowing machines, a hay rack and a grain binder, all of which we could use. Of teams we now had plenty, with two of our own and two belonging to the Blair place.

We hoped that our extended farming and cattle operations would make it unnecessary for is to spend the cold winter months hauling coal. Instead, we planned to bale the hay that could be spared after feeding our cattle, and to haul it from Peach Valley. It was our idea that by raising diversified crops, breeding and fattening cattle, and marketing hay, we would practically always be at work with our teams. We would now have about 235 acres under cultivation, as well as plenty of pasturage for cattle. To keep everything going at the home place, the Blair place, and the Peach

Valley ranch, would require careful planning.

Irrigation was an almost continuous process from March to the end of the year. The final irrigation in December was given in order to cover the orchard land with heavy ice to hold back the blooming of the trees in early spring. During most of the season we would get up at four o'clock to irrigate. In order to reach the different fields quickly, we used saddle horses. Since I supervised not only the irrigation but all the work of the three places, I was in the saddle a good deal of the time. It took much thought and effort to keep the teams, implements (which we used interchangeably on the different places), boys, irrigating water and ripening crops, all coordinated. During the busiest part of the haying season, I found it necessary to fire one or two men as temporary helpers.

We started plowing at Peach Valley early in March. One Sunday, Howard and I, in violation of the family's principles, were plowing there because we considered it extremely necessary to get the oats and alfalfa in early. Since we had not gone home on Saturday night, as was our usual custom, Mother must have become suspicious, for about the middle of the afternoon she appeared in a buggy. She was profoundly shocked that any of her sons would desecrate the Holy Sabbath.

We planted about fifty acres to oats and alfalfa in the eastern part of the valley and twenty-five acres to oats alone in the western part. Then we returned to Garnet Mesa and planted wheat and oats on the Blair place. Next, we set out a large garden on the Blair place.

About the first of April, the train load of cattle from Oregon arrived, and I went down to the stockyards to pick out our fifty heifers. The ones I chose were all shorthorn and half Hereford, with red bodies and white faces. All of them had been bred to

Hereford bulls and each would have a calf within a short time. We fell in love with them at first sight, and were proud to see them in our home field. We felt that now were really beginning to get into the cattle business. After keeping them on the home place for a few weeks, we sent them and our other cattle by Charlie Mundry to the Grand Mesa for summer pasture.

Again, we sold the apricots on the Blair place to the canning factory. Next, we started haying in Peach Valley, cutting all the large hay fields one at a time, racking and shocking it immediately. By the time the last part of the field was cut, the hay from the first part was ready to haul in. In order to handle the hay, we made ourselves a large derrick. A tall spruce mast was centered in a frame work of heavy spruce logs about fifteen feet square, which rested on the ground. Several braces running up from the framework fastened to a heavy plank, with a hole through which the mast ran. A stationary boom was fastened near the top of the mast, the tip of which was about forty feet from the ground. At the end of the boom was a single pulley through which ran a rope to raise the hay. One part of the rope went over to the mast through a double pulley, and down so that it could be drawn by a horse in order to pull the load.

An amusing thing happened as we got ready to thread the boom with the rope for the first time. We had thrown down several loads of hay, so that I would have an easy place to fall in case I lost my grip while crawling along the boom to its end. I admitted to the boys that I was rather afraid to attack the job. Louis, who was about eleven years old at the time, volunteered to thread it for me, for a dollar. He took the rope and inched himself along the boom. When he got to the very end, he said that he was scared and demanded an extra dollar to finish the job. I was glad to promise him this, although I regarded it as a kind of blackmail. He maintains to this day that he never got either dollar!

One day while riding back from our Garnet Mesa farm, near a large arroyo we saw a little half-grown coyote and immediately chased him. He tried his best to get back into the arroyo where I suppose his home was; but we turned him to the open adobes. For quite a while he kept running until his tongue was between his front legs and his tail between his hind legs. He was completely "tuckered out"; and finally had to lie down. I picked him up, held him in the front of my saddle and went to the cabin, to which I tied him with a chain. He was as quiet as a new born lamb. That evening, as a first step toward taming him, I started to pat him on the head saying, "Good little coyote, good little coyote." Suddenly he jumped up and bit me right through the end of my finger and finger nail. We attempted to feed him, but he would not eat. Finally, I shot a rabbit and tossed a raw hind leg in the air to him. He jumped and snatched it. I fed him this way for several days, but without any effect in making him tamer. Being soft hearted, we finally turned him loose.

Another day Howard and I, just for sport, rode after a coyote in the adobes. He was going mighty fast, but so were we. Suddenly my horse stepped into a prairie dog hole. Over he went head first and landed square on his back, splitting the light saddle on which I was riding. Luckily the momentum had thrown me far beyond him. As I had done a great deal of practice on horizontal bars, both at school and at home, and some trapeze work as well, I landed safely without hurting myself.

During the time we spent in Peach Valley we "bached," getting our own meals. We were not the world's best cooks, and the meals we concocted had a tendency to consist largely of bacon and eggs, pancakes, hot biscuit and such fruit as we had been able to bring from home. At first, we had great difficulty in keeping the food supplies from mice and pack rats. We finally made a large hanging shelf, suspending it in the middle of the room from the rafters of the shack with barbed wire. This proved a little too much for the sly marauders.

The heat of the shack was extreme in the middle of the summer, as it sat on the west side of the adobe hill. It did not cool off sufficiently to be comfortable even at night, so we slept out of doors on the bare adobe ground. The air was perfectly clear and the stars were brilliant. I enjoyed nothing better than lying on my back looking up at them. Sometimes on moonlight nights kangaroo rats would come out and appear to dance in the moonlight. They had very short legs in front and extremely long legs in back, just like those of kangaroos—hence the name. I have never seen rats like these anywhere else, although it is said that they are common in Arizona. We were not troubled by mosquitoes on the adobes, but in the wet alfalfa fields when we were cutting hay, there were so many that slapping the belly of a horse would make the hand red with blood.

Even before we had quite finished the first crop of hay in Peach Valley, we started cutting hay on the Blair place with a part of our gang. Following this, we cut the grain in Peach Valley and stacked it, and then the grain on the Blair place. As we had the binder from Peach Valley, I also cut the grain of several of our neighbors. Grain cutting was a rather jolting operation, for it was necessary to cross and recross hundreds of little irrigation ditches in the process. By the time all the grain was cut, it was time for the second cutting of alfalfa. Although there was enough water in the Loutsenheiser Ditch to irrigate a few acres of alfalfa in Peach Valley for the third crop, the Garnet Mesa Ditch had run practically dry and no third crop at home or on the Blair place was possible. What little water there had been in the middle of the summer, we had used for the orchard.

One day that summer, while we happened to be at home, we received news that Mr. W. A. Womack, the father-in-law of Mr. Neighbors, who had worked for Father on the lower Garnet Mesa ranch, had been shot and killed by a man named Mehaney up at the Grand Mesa Lakes. The killing brought to a head a very strained relationship that existed between the early settlers and the stockholders of the Surface Creek and Reservoir Company, on the one hand, and an Englishman who had leased the use of the Grand Mesa Lakes and reservoirs, on the other hand. The basic reason for the ill feeling was the difference between English and American hunting and fishing rights.

Early in the 1800's, William Alexander came to the Grand Mesa region and took up—under the preemption laws governing the former Ute Indian Reservation lands—160 acres near the body of water still called Alexander lake. A little later he took into partnership Richard Forest, for whom Forest Lake was then named. Alexander and Forest constructed a hotel and fish hatcheries, and in 1884 the partners began constructing dams and developing lakes in this neighborhood for the purpose of fishing and raising trout.

In 1886, Alexander and Forest made a contract with the Surface Creek and Reservoir Company to assist it in locating suitable sites for dams and in building dams. The company was engaged in developing a large storage system of lakes and reservoirs (the latter largely in slough areas), for the Surface Creek irrigation project. In return for the assistance given by the partners, the company granted them fishing privileges. Such privileges were not exclusive, as the stockholders of the Ditch and Reservoir Company retained the right to fish in the lakes and reservoirs of the system. In practice, almost everyone who wished to fish, did so.

Presently, Alexander disappeared under mysterious circumstances. and nothing was ever heard regarding him. Forest seems to have claimed ownership of the partnership property. In 1896, he sold the 160 acres of land, the hotel, fish hatcheries, and apparently the fishing rights granted by the Ditch and Reservoir Company, to an English barrister named William Radcliffe. The new owner began to treat the holdings as a private reserve, and to deny fishing rights to all others. He evidently interpreted his own rights as exclusive. However, the stockholders of the Ditch and Reservoir Company continued to fish in all the lakes of the system, as they were convinced that their rights were equal or superior to Radcliffe's.

During this time of hard feelings, the Colorado Legislature passed a Game and Fish Law (Colorado, Laws 1899, Ch. 98) which gave individuals the right to lease public lakes and parks as fish and game preserves. The fish and game in the leased area were deemed the exclusive property of the leasee. Where notice was posted, trespassing was made a punishable misdemeanor. Under this law Radcliffe leased certain lakes that the Ditch and Reservoir Company had developed. The Company protested, but Radcliffe's claim was supported by the United States Forest Service and the Colorado Game and Fish Department. Most of the fishermen in the neighborhood were unable to believe that Radcliffe had any real right to interfere with them. They continued to fish in the disputed lakes.

On Sunday afternoon of July 14, 1901, W.A. Womack and a

small party of ranchmen from Surface Creek Mesa were riding in the vicinity of Island Lake. As they were crossing a reservoir dam, Mehaney (Radcliffe's warden) came up holding a gun, and accused them of fishing on Radcliffe's preserves. Womack replied that he had not been fishing, but that if he should take a notion to fish, he had a perfect right to do so. Hot words went back and forth. Then Mehaney, suddenly losing control of himself, fired at Womack, wounding him so severely, that he died that same evening.

Deputies examine the site of the murder of W. A. Womack at Island Lake on July 14, 1901. (photographer unknown)

Before the others had quite realized what had happened, Mehaney left the scene and made his way by a roundabout trail to Delta. He arrived there on Monday morning, and gave himself up to Sheriff George Smith. During that day he was held in the jury room of the Delta County Court House. After the news of Womack's death had spread, numbers of men from Surface Creek Mesa rode into town late on Monday. The sheriff, fearing a raid and a lynching, instructed the deputy sheriff to try to move the

CHAPTER X: *Peach Valley*   223

prisoner to a safer place. At eight o'clock in the evening, while a case was being tried in the court house, the deputy sheriff spirited the prisoner down stairs and out of a back door, where a team was awaiting them in the alley. They went to the Smith ranch, about two miles up the Uncompahgre River, where the prisoner was held until the next morning. When the court adjourned after midnight, a mob of about 150 armed men smashed their way into the courthouse looking for the prisoner, and broke all locked doors in the hope of finding him.

At daybreak on Tuesday, the deputy sheriff drove up to Olathe with the prisoner, and caught the train to Gunnison. That night, a huge mob of armed men rode up to Alexander Lake looking for Radcliffe. Finding that he had escaped, they ordered all his employees to leave, and then set fire to the hotel and fish hatcheries. The entire plant was reduced to ashes. Only the icehouse escaped destruction, due to its contents.

A short time after the killing, rumor spread that Radcliffe was on his way back to the lakes. The settlers gathered to wait for him. However, he did not appear at the expected time. The reason was explained by Ula (Eulalie) King Fairfield much later. Her father, Judge A. R. King, who was taking the train for Denver, happened to meet Radcliffe on the railway platform at Montrose. The judge informed Radcliffe as to his probable fate if he tried to return to his Grand Mesa property, and urged him to go back to England. Radcliffe evidently took this sound advice, for he was never seen again in Delta County. Ultimately, through diplomatic channels, the United States government was induced to pay Radcliffe $25,000 in compensation for the destruction of his Grand Mesa property. Mehaney was tried in Gunnison, convicted of voluntary manslaughter, and sentenced to serve eight years in the State

Penitentiary at Canyon City.

Our first year in Peach Valley (1901) had been rather successful. We raised a large crop of oats and 100 tons or more of alfalfa hay. It was not too expensive to haul our oats to market, but the disposal of the hay presented some difficulties. We tried to get some cattlemen interested in buying the hay and feeding it to their stock in the valley; but since there was a large crop of hay all over the Western Slope, there were no buyers. The cattlemen preferred to buy hay for wintering their stock on Surface Creek Mesa, Tongue Creek and the Gunnison River Valley—both because these places were nearer the range and because they had much better water than we could supply. We had plenty of hay on the Blair place for our own stock, so we finally decided to bale the Peach Valley hay and ship it through a commission house in Delta to mining camps that had again started operations. We bought a second-hand baler and started to work.

Baling the hay did not present much of a problem, but getting it to a railroad station did. At first, we hauled it to the Delta station, but this meant a trip of at least nine miles each way, so that we could only take one load a day. As the hay sold for $7.00 a ton delivered at the track, and we could haul at best, two tons at a time, the hauling cost plus the baling cost made the returns negligible. Although we did not know enough of economics to realize it, we were faced with the producer's inevitable problem—location cost. This, I might add, was in general the most difficult problem for the Western Slope farmers. Mighty crops could be raised, particularly of fruit and vegetables, but the cost of getting them to market was so great as to make profits nearly impossible. We partly solved our immediate problem by hauling the hay down three miles to Reed—a freight station on the new branch of the Denver and Rio

Grande Railroad that ran up to the recently opened coal fields at Summerset.

After we had finished baling and shipping our own hay, we decided about the middle of December to buy more hay in the Gunnison Valley, bale it and ship it to the mountain mining camps. This meant hiring some help, as the younger boys were in school, Clarence was in the bank, and Arthur was in Boulder. We could buy the hay for about $3.00 per ton and could make about $4.00 per ton by baling it and putting it on board the cars at Reed. As we could bale and deliver five or six tons per day, this gave us from $20 to $24 for the work for myself, Howard and two hired men, plus two teams. We were not making our fortunes, but baling hay was at least better than hauling coal! We had to live in tents near the large hay stacks that we were baling, as it took too much time to go back and forth to our home on Garnet Mesa.

It was a very cold winter. Often the temperature would be as much as fifteen or twenty degrees below zero. We could keep the tents warm with little stoves as long as we were awake, but it was very cold there in the early morning. At night we drew cards or flipped a coin, to see who was to get up first in the morning to start the fire. When we started to dress, if we touched the wall of our tent, ice crystals would fall down on our backs. The pitchfork handles and the tongs with which we carried the hay felt like so much ice. We had to warm the bits before putting them into the horses' mouths. In about half an hour, after the sun had come up and we were working hard, we were quite warm. We must have baled two or three hundred tons of hay that winter.

Early that fall, I had purchased a beautiful yearling colt from Mr. Hunt. She was solid black except for a white star on her forehead. Her mother was a racehorse and she had been sired by one of Mr. Salisbury's famous black racing stallions. She was a beauty, with small clean-cut legs, graceful body, long arched neck, beautifully shaped head and large limpid eyes. I intended to use her for a buggy horse. I spent many hours in keeping her sleek and shiny, and grew fond of her as only a horse lover can.

I had not had her very long, when a man saw her and wanted to trade for her. He offered me two full grown horses for her: a good saddle horse weighing about 1,000 pounds and a fine mare weighing about 1,200 pounds. We needed a saddle horse rather badly, and could use another horse in farm work. And since I was beginning to feel that we had no business to keep a potential race horse, I agreed to the trade very reluctantly. The man said he would trade only on condition that the colt could be driven immediately, so I hitched her up to the racing sulky that he was driving and started her off. Although she had never had a harness on her before, she went along beautifully. We made the deal then and there.

That afternoon, I hitched up the new mare to the wagon with Topsy. She refused to budge. I called Howard, who was cultivating with another team. We hitched Howard's horses on as a lead team, and hitched Topsy's stay chain back so that she could do all the pulling on the double tree. I got into the seat and spoke to both teams. They started out, but the balky mare refused to budge. I cracked the four-horse whip and away the other horses went. At first the mare braced her feet and half dragged, half walked along. Presently, she lay down. We dragged her along until she finally decided to get up. She became angry and threw her front feet over the neck yoke. It made no difference to the other horses. She had to come along as best she could. After she became weary of being pulled, she was willing to go along. The next morning, she tried the same old tricks with the same results. I think she soon found that she was conquered and gave up. I put her to work on the baling press where there was steady pulling. She became a fine steady horse and almost never afterward caused trouble.

It is perfectly remarkable to see what can be done with a "bad" horse in a four-horse team, when the other horses are well trained. Very often after this, Howard and I would trade for, or buy, wild, mean, or balky horses that none of our neighbors who used only single teams could handle. We would usually get them at about one-half what they would be worth if their dispositions and conduct had been different, break them well, and then sell them profitably, or trade them for other wild horses, receiving a bit of cash to boot. This seemed to us to be very legitimate horse trading—and so, it was.

The cattle came down from the mountains rather late that fall, almost every cow being followed by a fine fat calf. The young stock also looked well. We placed the calves in the corral for weaning. They bawled, seemingly in anguish, for several days and nights. But as we fed them with juicy third cutting hay, they soon became reconciled to their lot, and within another few days, had even forgotten who were their mothers.

We were unable to rent the Blair place for the summer of 1902, as we wished to do, but we arranged to take the Peach Valley ranch again. However, we knew from experience that our home place and the Peach Valley ranch were all that we could handle without hiring help. The younger boys would be able to do farm work during the summer, and perhaps we should come out just as well in the end by doing all the work ourselves, instead of having hired men part of the time as we had done the summer before. About one hundred and twenty-five acres of Peach Valley land were now in alfalfa, and a heavy crop was to be expected.

Sometime in March, I had a chance to go to Denver by train, free of charge, with a load of cattle that were being shipped by two cattle buyers. It was always necessary for several men to accompany each trainload of cattle, to see that they were properly fed and to examine them whenever the train stopped, so that any which had lain down and might be trampled by the others could be made to rise by means of prodding with a long pole having a sharp nail in one end. We rode in the caboose of the freight train going to Denver, but had a ticket back in a regular coach. I did not at all mind riding in the caboose. It had a little bunk where we could take turns lying down or sleeping. Most of the time, however, the men played the card game "sluff."

The train had a hard pull up the Western Slope. At one place where it had to zigzag to get up the mountain, we got off and walked directly up the mountainside, easily catching the puffing little narrow-gauge train as it finished its long journey to make a few hundred yards up a steep grade. In the middle of the morning, we arrived at Salida, where we unloaded, fed and watered the stock. Late in the afternoon we started on a down-grade toward Canyon City. Much of the night I sat on top of the caboose and watched the glory of the Royal Gorge of the Arkansas, ghostlike in the moonlight.

Every once in a while, the train would stop on a siding to let another train pass. At each stop we would get out and look over the cars of cattle that were assigned to us. Just before we reached Pueblo, the train stopped and we got off to look at the cattle at a place where there were double tracks. I was poking a critter up, when I heard a roar and saw a fast passenger train practically upon me. I jumped towards the cattle train, and was nearly blown off my feet by the concussion of air as the passenger train blew by.

On Easter Sunday morning, we went slowly through Pueblo, the steel city of the West. Italians and other foreigners were starting on their way to church all dressed in their colorful costumes. "The God-damned Dagoes are going to overrun this country," remarked one of the cattlemen. The others agreed. I shared their instinctive feeling against foreigners, though I don't know why. How little did I comprehend then of the whole social, economic, and political situation at the steel mills!

We arrived at Denver on Sunday evening, and after leaving the cattle to the tender mercies of the stockyard owners, went to the Brown Palace Hotel. "Nothing is too good for cowboys," remarked one member of the party. I was rather dumbfounded by the splendor of the place. At dinner that night Mark Beckly, looking over the long bill of fare, startled the waiter by remarking, "You don't have to bring me over one-half of the stuff there, waiter; I am not particularly hungry."

After dinner we started to see the sights. The cowmen insisted on going to the Alcazar, which proved to be staging a thoroughly rough vaudeville show. Toward the middle of the house, a fight started between a man and a hard-looking woman. She kicked him in the groin. In a moment all was in turmoil. Police began to pour in. We made an exit as rapidly as possible. Some of the men went to visit houses of ill fame, but they advised me to go to my room and save myself a lot of trouble. I followed their advice.

The next morning, we went to see the stockyards and the packing plant. Much of my enthusiasm for the cattle business died right there. To think this was the end of the perfectly beautiful cattle I was raising!

That afternoon I took the train for Boulder, where Arthur was taking his medical course at the University of Colorado. I was charmed with the place. The University is on a mesa, gently sloping up to the foothills of the mountains. Some of these foothills are in the form of flatirons and are quite high. Boulder Creek, which runs north and east from the mesa where the University is located, comes down a beautiful canyon from the Arapahoe peak and the Arickarees. To the east of the University, one can look off for miles into the prairie country. The grass and early flowers were just coming out. The campus was alive with students of both sexes, all seeming to be lighthearted, happy and gay. What a contrast with the barren Peach Valley: trees, grass, girls, laughter and song!

I found that Arthur was very happy in his work. He made expenses by taking charge of the cadavers and helping in the laboratories. He was much interested in anatomy at the time, and was always handling human bones and making dissections. I quickly made up my mind that such work was not for me. Arthur and two other medical students were "baching" in a little building near the campus, to cut down expenses.

I have never known just how Arthur managed to get into medical school, for I believe that he had never graduated from high school, unless he had taken some secondary work while at Paonia. He was, however, an extremely good student with a phenomenal memory. At this time Arthur planned to become a medical missionary like our grandfather Bradley. He took me to one or two sessions of the Student Volunteers, an organization of prospective missionaries. I liked the students belonging to the organization, but I must confess that when the circle engaged in prayer, each one praying aloud in turn, I was much embarrassed. When my turn came, I remained silent.

I looked around a bit to see if there might be an opening in Boulder, in case we should sell our cattle and come here to educate the family, as Arthur and I thought it possible to do. This undoubtedly would have been a good move, as we probably could have sold all our Delta holdings for $3,000 to $4,000 clear, which would have been enough for a start. However, although I wanted to move to Boulder, we finally decided that it might be better to continue farming and cattle raising for a few years, and then to come with more money ahead.

This trip gave me my first intimation of what a college or university really is, and also increased my uneasiness as to my educational position.

When I returned to Delta, I found that the neighbors were getting ready to spray their fruit trees with whale oil soap to get rid of some new pest. I arranged with Mr. McGrannahan, who had a forty-acre orchard near us, to help him in return for the use of his spraying outfit on our trees. This whale oil mixture was fearful smelling stuff. By night one's clothing would be fairly saturated with it. Later we sprayed with Paris green and other mixtures. The experience of spraying trees several times a year further convinced me of the undesirability of orchards.

Shortly after the first spraying of the fruit trees, we received notice that all the cattle in the county would have to be dipped in a chemical solution to prevent injury to them by the Mexican screwworm. I thought the order reasonable, as I had noticed several cows with holes eaten right through their hides by these grumps. Hence, I made plans for the dipping of our cattle. When this had been completed, we drove them up on the range.

The dipping process required rather costly equipment, which no small cattle outfit could well afford. Hence, we paid a nominal fee to use the dipping vat of the Henry Kohler outfit. This vat was fifteen or twenty feet long, six feet deep, and about four feet wide.

It was filled with a sulphurous solution kept hot by the steam from the boiler of an old threshing machine engine. Just before the entrance to the vat a curtain was hung. The cattle, one by one, were driven into a narrow enclosure leading to the vat. Each animal, assisted by a sudden sharp prod, was forced toward the curtain, which gave way as the cow-brute plunged into the deep vat head-first. The surprised critters found their whole bodies submerged in the solution. They were supposed to swim through the smelly stuff until they were able to come out at the other end of the vat by means of a ramp. My particular job was to stand beside the vat and urge the animals through as rapidly as possible. As I was doing so one day, a very large bull suddenly threw up his head and caught one of his long horns in the bottom of my trousers, almost pulling me into the vat with him. If that had taken place, the results would have been sad to contemplate.

The work in the valley and on the farm proceeded this summer much as it had done the year before. Two or three events deserve mention, however.

Howard and I spent a night in the Black Canyon. On our way down the extremely steep trail, we heard the tinkling of sheep bells. When we came toward the bottom, we saw a few sheep grazing on the grass that had sprung up in the narrow flood bed of the river and in little breaks along the canyon sides. That night we were awakened by blood curdling cries. First, they sounded like a woman in travail, then like a person screaming for help, then they diminished to a sort of moan. The canyon walls echoed the ghastly cries and intensified their weird quality. We finally decided that the sounds were caused by a pair of mountain lions attracted by the sheep.

On our way back we happened to pick up some shale rock. To

our surprise it smelled like petroleum. We thought that it might be oil-bearing shale and took it to Delta, where upon examination, we proved to be right. Several of us immediately filed on claims along the lower edge of the mesa. There appeared to be the possibility of oil wells in the region, and we thought that we might become rich. This happy dream never realized.

When we were making the second cutting of hay in the valley, I put the top on a stack about thirty feet high, and told the boys and a hired man to let me down by the sling that we used to handle the hay. I caught hold of it, expecting to move the derrick boom free from the stack and bring me down. Instead, they swung the derrick boom out over a team of horses, and kept me hanging high in the air. I yelled to them to let me down, as my hold on the sling was none too good. They did not move, but laughed at my predicament. My grip was giving way. At any moment I might fall upon the team. Just about the time I could stand it no longer they swung me clear of the horses and let me down. I have never been so infuriated in my life. I picked up a pitchfork and started for them, with murder in my heart. Luckily for them, I was so exhausted that I could not run as fast as they could, and my temper soon cooled.

One day shortly after this, when riding toward the northern end of Peach Valley, I saw some twenty miles away over the western part of the Grand Mesa, a dark cloud drifting very rapidly in my direction. Its course was marked by a broad white strip that lay on the ground behind it. As it approached me with a roar, I saw that I was directly in its path. I set spurs to my horse and was barely able to get beyond its jurisdiction when it swept past, leaving hail stones the size of eggs piled three inches deep. As I rode down the Gunnison Valley, I saw alfalfa fields that had recently been irrigated, with the crop completely driven into the ground, and trees stripped bare of their fruit, leaves, and even small twigs. Farmers told me that the hail had killed many of their chickens, pigs, and young calves. It so happened, however, that the storm missed all the land we were cultivating.

The terrible glare of the sun shining on those bare adobe hills, together with the adobe dust, began to affect my eyes. One day when I was riding to Peach Valley, my eyes suddenly began to pain, and continued to do so for several days. I went to town and was fitted for glasses. Although they were necessary, the glasses proved to be a source of considerable annoyance and embarrassment to me in connection with the rough work that I was always doing.

Toward the middle of the summer, the water in the Loutsenheiser Ditch became very scarce and finally failed. It began to appear that our oat crop would not "make," and that we would have no second cutting of hay. Something had to be done. I got on my horse and rode along the ditch to Montrose, about twenty miles away. There I found, as I had suspected, that the people on the upper end of the ditch had plenty of water. I had a long talk with the President of the ditch, who finally consented to let me have one of the keys to the headgates along the ditch, in order that I might shut off all those located toward the upper end.

Down the ditch I rode that night, shutting off the headgates, fearing that at any moment I might be met by some irate farmer whose water was cut off. I recalled the story of Mr. Payne, who had been the ditch walker along a similar canal. One day as he was shutting down the headgate of a person who was stealing water, that individual came riding up furiously on horseback and threatened to shoot him. Payne said, "Just hold on a moment partner. Let's look at that headgate again. Perhaps I have made a mistake."

As the threatening one was bending down to look at the gate, Payne seized his gun and threw it into the ditch.

All night I met no one, however; and toward morning I arrived at the valley in safety. For several days we had plenty of water, enough at least to guarantee a second cutting of hay and a crop of grain. The second day that the water came, I was walking up to the place where the headgate divided our water from that of one or two neighbors who lived farther down on the ditch. There was old man Myers. As I approached, he began to curse and to accuse me of stealing water. Finally, he raised his shovel and ran toward me threatening to kill me. "Look here, old fellow," I said, raising my own shovel, "I am a much younger man than you and much stronger; if you try to hurt me, you will be the one killed." He saw the error of his ways.

I began to talk to him. He finally admitted that the headgate was all right when he had first seen it; but, he asked, if I had not been stealing water, how was it that he got so little at his place, three miles away? I explained that a small stream of water running three miles through the hot sun would almost entirely evaporate. "Let us walk down the ditch for a mile or so to prove it," I said. We did, and he was finally convinced.

Poor old Myers was a marginal type of farmer, extremely ignorant, probably moronic, and shiftless. His place was toward the very end of that long twenty-five-mile Loutsenheiser Ditch, and was located on extremely poor land. But he seemed satisfied with his life. "What more can a man want than I have?" he would say. "My wife, she sells enough eggs to get groceries. My cow gives enough milk. I have plenty of overalls and my wife makes me shirts. What more can a man want?"

The summer of 1902 was extremely hot. After dinner at noon, it seemed as though the sun would blister us when we first went out into it. Soon after we began to work, however, we would be wet from exertion. As the water on our skins evaporated rapidly because the atmosphere had no humidity, we would soon feel quite comfortable. On Sundays, when we were not working, we suffered most from the heat. We would go home and lie flat on the floor or under the orchard trees to keep cool.

Toward the end of summer, there was no rain for some weeks. The ditch ran dry. At last came the rain in the mountains, and the ditch began to run again. We went to make repairs where the water was coming down the ditch for the first time in two or three weeks, for we knew that the hot sun had made many cracks in the ditch bank and that unless these were attended to immediately the water would soon cut large holes there and escape, particularly along hillsides. After stopping up holes for two or three miles, we came to a place where the ditch ran along a slope. Unluckily, here was a very large crack, with water starting to pour through it. Howard and I began to shovel. We never worked so hard in our lives. Just as it appeared that we were getting the better of the hole, it would break through again. Faster and faster, we worked, but the water was too much for us. Both of us sat down and began to cry from complete frustration and exhaustion. When we were a little rested, we had to go up stream, cut an opening in the side of the ditch where the ground was more level, and put a temporary dam of brush in the ditch to cut off the stream from above the break. Then, with no water to bother us, mending the large crack was not too difficult a job.

The heavy rain in the mountains assured us a good third cutting of alfalfa, but we saw that we could no longer trust even the Loutsenheiser Ditch in dry seasons. There were light crops on Garnet Mesa that year, except for the grain which had ripened before the drought began.

An incident occurred that summer, not far from Peach Valley, that showed the bitter feeling existing between the sheep men and the cattle men. The two groups had agreed that sheep should not go west of a line running almost north of the Gunnison River bridge at the end of the Black Canyon up to the cedars, and that they should not go up on the cattle range farther than the cedars. One of the sheep herders broke the agreement and was found with about 3,000 head of sheep in the cattlemen's territory. The "greaser" tending the sheep was tied up, while many of the sheep were driven to the rim of the Black Canyon and forced over the edge of a precipice a thousand feet high. They all perished. Public opinion did not condemn the cattle men, since the sheep ruined the range for cattle. They would bite off the grass down into the ground, pack the range hard with their thousands of sharp little feet, and litter it with sheep manure, which cattle hated. A bunch of sheep could ruin the range permanently, absolutely killing off the grass, which in that dry country had a hard struggle for existence anyway.

A year or two before, I remember, a great flock of sheep had passed our place on Garnet Mesa. The owner said that they had come from Utah and were heading for the upper Gunnison country. I advised him against the move, on the ground that his sheep would probably be killed. Within a week or so I heard that my prophecy was but too true. By the way, the only experience that we ever had with raising sheep occurred after an ewe from this same flock gave birth out of season to two little lambs in front of our place. The owner, not being able to take the trio along, gave the lambs to us. After they became large and fat, we sold them for three or four dollars apiece.

Despite the scarcity of irrigation water that summer, we had a very good crop in Peach Valley. We put up about 250 tons of alfalfa hay and about a thousand bushels of oats.

On the home place we raised, as usual, enough wheat for Mother's chickens and nearly enough hay for our horses and milk cows. The orchard was almost a failure this fall, and so was our winter garden, which was practically burned up. Ordinarily, by having a large garden and a full cellar of vegetables and fruit in the fall, and by trading in eggs or selling them by the crate, we were able to keep our grocery bills down to about $20.00 per month. That winter, however, we would have to spend more.

That fall, the price of hay was again low, about three dollars per ton in the stack, and five dollars delivered. We felt the disadvantage of not having the hay from the Blair place, which we had formerly been able to haul into town for merchants and livery stables, or to sell in the stack. No one wished to buy the hay in stacks in Peach Valley, and hauling it ourselves the long distance to town would cost us almost all that it was worth. Nor had baling and shipping it to the mining camps proved very successful, financially. We tried again to sell the pasture and hay to cattlemen, and again we failed. Not much of the hay was needed for our own cattle, as our pastures and straw stacks—plus a very little extra hay in March and April—would carry them safely through the winter. Hence our inability to sell would mean a loss of much hard work and anticipated income.

As hay and cattle prices were both very low that autumn, several cattlemen decided to fatten steers on alfalfa hay instead of shipping them to market. We had read in the *Colorado Stockman*, a weekly that we took, as well as in another farm paper, of experiments that had been made by the State Agriculture College at Fort Collins of fattening cattle on alfalfa. It was claimed that a first cutting of alfalfa hay, even though steers were given no other food with it, would put a pound or more of fat per day on them; and that after three or four months of such feeding, the animals would bring nearly as much as corn fed steers.

The plan appealed to us, but how were we to get the money to finance the purchase of 50 head of steers, which we figured would be necessary to eat our surplus hay? I talked the matter over with several cattlemen. Clarence Mower offered to let me take my pick of his large herd of three-year-old steers for $35 per head, and to postpone payment, except for $500, until I sold the creatures after fattening them. The $500 he would have to have in advance. I went to the Farmers and Merchants Bank, of which my father had been cashier and co-owner at the time of his death, and talked over the matter of borrowing the money with H. H. Wolbert, then cashier. He considered the proposition of feeding steers very risky, since the price of cattle might go down still more, and since in any case, fattening steers on alfalfa was hardly beyond the experimental stage. I was very much disappointed at not getting the money. Realizing that something had to be done with the great stacks of hay we had in the Valley, I went over to the rival bank, the First National. Dr. Stockham, who acted as minister for the Baptist Church, was the cashier of that bank. Stockham readily consented to let me have the money on my own note without security. He said that he had heard many good things as to our family's ability, hard work, and integrity, and that he was therefore perfectly willing to lend us the money.

We deepened the pond in Peach Valley in order to have

plenty of water, and built a large log corral so that there would be no possibility that the steers might get out. When Mower had collected his cattle from the range and brought them down to his father's ranch on Tongue Creek, I rode up with him to pick out our steers. I had never before had an opportunity to judge steers on a commercial basis, but I had read a great deal concerning the desirable points, and had habitually kept my eyes open in looking over bunches of cattle. I did not doubt my ability to "top the bunch." The cattlemen expressed surprise that a "kid" could pick out so many of the best steers. They were beauties. We judged that they weighed over a thousand pounds each.

We drove the steers to Peach Valley and put them in the corral for full feeding—that is, we gave them all of the first cutting of alfalfa hay that they could possibly eat. They began to fatten rapidly. My brother Clarence stayed in the valley to feed them and to look after and feed the rest of our cattle. He spent a miserable winter in that God-forsaken valley—he has told me since. However, he had a great deal of time on his hands which he used to good advantage by studying Latin and mathematics. Probably it was this time spent in study that enabled him to enter an advanced class in Grinnell College when he left for Iowa the following fall.

Toward the spring of 1903 our supply of first cutting alfalfa hay began to run short, and the water in the pond was not as good as it might have been. We moved the steers to a better source of water in the Gunnison Valley. Then we bought several tons of hay to continue the fattening until others were ready to ship their cattle. The hay cost us $3.00 per ton, I think. About the time when this hay was exhausted, several cattlemen decided to ship their hay-fattened cattle to Denver or other packing house centers, according to market conditions. I planned to ship ours with them. One day, however, Mower offered me $45.00 per head for the cattle just as they stood, now weighing better than 1,100 pounds on the average. I accepted the offer. He told me later that the market fell between the time when he bought the cattle and the time when they reached Denver, so that he lost money on the deal. I was somewhat skeptical, for as one cattle-raiser later remarked, "Clarence Mower never lost in a cattle deal in his life." However, market quotations for that period show that "top steers were selling at only $4.25 to $4.75 per hundred pounds; so, it is certain that Mower could hardly have made much profit after paying costs of shipment. The net result of this venture to us was, that after paying the bank loan with ten per cent interest, paying our debt to Mower, buying the extra hay in the Gunnison Valley, and using Clarence's time in feeding the steers, we sold our large crop of hay transformed into beef cattle at only about $2.00 per ton. This was not much, but considering the hay market in the fall, it was satisfactory to realize that we had at least broken even.

Almost as soon as we sold the steers, Clarence secured a position in Hotchkiss. He became manager of a commission house there, which was a branch of an established commission house in Delta.

During the previous fall, I had become involved in a mining venture which appeared to be promising. Ben Elliot, part-owner of the best men's clothing store in Delta, who was regarded as a "financial wizard," told me of a gold mining adventure in which he and several others were interested, and asked me to take a tenth interest at $300. The mine, called the "Cleveland," had been discovered by an old prospector who was to retain a twenty percent interest. It lay, so the miners said, in an outcrop of the same vein on which the famous Camp Bird Mine was located. The gold content of the quartz was increasing rapidly as the tunneling went deeper.

I did not think that I ought to participate in the venture, but promised to go with the old prospector to look the mine over. We drove up above Montrose, and at Ridgeway we took the road toward Telluride. Near the top of the range, a branch road led toward the north side of a high mountain. After we had followed this road for a few miles we had to get out of the buggy and walk a narrow trail along the steep mountainside. We finally came to the camp, where we saw two men who were working the mine. There we stopped for lunch.

After lunch we went to see the mine. In order to do so, it was necessary to ascend a precipitous cliff. In places, we were compelled to climb up a narrow crevasse. I did not dare to glance down. Finally, when we reached the top and moved toward the mouth of the mine, we could see outcrops of quartz that certainly appeared to run in the general direction of the Camp Bird Mine. On entering the mine, we saw that a shaft had been driven in about a hundred feet. The miners themselves were enthusiastic about the prospects. They felt that it would be only a short time until they struck quartz that would yield as much as $100 per ton. If that materialized, we should all be rich soon.

The old prospector told us many tales of people who had "struck it rich." We had several examples in our own community. As I heard the old man's stories, and remembered actual instances of mining luck, I found myself interested in the present mining project—even against my better judgement, which told me that more fortunes had been lost in mining than had ever been made.

After looking at the mine, we stood for a few moments gazing at the wonders of the landscape around us. Far to the right stood a mountain peak that glistened strangely. It contained a great deal of rock salt, someone explained. Northward, we could just see over the slope of the mountain on which we stood. In many very steep places, there were great bare strips in the timber, where giant snow slides had carved their way through spruce forests. Beyond lay the beautiful bottom lands of the Uncompahgre Valley with its hay fields and orchards. Immediately to our right stretched the desolate adobe country, and next to it the outlines of the Vernal Mesa and the Black Canyon of the Gunnison. Far in the distance we could see the silhouette of the Grand Mesa against the sky, its horizontal lines forming a striking contrast to the rugged country around us.

On returning to Delta, I talked with the man who had suggested that I go into the venture. I rather wished to take a chance on the mine, but had no money. Finally, he agreed to act with me as co-signer of a note at the First National Bank. We borrowed $300 and used it to buy stock in the mine. Several times during the winter and the next spring, reports of a very cheering nature came to us. Every foot driven into the mountain made quite an increase in the gold content of the quartz. It began to appear that we might be rich. Why not?

That winter, as usual, Howard and I hauled coal a part of the time and looked after the home place. We rented the Peach Valley ranch again for the season of 1903, but planned to operate it in connection with the running of the cattle on the range. We figured that most of our planting of oats and wheat, as well as the orchard work, would be done before we took the cattle to the range, and that I could manage the cattle there, since Clarence, Howard and the boys were able to operate the home place and Peach Valley in the summer, with such help as I could give them between the spring, summer and fall round-ups. But in order to justify using so much of my time on the range, it was necessary for us to have more cattle of our own and to care for a large number of our neighbors' cattle. That spring, counting young stock and calves, we had about 175 head of cattle; but we decided that we needed more. Mr. Cabrill had sold most of his cattle, but had some thirty head remaining, in addition to any which might have wintered on the range. He offered all these to us at what seemed a reasonable price; and said that he would throw in his registered brand, which was Lazy H Box (⊥▢). Cabrill's brother, who also had a few head of cattle, offered to sell them to us along with his "TIT" brand. They both were to take my notes for the whole price. We now canvassed many of our neighbors and thus secured some two hundred additional head of cattle. This combined herd of more than four hundred cattle would mean that my time was used to advantage.

We had only two or three saddle horses. As it seemed necessary to have six or seven horses on the range, so that they could rest between strenuous rides or recover from any bruises or lacerations which they might receive, we finally obtained three unbroken colts. One was an apparently mild-mannered gray. Another, called "Koppy" by the man who sold it to us, was a brown that proved to be as wild as the devil. The third, which we named "Brownie," gave us much trouble when we were breaking him. Our "string" was completed when we obtained two horses that were already broken. One was a light bay, highly nervous and as quick as chain lightning. Though he seldom bucked, he would jump so quickly when startled or when turning a cow, that he would almost break his rider's back. The other was a large roan horse that was of little use as a cow horse, but was valuable in riding back and forth between our camp and the range. He had four gaits; he could pace, fox-trot, single foot and lope. The only difficulty with this critter was in getting on him. If the reins were held tightly, he would rear back on his hind legs, threatening to throw the rider on the ground with the horse on top of him. If the reins were loose, just as one put his foot in the stirrup, the horse would take a mighty jump ahead. Once mounted, however, he was tractable enough.

We had some interesting experiences breaking the aggregation of colts. Howard, who prided himself on being able to ride "anything that had hair," picked out Koppy as his first colt to break. I picked out the gray colt, whose name I have forgotten. Koppy bucked furiously, but Howard could easily ride him. He began to seem fairly well broken in a few weeks, but we never trained him completely and finally traded him off a couple of years later. The gray colt never bucked with me while I was breaking him in, as I treated him very gently.

I had ridden Brownie several times and he had bucked quite viciously. The first time I rode him he threw me off. I got on again and pushed the spurs into him in order to stick on better. He bucked and bucked but could not throw me off. He then began to "swap ends," that is, to whirl about. When this did not unseat me, he threw himself on the ground in a furious rage, and started to roll. I saved myself as best I could, and he stood up. With the help of Howard, who snubbed Brownie to his saddle horn, I mounted him once more and rode him until he was completely subdued. He never tried to buck me again.

Before we were sure that Brownie was conquered permanently, Howard and I decided to ride him and the gray colt up to Peach Valley. We had a long argument as to who was to have Brownie. I must confess that I was rather terrified at the prospect of riding him again. Howard, despite his claims of superlative horsemanship, vowed that he would not ride him, so, I finally consented to do so, trembling in my boots.

We started off. For some unknown reason, the gray colt did not like Howard. No sooner was Howard on his back than he began to buck, swapping ends and acting like a "regular bad horse." First, Howard's hat was bucked off, then one boot, then another. Finally, off came Howard himself. He collected his clothing and got on again, holding the colt's head up so high that it was difficult for him to buck. For miles, the colt tried every few hundred yards to throw him off. Howard finally pleaded with me to trade horses, as he was absolutely worn out. Brownie through all this time had been behaving himself like an old work horse. I hated to trade him for the gray, but finally did so, and his conduct for Howard was as good as it had been for me.

When I got on the gray colt and loosened the reins, he behaved like a perfect saint, and continued to do so all day long. I rode him quite regularly for months without the least trouble. One day on the range, however, he departed from his good behavior. We were riding along in a large open space. As the other men's horses were going at a running walk, I wanted to train the gray to do likewise, so I held his head rather high and applied the spurs gently at almost every step. He decided to take offense. Suddenly he pulled down his head and began to buck violently, taking me entirely off guard. The leather belt holding the two legs of my "chaps" together got over the saddle horn, and I thought I was about to be ruptured by the pounding. Some of the men saw what had happened and roped the colt, snubbing his head to the saddle horn, thus allowing me to get off. I was so weak that I had to lie down on the ground several minutes before I was able to ride again.

CHAPTER X: *Peach Valley*

That spring Howard and I and one or two boys of the neighborhood tried to improve our horsemanship by practicing on the bunch of wild horses that roamed over the adobes and lived on grass growing along the canals and on the Vernal Mesa. At an angle in the fence of the Peach Valley ranch, there was an arroyo twenty or thirty feet wide, with perpendicular banks about ten or twelve feet high. Someone, before we came to the ranch, had put a log fence in two places across the arroyo, thus making a corral of sorts, and had cut an opening into it. We would run the wild horses into this improvised coral, then, roping and saddling one of the horses, we would drive it out on the adobes and ride it. I was never as enthusiastic about this sport as the others were.

One day, Howard got on a particularly bad colt and rode him in the corral. Then he asked us to help in making the animal go out to the level ground. I had a hackamore around the colt's head, and by means of pulling and slapping him, we managed to get him out in the open. He began to buck furiously. In some way or another my hackamore rope slipped off my saddle horn, so that I had no control over him. The colt started to buck and run at the same time, and came nearer to the steep bank of the arroyo. I was afraid he would jump down. Howard was yelling at us to do something for God's sake. I reached down off my horse and managed to catch the rope and snub it around the saddle horn again, just in time to save Howard's horse from going over the edge. Howard was white with anger. He thought we had let the colt loose on purpose.

CHAPTER XI

Struggle for Water

When the Uncompahgre River Valley and the surrounding mesas were first settled, it was generally believed that the river and its tributaries would supply enough water for all irrigation and domestic purposes. A rather wide system of irrigation canals and ditches had been established almost immediately. In the spring and early summer, the river had a flow much larger than was required for irrigation, and at first the water seemed adequate even in late summer. When there was any failure of water in the early days, people believed that it was primarily due to a light fall of snow in the mountains during the preceding winter. Sometimes a suggestion was made that those at the upper end of the irrigation system were stealing water.

However, there were several factors involved, which at first, we did not quite comprehend. We tended to overlook the prior appropriation of water by settlers under the San Juan Treaty, which included not only the mountain mining region, but also the upper part of the Uncompahgre Valley. Since these settlers had appropriated the river water even before 1881, when the Indians had been driven out, their claim was superior to ours. Again, it was a long time before we realized that as most of the timber was cut off the high mountains at the headwaters of the river for mining purposes, the beneficial effects of forests as water retainers and distributors were lost to us. Now the snow tended to melt at a rapid rate early in the season, causing a greatly flooded river whose waters were largely going to waste, but an almost dry stream in the late summer and fall when crops needed it most. Finally, each year more land had been taken up and water rights given, until the rights claimed exceeded even the maximum capacity of the river.

The years from 1895 to 1899 had been particularly bad. The First Annual Report of the United States Reclamation Service in 1902 gave the maximum and minimum discharge of the river for that five-year period, as follows:

Maximum Discharge			Minimum Discharge	
Year	Date	Cubic ft per sec.	Date	Cubic ft per sec.
1895	June 29	1,535	Nov. 6	25
1896	May 27	3,375	Aug. 15	10
1897	June 15	1,467	Sept. 15	5
1898	June 24	985	Aug. 31	5
1899	June 15	1,163	Sep. 10	4

As a result of the lack of water in the late summer and early fall, large acreages of crops that had been planted optimistically in the spring, withered and burned up toward the end of the growing season. Although about 118,000 acres of land had been taken up and patented, less than 30,000 acres were under cultivation and there was not really enough water for more than 10,000 acres. Foreclosures had been made on about 20,000 acres of land now held by loan companies. Evidently something had to be done.

The thing that was finally done was initiated by a dream. A rancher named F. C. Larzun, who had once been a miner and was therefore well acquainted with tunneling, claimed to have dreamed of a tunnel through the Vernal Mesa, bringing water of the Gunnison River Grand Canyon into the Uncompahgre Valley.

People tended to consider the man a little bit "off." However, he urged the building of a tunnel for about ten years, by day and by night. In 1894 he finally got the people of Montrose sufficiently interested to raise a small sum of money for investigating the possibility of such a project. A survey was made by Walter Flemming of Montrose and Richard Whimmeral of Ouray. By running levels, they found that the Gunnison was so high above the Uncompahgre Valley that if a channel could be developed, the water from the Gunnison would flow down in sufficient quantity to irrigate most of the arable land. It was not possible, however, to bring water by canal. The only possible type of channel was a tunnel through the wall of the Grand Canyon (now called the Black Canyon). The surveyors did not encourage the idea of such a tunnel, for they believed that the cost could not be borne by the farmers and ranchers in the Uncompahgre Valley.

The fact that a diversion of the Gunnison waters for irrigation purposes had been declared possible, however, caused the development of a strong public opinion in favor of attempting it. The people of the valley, through their representative in the Colorado Legislature, applied for State aid. On April 11, 1901, a legislative act appropriating $25,000 for the project became effective. Though the appropriation was small, a construction committee was appointed by the Governor. In December, 1901, the work was started on the basis of surveys made by the United States Geological Survey. After 900 feet of tunnel had been driven, no further work was done by the State, as it appeared that the Federal Government was preparing to take over the project. In 1903, the State gave over to the Federal Government the work that it had already done.

Although there had been much talk of the tunnel, and some little progress toward developing it had been made, to many on Garnet Mesa it seemed merely a dream, or at least a distant event. In order to secure water immediately, the farmers on the Mesa met and decided to build a rather large reservoir in the adobes above the Garnet Mesa Ditch, using the water to fill the reservoir in the winter or during the spring freshets when it was not needed for irrigation. It was decided that a company should be formed to carry out the project, and the organizers hoped that every farmer would take out stock in the enterprise, roughly proportionate to the number of shares held in the Garnet Mesa Ditch. One could either pay in cash for his shares or work out their value on the project itself, using teams, plows, and wheeled scrapers[6], at the rate of $3.00 per day for man and team. Our family decided on the latter method of payment, giving up coal hauling for a month or six weeks during the time the roads to the coal mines were at their worst. Both Howard and I participated in the work, but Howard did the lion's share. With other workers, we lived in tents at the site of the project.

The place where the reservoir was to be made was an abomination of desolation if there ever was one. The valley toward the center had a coating of white alkali, through which ran a tiny sluggish red rill consisting of alkali dissolved in seepage water from the farm lands about. Toward the sides of the valley grew a few grease weeds and salt weeds. The hills on either side were grey adobe without a sign of vegetation.

The weather was bitterly cold. Every morning it was necessary to put four or six horses on the plow, to break up the frozen earth that was to be hauled in the wheel scrapers for making the dam.

---

6   Scrapers on wheels with long handles in the back, which could be used to raise the scrapers up or down.

We wore heavy red flannel underwear and heavy woolen socks, and kept them on by night as well as by day.

The dam, as I remember it, was about seventy feet wide at its base and twenty feet high; it would back water up the valley for more than a mile. It was finished in the first part of March, and the water was turned in. Everything seemed to be in good shape. I saw the dam once when the reservoir was nearly full. It appeared that there would be sufficient water for our needs.

One morning, only a few days after I had viewed the dam, news came that it had gone out, seriously flooding the river bottom lands below. The water evidently had seeped through the sides of the hills against which the dam rested, and had so softened the soil there that the dam had no support and simply slid out. This was a severe blow to us, for we not only lost our work and our water supply, but we feared that we might be faced with the possibility of damage suits. Luckily for us, this fear was not realized.

It now appeared that our only salvation was the proposed tunnel to bring water from Gunnison River into the Uncompahgre River Valley. In order to understand this project, it is necessary to know something about the two river systems and their relationship one to another.

The Uncompahgre River rises in the high San Juan Range of mountains in southwestern Colorado. About its headwaters are mountain peaks, some of which have an elevation of more than 14,000 feet. Their deep crevasses are said to hold eternal snow. The drainage area of nearly 5,000 square miles is in general, very steep and rugged, and offers no places where storage basins could be constructed. As the figures above show, the stream in late spring and early summer had a capacity of from 1,000 to 3,000 cubic feet per second; but in late summer and early fall, its flow diminished to a few cubic feet. However, the flow varied considerably from year to year, depending largely upon the amount of snow in the mountains.

About twenty miles east of the Uncompahgre Valley is the Gunnison River. This large stream flows for nearly 35 miles through the deep, narrow Black Canyon. Above the water are almost perpendicular canyon walls, which in places reach a height of more than 2,000 feet.

There is a vast difference between the two rivers, although they run so near each other and even meet at Delta. The Gunnison rises in high mountains on the western slope of the Rockies. It has nearly eight times as much drainage area as that of the Uncompahgre. There are several places on its tributaries where reservoirs can readily be constructed, and it has a large volume of water, even in late summer.

Yet before the tunnel was built, very little land was served by the Gunnison River. In the many miles of the deep Black Canyon there is no land to irrigate. After the stream breaks out of the prison walls of the canyon, it flows through the Gunnison River Valley for ten or twelve miles; but this valley is only a mile or so in width and consequently requires little water. After the Gunnison is joined by the Uncompahgre at Delta, it flows through a wild area cut by numerous canyons, until it unites with the Colorado River at Grand Junction.

A narrow formation called the Vernal Mesa, with an average height of about 8,000 feet, divides the Uncompahgre River Valley from the Black Canyon of the Gunnison. The walls of this canyon, one of which is also the eastern wall of the mesa, consist of sold granite and even harder rocks. But on the west side of Vernal Mesa, no granite is seen. In some early age that area evidently dropped for a distance of several thousand feet, so that the entire Uncompahgre Valley region lies in the so-called Colorado shale. The mesas that border immediately upon the Uncompahgre River, however, are covered to a depth of some fifty feet by alluvial gravelly soil washed over the shale from the high plateau to the southwest, the Uncompahgre Plateau.

Here then was a large territory, the Uncompahgre River Valley, burning up in the late summer and early fall for lack of water; while only a few miles away was a large river capable of supplying all the water that the valley could use. That river, however, was confined in a deep canyon and was separated from the Uncompahgre Valley by a high narrow mesa. If a tunnel driven through this mesa could be made to divert the Gunnison water to the valley, our desert might blossom as the rose.

Although the Black Canyon was deep, the riverbed was considerably above the bed of the Uncompahgre, which was down in the dropped area. Hence, if a tunnel would connect the two streams, water would flow by gravity from the Gunnison to the Uncompahgre. But could such a tunnel be built? Was it a reasonable, or even a possible undertaking, in view of the geological structure of the region and the cost involved?

In the fall of 1900, a group of Delta and Montrose ranchmen organized a party with the hope of stirring up general interest in the matter, and ascertaining definitively whether the tunnel was feasible. The party consisted of J. E. Pelton, who was the leader, J. A. Curtis, the Delta County Surveyor, E. B. Anderson of Garnet Mesa, and M. F. Hovey and W. W. Torrance of Montrose.

This group fitted out two flat bottomed boats with enough supplies to last a month. They went by train to Cimarron, where the canyon could be entered easily, and started their exploration.

Observers were stationed on the west rim of the canyon to note their progress. As the explorers went down the river, they began to be confronted with great difficulties: there were rapids, piles of driftwood, and boulders, which at places so blocked the river that the boats had to be dragged over them. On the second day out, the party lost one of their boats and half of their supplies going over a small waterfall, which they named the Falls of Sorrow. For five days, the observers on the rim of the canyon were unable to see their whereabouts.

The farther the explorers went in the canyon, the greater became their troubles. They finally came to a place where the large column of water was forced to flow through a very narrow channel with incredible speed. As it seemed almost certain death to chance this whirlwind fury, they decided to abandon their investigation. They had progressed only 14 miles in 21 days. To climb out of the west side of the canyon was not possible. Finally, the party had to leave their boat and supplies, and working themselves through the cracks and crevices, crawl from crag to crag up the almost perpendicular wall on the east side of the canyon, which was more than 2,000 feet high. To make this climb took them from eight in the morning until late at night. Even then they were dozens of miles from civilization. After a night on the bare ground, they managed to reach the nearest little town the following day.

Although this expedition did much to interest the public and the Federal Government in the diversion plan, it had not shown that the plan was practicable. Meanwhile, the Federal Government had been considering the problem. The first definite Federal step toward the realization of this project (as well as many others) had been taken when Major John Powell made an irrigation survey and report as early as 1879. Largely through his efforts and reports, the Government was encouraged to continue investigations. In 1888, Congress made an appropriation of $100,000 to be used for making hydrographic surveys of the Western States by the Geological Survey.

In 1900, Abraham Lincoln Fellows, a division chief and hydrographer of the Survey, had recommended a study of the Gunnison diversion project to Chief Newell, who authorized him to make the study. This included a topographical survey of the Vernal Mesa and the exploration of the Gunnison Black Canyon. Although it was accepted in a general way that the diversion of water from the Gunnison into the Uncompahgre Valley was possible, a suitable location for the tunnel that would accomplish this had not been established. In the summer of 1901, Mr. Fellows was instructed to begin a systematic survey, with the cooperation of C. H. Fitch, topographer and consulting engineer. Fellows immediately began making plans. It was his opinion that the exploration should be made by himself and a companion alone, and that the best way to make the trip was by foot and by swimming where necessary. He decided to use no boats. Every care was taken to make the load of supplies, which had to be carried, as light as possible.

The story of the expedition told here is based chiefly upon a statement written by Mr. Fellows, and contains several direct quotations therefrom.

Fellows specified that his companion should be young, extremely strong, without dependents, and a powerful swimmer. These chief specifications were met by William W. Torrance, a young man of thirty who had been in the Pelton party a year before, and who was full of enthusiasm for the adventure.

The outfit prepared for the expedition included a pneumatic rubber mattress, to be used as a raft for carrying equipment, and as a bed at night. In addition to food, the men had with them surveyors' instruments, a Kodak camera, silken ropes, and hunting knives. They wore on their persons waterproof bags for notes and valuable instruments.

Fellows, who had made a thorough study of the western rim, selected three places where it was possible for a man to climb into the canyon. He arranged that his friend A. W. Dillon of Montrose should convey supplies of food to these three places, "awaiting at each in turn until we should have arrived, or until there was no longer hope that we should arrive."

The journey was finally commenced on August 12, 1901, at the mouth of the Cimarron River, where the explorers had come by train. Fellows and Torrance went down into the Black Canyon of the Gunnison carrying packs on their backs, and began to travel along its length. It was frequently necessary for them to wade through deep water or to swim. All walking was done on masses of boulders which lay along the canyon walls. Often, they had to swim from one side of the river to the other, when it was absolutely necessary to cross. The surroundings were of the wildest. "The roar of the waterfalls was constantly in our ears and the walls of the canyon towering half a mile in height above us, were seemingly vertical. Occasionally a rock would fall from one side or the other, with a roar and crash, exploding like a ton of dynamite when it struck bottom, making us think that our last day had come. At times, the canyon would become so narrow that it would almost—but not quite—be possible to step across the river. At times, great gorges of rock that had fallen from the sides would hem in the water to such an extent that it would be nearly concealed" … "Our most dangerous work, possibly, was that of climbing along the sides of the precipices, traversing old mountain sheep tracks at points where it was impracticable to swim without too great a danger to life and limb."

At one place, Fellows had a fall of about twenty feet, but made a safe landing in a bed of wild gooseberry bushes. On the third day, the men arrived at a place where Dillon met them. They were glad to send him to Montrose for new shoes and fresh supplies. "We remained at this point two nights and one whole day, sleeping nearly all the time." On the morning of the 16th they started out once more. "I have availed myself of the opportunity to send out my rolls of films containing the photographs taken so far, together with my notes, in order that they at least might be saved."

The canyon became more and more rugged. "At times we would traverse along reaches looking like mill ponds with the sky and canyon walls reflected in depths of blue water, but again we would come to rapids and waterfalls as turbulent as the waters of Lodore[7]. The canyon walls appeared more and more to be hemming us in from the outer world." … "One remarkable point which we passed on the 16th I called the Giant Stairway. The walls looked almost as if cut into enormous steps by some Titan of old, while statues, turrets and pinnacles adorned the rugged precipices on either side."

That evening the explorers reached a spot they named Beaver Camp, for here beavers had cut down some of the great trees growing in a little flat area. On the 17th they reached the point where the Pelton expedition had given up. They made great bonfires of the driftwood that lay along the stream, to indicate to Dillon on the rim of the canyon that they had passed this point. Here they found provisions and supplies, and the boat abandoned by the Pelton party.

---

7   The Lodore river, so named by Powell after the famous English poem "The Cataract of Lodore" by Robert Southey, was synonymous with an impassable waterway.

They saw before them "the mighty jaws, past which there was to be no escape." Fellows said to Torrance "Will, your last chance to go out is to the right. You can make it there if you wish, but if we cross the river at this point there can be no return, we must go on. I do not ask you to go, but leave the decision entirely to yourself. As for me, I am going through." … "Torrance said 'Here goes nothing,' and commenced to pull off his coat."

"Nothing further was said. We swam the river, reaching a point of rocks on the other side, but still above the gorge. And, lo, we beheld a beacon of hope through the narrow opening, where the water was of unknown depth and velocity, and below which it was believed there were high falls, a bonfire kindled by Dillon on a large rock below the jaws of the canyon. He had come down by a most precipitous path, risking his life and limb for our encouragement. The very sight of this man in the jaws of the gorge was a wonderful inspiration. Again, we plunged into the foaming water and in a few minutes, we had passed through the jaws of the gorge and were safe among the enormous boulders below."

The explorers lunched heartily upon provisions brought by Dillon, and started on their way again. There was another gorge apparently as dangerous as the first, but they passed through it in safety. They were now confronted with enormous boulders near the water, which could not be climbed or passed in any way. Hence, they had to climb the sides of the canyon and move along precariously until the boulders were left behind. They "made camp under a huge shelving rock against which the roaring river reverberated and echoed like demons howling over their prey."

Still, they worked along the canyon. On the morning of the 18th they came to a gorge where gigantic boulders had fallen from the cliffs, the water flowing one hundred feet or more beneath them.

"They were packed closely enough, however, so that they formed a dam in the high water. The boulders were smooth and polished to such an extent that it was only with the greatest difficulty they could be surmounted. It took us six hours to traverse less than a quarter of a mile. At times it would be necessary for one of us to climb upon the shoulder of the other, clamber to the top of some huge rock and draw our supplies and the other man up by means of the rope which we carried with us. Again, on the other side there might be a deep pool where we were obliged to swim, into which the water boiled from the cave above and was sucked out again through the crevice between the boulders below. In one of these pools, I was completely drawn down under the crevices below, but by dint of the hardest kind of swimming, succeeded in getting into still water. At this time, Torrance felt that he would never see me again."

The men were now out of provisions, "having lost or spoiled those with which we had been supplied. We were hungry, sick and exhausted and were losing flesh, as we had through the entire trip, at the rate of about two pounds per day. At this critical stage, while climbing along the side of the canyon thirty or forty feet above the stream, I stepped out from behind a large rock to a spot where there were some small bushes. As I forced my way through these bushes, up sprang two mountain sheep which apparently had been lying asleep and which I had come within three feet of stepping upon. One of them was so dazed that it sprang over the cliff and broke its shoulders upon the rocks below. It was hard on the poor sheep, but I could understand why it had been so frightened when I saw the reflection of myself in a mirror after we had reached civilization. Although hard on the sheep, it was our salvation. Though the game laws of Colorado forbade one having any portion of a mountain sheep in possession, a hind quarter was immediately added to our supply and a goodly portion was cooked and eaten."

Soon after this they came to a succession of falls that Fellows named Torrance Falls. On they trudged through the rain, expecting to reach Red Rock Canyon where Dillon was to meet them. This proved to be impossible. They camped for the night under a sheltering cliff, pulling up their rubber sacs to keep off the rain, and making an enormous fire of driftwood.

The weather was rainy and cold next day, the 19th, but the men pushed on. They had to swim the river again. At about ten o'clock they found Dillon waiting for them. By noon they reached a camp that had been made for them where the Red Rock Canyon meets the Black Canyon. They were tempted to end their explorations at this point, as it was below any spot where a tunnel could be made. But the next morning they started down the canyon again, hoping to reach a ranch house which they had erroneously thought was about eight miles away. They travelled eight or ten miles without finding it. "At night we camped without bedding and without food or water upon a bleak hillside." As they had now passed through all of the canyon that interested them, when they came to a trail leading out, they followed it and started for Delta down the Vernal Mesa and over the adobes. "We were," said Fellows, "strange looking objects. Our clothing and shoes were ragged, and with a luxuriant growth of beard and a covering of dirt acquired in the last few miles of our trip we would hardly been candidates for positions in polite society." "...We had been obliged to swim the river, the water of which was as cold as ice, seventy-six times. We were bruised from head to foot. Each of us had lost at least fifteen pounds in the ten days trip."

CHAPTER XI: *Struggle for Water*

As Howard and I were mowing hay that August morning in Peach Valley, I noticed coming toward me over the adobes on the side of the hay field, two of the most bedraggled men whom I had ever seen. At first, I took them to be tramps. However, as soon as they began to talk, I knew that they were educated men. They told me a bit regarding their trip, and asked if I could provide them with food and take them to Delta. I replied that I could not leave my work, but that they would find something to eat in our shack right over the little ridge which divided the two sectors of Peach Valley. They were welcome to take whatever they wanted. In the stable, I told them, they would find a horse and buggy which they could use for driving down to Garnet Mesa, and could leave at Mother's place. At noon when we went back to the shack for lunch, we found that the two pies, the cold meat and other good food that Mother had left us the day before were gone. But on the table lay two silver dollars and a calling card inscribed Abraham Lincoln Fellows, Division Director and Hydrographer of the United States Geological Survey[8].

---

8 More on the history of the tunnel project can be found in Appendix III

CHAPTER XII

Cattlemen

As soon as our cattle and those of our neighbors had been dipped in Henry Kohler's vat to prevent Mexican screwworm, I gathered them together and started driving them up Tongue Creek and Oak Creek toward the open range on Grand Mesa. A few words should be said as to the nature of this "open range." Before 1891, the public lands in the high mountain and forest country in Western Colorado seem to have been given almost no attention by the Federal government. Settlers took up land suitable for farming and capable of irrigation, to a height of a little over 7,000 feet. But at higher levels, on the Western Slope at least, the country was not only too steep for farming, but was also too cold for most crops. Above this line, as well as on the lower mesa and adobe areas where no irrigation was possible for lack of water, these lands were regarded by the settlers as a kind of common property. The upper lands were used as the source of timber or wood, or were employed for such purposes as the grazing of livestock, hunting and fishing, or for the building of reservoirs for irrigation purposes. With minor exceptions, no areas there had been granted by the government to particular individuals.

There was a general understanding, and even agreement, that sheep could not be brought upon certain ranges. But there were no rules or regulations as to the number of horses or cattle that could be put on the range, or as to deforestation. Anyone who wished to carry out timber, logging or cattle operations on the open range simply did do. It was possible to fence off portions of the range for particular purposes, such as the fattening of beef animals in the fall, establishing fenced pastures for saddle horses, and building cabins. Such activities were recognized as giving a sort of indefinite proprietorship. There was also a common understanding that certain portions of the range "belonged" to certain individuals and companies who habitually used them. Thus, although some inevitable intermingling of cattle and horses occurred, it would have been considered a grave matter if one outfit should attempt to bring too many of its cattle into the preserves of another.

At the time when I began to run cattle on the range, this primitive situation was gradually coming to a close. A law of 1891 gave the President of the United States the right to provide for forest reservations. Acting under this law, in 1892 the President established the Battlement Forest Reserve, which embraced a large part of the Grand Mesa. Although rules and regulations governing Federal forest reserves were established in 1897, they had little or no effect upon existing conditions, for they provided that the pasturage of livestock in the forest reserves "will not be interfered with as long as injury is not being done to the forest growth and the rights of others are not jeopardized.[9]"

In 1902, an amendment to the rules and regulations provided for much more effective control. The owners of livestock were now required to secure grazing permits if they wished to pasture their animals in a Federal forest reserve. They received permits subject to the express condition and agreement that they would comply with all legal requirements. In every case where a permit was granted, it was the duty of the Secretary of the Interior to determine the number of cattle and horses that could be pastured in the area concerned. The number of livestock that any one individual

---

9 See ORGANIC ACT OF 1897, section 13

could run on the range was greatly limited, and fees were to be charged at so much per head. Private fencing of pastures was prohibited.

Although these regulations were in effect when I started to ride the range, most of the neighboring cattlemen refused to recognize them, particularly as there seemed no one at hand to enforce them. After talking the matter over, we came to the conclusion that we would let things drift until someone started to make trouble. We did not apply for permits. We did not limit the number of cattle on the range. We did not tear down our fences or pay fees. It is true that we were always fearful that these rules and regulations might be enforced against us at any moment. However, for some reason or other, the Forestry Service took no action until 1905, and it was not until 1912 that effective control was established.

Our range was on the Grand Mesa, and lay chiefly within the area now known as Grand Mesa National Forest. It started in the unsettled foothills and mesas a few miles north of Delta, and went along the unoccupied lands bordering many little streams that ran down from the mountain: Kannah Creek, Point Creek, Doughspoon, Oak Creek, Dirty George (now revised to Gorge Creek), Ward Creek, Tongue Creek, Surface Creek, and numerous others further east on the mesa. The valleys of these creeks—along some of which ran rough roads used by farmers—served as thoroughfares up which the cattle were started toward the range in the spring, and down which they drifted in the fall after the cold autumn rains came or the snow began to cover the mountains.

On most of the creeks, except toward the western end of the Grand Mesa, where the streams usually ran dry in the summer, were farms given over chiefly to the raising of alfalfa hay, which was used to feed the cattle in the winter. A few miles above these creeks the country became very steep. The slopes were covered with sage brush, scrub cedar, pinon, scrub oak, quaking aspen, and spruce, ranged in tiers according to the elevations best suited to each. The cedar and scrub oak country was particularly steep and covered with rocks and boulders. The quaking aspen country was generally less steep, and was interspersed with large open places that were comparatively level. In these open glades we placed rock salt for the cattle; and they became salt licks and "stamping grounds"—places where the cattle naturally tended to gather. Just below the top of the mesa on its south side was a long valley-like formation running east and west. It was filled with dozens of beautiful mountain lakes and reservoirs built by farmers for the storage of irrigation water. The creeks above the scrub oaks, and the lakes and reservoirs, were filled with varieties of brook, speckled and rainbow trout.

The top of the Grand Mesa is a great plateau from 10,000 to 13,000 feet high, which is one of the largest high table lands in the Rocky Mountains, if not the world. Much of its face is almost perfectly flat. It is covered by large pastures and beautiful groves of spruce. The most interesting feature of our range there was a twenty or thirty mile stretch of rim rock around the western third of the Grand Mesa. This formation was from two hundred to a thousand feet high, and in many places it was nearly perpendicular. It was evidently the result of a great lava flow from an old volcano, whose crater still could be seen. The western top of the area enclosed by rimrock was known as the "Big Pasture." A short fence across the Mesa, where the rim rock ceased, was sufficient to contain many thousands of acres, all covered with grass that was more than a foot high in the early summer. This pasture was used by all the cattlemen on the western half of Grand Mesa as a place to take steers or barren cows to fatten for a month or so before shipping them. Because of the rimrock, the only easy access to the Big Pasture was from its eastern side. A single steep and difficult trail known as "Shirt Tail Trail" led to it at the western end of the mesa.

The flowers and trees on the Grand Mesa were wonderful. There were millions of beautiful Rocky Mountain columbines, blue and fringed gentian, purple asters, harebells, shooting stars, Rocky Mountain bee plants, and many other blossoms. Most of these flowers grew high up in the mountains. There were also great forests of Engelman spruce, blue spruce, Alpine fir and Douglas fir, all of which made splendid settings for the crystal-clear mountain lakes. The animal life found on Grand Mesa was of many varieties—badgers, martens, beavers, coyotes, wildcats, plenty of mule deer, elk, jackrabbits, squirrels, and an occasional bear. The grouse was the most plentiful of game birds.

The views from the top of the mesa were spectacular. At the western extremity one could look into the seemingly interminable deserts of Utah. Faint against the sky could be seen a range of mountains in the distance, which looked almost ghostly. To the southwest was the Uncompahgre Plateau, with deep, rugged canyons sloping down from it to the Gunnison River. In the same direction could be seen the little town of Delta. Toward the south were visible the green Surface Creek Mesa, the Gunnison River Valley, and Garnet Mesa. Behind them were the bleak adobes, and in the distance rose the mighty San Juan Mountains, covered with snow. To the southeast one could see the Vernal Mesa and the Black Mesa, with an outline of the Black Canyon sharply cutting them apart. To the east were the noble peaks of Mount Lamborn and Land's End, which stood like sentinels guarding the West Elk Mountains lying beyond.

Each different cattle "outfit"—of which at this time there were only a few on Grand Mesa—had two camps: a spring camp located at the edge of the quacking aspens, which was used for the first roundup before the snow had melted on the higher levels; and a summer camp under the rim rock, which was used during most of the summer and fall. These camps were built of logs. They were established in locations where rim rock formations or other natural obstructions, such as slide rock, could enclose pastures for our horses with little need of fencing. Another prerequisite of a good camp site was that it should be near a creek to furnish water, and a cold spring to serve as a storage place for butter, milk and other perishables.

The camps were supplied with bedding, wood stoves, and cooking utensils which had been brought up by pack horses or mules. They were always stocked with provisions consisting largely of flour, ham and bacon, and canned goods. We never locked these camps, and any cattleman or hunter was welcome either to join us at our meals or to come and cook his own meal. There was only one condition attached: that he should wash the dishes and clean up after leaving.

Harry Stockham and I had our summer camp about half a mile from the source of Ward Creek. This was a beautiful rushing mountain stream filled with brook trout, for it had been the practice of cattlemen to go over to the fish hatcheries at the Grand Mesa Lakes only four or five miles away, and "pack" over in large milk cans thousands of little trout about an inch long, to stock the stream. In bringing the little trout over to the camp, it was necessary to stop quite often to pour fresh water into the milk cans, as the great number of fish soon exhausted the oxygen in the water surrounding them. As Harry and I continued this process, it was possible to go down at any time and get a mess of trout quickly.

The camp pasture for our horses and milk cows lay between two ledges of rim rock formation which could not be crossed by horse or cattle. Thus, we had a pasture of three or four hundred acres, without more than a hundred yards of fencing.

Although cattle bearing different brands roamed more or less everywhere, the range was by some common understanding divided into several sections. The area below the rim rock, from its western end nearly to the Grand Mesa Lakes, was the general territory of three men: Clarence Mower, with his DW— brand; Charles Mundry, who possessed only a few hundred head of cattle, but ran several small bunches for farmers; and Henry Hawker, who also ran cattle owned by other persons—chiefly those of Mr. Howard, a grocer in Delta who had that spring moved his cattle to the range from the San Luis Valley country. Next was a rather narrow strip near the Grand Mesa Lakes, which Harry Stockham and I considered primarily our range. Finally came the land used by Henry Kohler's 'open A bar I' (L—I) outfit, a very large area that extended from our preserves indefinitely eastward. There probably were some cattlemen on the far eastern end of the mesa; but we did not ride the range with them in roundups, and so far as I can remember, I did not even know their names.

There were three general roundups: Spring, Summer and Fall; with various others in between. On roundups the men of all the outfits that I have described would ride together. We usually started at the Mower, Mundry, Hawker camp first. After riding five or six days, branding the calves—or later in the summer picking out steers and fat cows without calves to drive up to the big pasture— we moved to our camp. When we had finished there, we went on eastward to the L—I camp, where we spent a week or more.

I came to know these cattlemen and cowboys rather well. Clarence Mower was by far the most distinguished looking man on the range. He was well over six feet tall and rode like a knight of old. He always wore a fine soft wool shirt with a white silk handkerchief around his neck. He had been sheriff of Delta County and was an influential politician as well as a cattleman. Besides owning and running cattle, he was engaged in buying and selling them. He was a fine rider and an excellent roper, and could read brands as a school teacher would read a primer. Unless Tom Moore happened to be with us, Mower led in roping the calves and dragging them to the branding fire, or cutting out fat cows or steers from the bunch. He always had a "top" horse which he handled very well. His favorite mount for roping or cutting out cattle was a beautiful old buckskin horse that he claimed could read all the brands on the range. At last, much to the grief of us all, this horse became blind. He was put in the big pasture; but after he had been there for a week or so, we never saw him again. He must have fallen over the rim rock.

Mower's father, Tom, had a large hay ranch on Tongue Creek. He would often come up to ride with us, although at that time he must have been sixty years old. He was quite as good looking as Clarence, and despite his years, he sat in his saddle as straight as a mountain spruce.

Charles Mundry, I had known ever since that first Christmas night on Oak Creek. He was a typical Yankee from Connecticut who had come to seek his fortune in the West. He had assisted us in building our house at "The Elms," had worked in the Delta Flour Mill, and was now just starting to build up a little herd of cattle of his own. He also ran several hundred head of cattle for others. He was a small wiry man and a very hard worker. Although he was never much of a rider, he was an expert at handling the branding iron, ear-marking, dew lapping, and so on.

Henry Hawker was a newcomer on the range. He was large, very red-faced, and shy. He hardly ever talked, but would sit on a log singing cowboy songs by the hour. He knew all the stanzas, and I always suspected that he added some of his own compositions. From him I learned most of the songs that have appeared in the Lomaz collections or in Sandburgs' "American Songbag," such as: "Bury Me Not on the Lone Prairie," "Sam Bass," "Get Along Little Dogie," and "Don't Take My Boy to Prison."

Harry Stockham was the son of Dr. Stockham, cashier of the First National Bank of Delta and parson of the Baptist Church. Harry had just started in the cattle business the year before. He was about twenty-two years old when I first knew him—a long, lank individual with a thin face which he could draw up in comic wrinkles. He was witty and poetical by nature, and I believed composed some of the songs he sang. I enjoyed camping with him and found him a mighty good companion.

The most striking man on our range was Frank Moore, the foreman of the Open A Bar I outfit. He was large, very well formed, and had dark eyes fairly burning with life and energy. There was current belief in a story that he had been a "big cattleman" in Texas but had found it advisable to skip the country after killing a sheriff. How true the story was, I do not know. None of the men ever talked of their past except to relate experiences with horses, cattle or wild women; and one was never expected to take these tales at their face value. Frank was by far the best rider and roper on the range. Even Clarence Mower had to yield when he was around. Frank practically never missed a critter toward which he threw a rope, and he could catch up a calf by the feet as easily as by the neck. I never knew him to pick out a calf for branding that did not belong to the right cow, as others sometimes did. He could easily take out of a large bunch, any cow that he chose. His motto was, "Turn the cow or kill the horse." When some tenderfoot asked him as to the value of a cowboy's life under such conditions, he laughed and replied that there were plenty more cowboys where these came from. Frank nearly always took part in rodeos held at the Delta County Fair, or in other events where good horsemanship was at a premium. He was full of the devil and would play tricks that were grotesque or even dangerous. If Frank had had an education, he would have been a leader in any group of men.

Mort Beckly, one of the Open A Bar I outfit, was the least prepossessing of the group. He was short and rather fat, with a red face. He was as strong as a bull, a very good rider of bad horses and a fairly good roper. Hawker, Beckly and Moore were considered cowboys, as distinguished from "cattlemen" who owned livestock.

Two men who were primarily cattle buyers were up on the range with us quite often; and we also saw them at Wilson's Harness Shop in Delta, which was a favorite hangout of cattlemen and cowboys. The first was a small, keen-faced man named Al Botsford, a brother of Miss Botsford the singer. He had been a reporter in New York City, but had come west, whether because of this health or because he loved excitement. He was considered to be rather shrewd in his dealings for cattle with the farmers. He was a very bright and witty person.

The other buyer, Tom Mostyn, was an aristocrat in bearing, manner and speech. Where he came from, I never knew, but I believe from England. He was tall, graceful, had a wonderful command of language, and impressed me as being perhaps the younger son of a good English family. He had the reputation of knowing his business of buying and selling cattle, and especially of having the ability to guess the correct weight of a critter, and to determine how much it would bring on the market.

One of the first things we had to do after turning the cattle up on the range in the spring, where they would gradually work higher and higher following the rapidly receding snow line, was to haul rock salt and pack it to the salt licks. The salt licks were placed along the range two or three miles apart, on a more or less level area that ran along the mesa at the central part of the quaking aspen belt. They were located in openings several hundred feet across, in order to give enough space for handling a large bunch of cattle. The salt licks served several useful purposes. As the cattle needed salt and tended to go where it was available, they could easily be assembled at the licks when we wished to brand the calves, pick out cattle to put in the big pasture, or treat any animal that might be sick. The salt licks also served as a place where the cows and bulls could come together to mate.

Getting the salt to the various licks was no easy task, particularly at our end of the mountain. It was necessary to haul the large lumps of rock salt, which we used in preference to the prepared blocks, from Delta up the mountain as far as there was any road. After this we had to pack it to the various licks on mules or pack horses.

My share of the salt, so it was figured, was two tons, to be placed near the extreme western end of the range. I planned to haul it over the adobes, across the mesa just south of Oak Creek, then up the old Baldwin milk ranch road. I put four good horses on the wagon loaded with salt and started out. In the adobes, I came to a place where a heavy rain had washed down one rut in the road and left it very soft. The right wheels sank down until the axles dragged. The team could not pull the load out of this hole. I unloaded many of the lumps of salt, which weighed from one hundred to one hundred and twenty-five pounds each, and carried them to the side of the road beyond the soft place, about seventy feet from the stalled wagon. The team was then able to pull the balance of the load out of the mud.

I loaded the salt back on and proceeded on my way, rejoicing, over the mesa and along Oak Creek. I went up the right side of the creek for several miles beyond our old place, to a point where the road crossed the creek. On the outer side was a very steep grade. I managed to drive the team almost to the top, but here the grade was so steep that I could not go farther. I unloaded five or six lumps of salt, and finally was able to persuade the team to haul the balance to the top. Then I walked back, rolled and carried up the pieces that I had unloaded, and placed them in the wagon. Just as I had finished this job, along came two or three cowboys. Had they come only a few moments sooner they could have helped me by hitching a rope to the wagon tongue and letting their horses help pull the load.

Next, I started along a rather steep hillside by the creek. A so-called road had been cut out about twenty feet above the stream. Suddenly a grouse started up with a mighty whirr from the upper side of the road near the lead horses. The horses shied suddenly toward the creek, the right wheels went off the bank, and the wagon box with its entire load of salt when down into the creek below. I hitched a log chain to the wagon box and pulled it out; and by almost breaking my back, lifted it into the running gear. I then rolled or carried the lumps of salt up the bank and loaded them on again. By that time, I was as weak as a cat and was doing just a little bit of swearing. One of the cowboys rode up, and after I had told him my story, said: "The good Lord will certainly forgive you for such God damned profanity."

We had to leave the wagon at the end of the road, and undertake the task of loading the mules and pack horses with salt. We would place three lumps on each animal, one on each side of the pack saddle and one in the middle. Around all of them we would throw the "diamond hitch," which I was just learning to make. Only one difficulty arose during this process: a horse lay down with the salt on his back. I had to unpack the salt, bring the beast to his feet, and load him up again.

It was necessary for us to pack all our camp equipment and staple foods up to our spring camp, and later to our summer camp. The "grub" was varied with the trout we caught, and quite often with grouse. I made an arrangement with "H.E. Horsewrangler," as Harry Stockham was called by the cowboys, that I should do the morning cooking while, he "wrangled" the horses from the pasture into the small corral with the aid of a "night horse"—one which was kept in the corral at night for use in the morning.

We also arranged that Harry would wash the dishes if I would keep all the horses shod. I had never shod horses before, but having often seen it done, I did not doubt my ability to do it. I got several different sizes of horse shoes, a rasp, a hoof knife, several pairs of pincers and a small nail hammer. With this equipment I was able to shoe the horses quite satisfactorily after a little practice. We had one or two rather wild horses that summer, and at times we would have to throw them down and "hog tie" them before getting the shoes on.

From my Poverty Flat and Peach Valley experiences, as well as those at home, I had become an expert biscuit maker. These experiences were reinforced by a trick or two that I learned from Mower. After cutting out the biscuit, he would dip them in butter or bacon grease just before placing them in the oven. They would bake with a perfect brown crust. It was not difficult to cook trout, grouse breasts, or steak. Every once in a while, during roundup, a yearling calf would be butchered and divided among the camps.

Once, a couple of eastern banker friends of Dr. Stockham came up on the range to visit us. Horsewrangler told them that I was a chef from the Brown Palace Hotel at Denver, taking a vacation. As I had to live up to that reputation, for supper the first night I prepared light baking powder biscuits, fried trout cooked in butter after being rolled in flour, grouse breasts cooked to a beautiful golden brown, hot coffee with cream nearly a half inch thick from the shallow pans of milk cooled in the spring, and wild gooseberry pie. The bankers swore it was the best meal they had ever eaten. Mountain air and exercise improve the quality of food. The next morning, we had flap jacks about eight inches across and turned them by flapping them in the air. We also had more trout and hot biscuits.

Most of the cowboys who became experts in biscuit making used the following system: They would take a large pan and heat some water in it. To this, they would add some shortening, usually lard, and let it dissolve. They would stir in the flour until a rather thick batter was formed. Into this batter they would mix a good deal of baking powder and a little salt, and would then add flour until a dough of the right consistency was developed. They would roll out bits of dough to the shape of biscuits in their hands. These would be dipped in melted butter or lard and laid in the baking pan. The resulting biscuits were delicious!

The most primitive biscuit maker I ever saw was Tad Barkley. Tad, who ran cattle on the Escalanta range and was about the best roper and pistol shot in the country, would open up the top of a sack of flour, make a nice large hole in the flour, partly fill the hole with water in which lard or butter had been melted, and throw in some salt and baking powder in accordance with his experienced judgement. Using his fingers, he would work the ingredients into a dough that would be lifted out of the remaining flour. He rolled biscuits of this dough in his hands, dipped them in melted lard, and cooked them in the skillet over an open camp fire. This process he would call, "building up a gorge." The biscuits were good, despite Barkley's unusual method.

My first experience with roundups occurred that spring, about the latter part of May or the beginning of June. We started at Mower's camp with about eight men in the gang. Pairs of men would scour four or five square miles of country, driving in the cattle along the trails to the nearest salt lick. The cattle were quite wild, and a few whoops would start bunches of them scurrying out of the timber along the trails. The bunches would increase in size until the salt lick was reached. The first men at the salt lick would build a fire and start heating the branding irons, which were always carried fastened to the saddle. It was quite exciting to see the different bunches of cattle come in.

In nearly all instances, the first bunch would be headed by a large bull. Soon there would be heard in the distance deep bellows or shrill notes of other bulls coming toward the stamping ground. The bull already there would answer with an angry roar, and would begin to paw the ground in rage, throwing the dust up over his back. Presently, another bull would appear on one of the several trails leading to the lick. Almost instantly the two bulls would charge at each other. But just before striking they would turn and stand still, evidently sizing each other up. Then, like a flash, they would rush at each other head first. They would strike forehead to forehead with a sound of thunder. Each would then brace and push. Often, they would remain in this position for several minutes, until one or the other weakened in the legs and was pushed back, usually at an angle. The one that had succeeded in pushing the other backward and sideways would make a furious lunge and send his long, sharp horns along the side of the vanquished, sometimes making a cut so deep as to leave a bloody line, and sometimes tearing off a streak of hair two feet or more in length. The defeated bull would rush off through the trees with bloodshot eyes, bellowing in rage. Woe to anyone who was in his path. Most of the younger bulls knew enough not to challenge the old warriors, but from time to time a young bull would attack an old bull and defeat him. We always left horns on the bulls so that they could protect themselves, the cows and calves, and could keep the large steers from molesting the cows, trying to perform the function of a bull for which they had no capacity.

To prevent fighting bulls from injuring each other, we would often "sic" the two dogs on them. As they felt their hind legs or tails bitten, the gallant warriors would turn their attention from each other to the dogs, who were always able to escape.

One day we found a bull of Kopp's by a stamping ground with a broken front leg. There seemed nothing to do but to put him out of his misery as quickly as possible. I took my six-shooter and emptied all shots right into the bull's forehead. This did not seem to affect him at all. Harry Stockham then aimed at this side and shot him through the heart. Kopp was furious that we had killed his bull. He maintained that we should have set his leg and cared for the bull until he could walk again—a likely operation, on the range!

State law provided that there must be one bull for every twenty cows, and that no bull should be allowed on the range that was not at least 7/8 purebred. It further provided that no bull should be kept on the range for more than three years, lest inbreeding take place if one should happen to mate with his own daughter. In compliance with these regulations, the cattlemen on our range shipped in pure blooded young bulls from Missouri or Kansas almost every year, to take the place of the old bulls that were shipped off to Denver and other points east. These rules were vigorously enforced, not by officers of the law, but by the cattlemen themselves who were interested in producing money making cattle of the highest quality. So well had this process of breeding from superior sires been carried out that instead of the scrawny longhorns from Texas that had first been placed on the range only two decades before, most of the range herds now contained nearly purebred cattle. About the only exceptions were a few mongrel Jerseys and Holsteins, who were the offspring of milk cows.

On the roundup, Mower and Moore generally did the roping of the calves, as they were the only ones who could read the brands with a high degree of accuracy and always pick out the right calf belonging to the right mother. As a rule, the mother would follow the calf, which was being dragged to the fire protesting in fright and terror, and at times an anxious cow would even charge upon the men who were doing the branding. The position of the roper was a responsible one for other reasons than correctness of the branding. If calves were missed two or three times by the rope, they became wild with panic and might leave the bunch and take to the tall timbers. Furthermore, too much roping would disturb all the cattle and make them restless and hard to hold. Valuable time was lost whenever the roper missed his chosen victim.

Harry Stockham was usually assigned the job of holding the cattle together by riding around and around the herd. Hawker and I took upon ourselves by virtue of our strength—or were assigned, I do not remember which—the job of "wrestling" the calves. Occasionally Mort Beckley would also tackle this job. As a calf was pulled along toward the branding fire, Hawker or I would follow down the rope until we reached its neck. Then, holding the rope at its neck with the left hand, we would seize its flanks with the right hand, give a might heave, and down the calf would go. One man sat on its head, which he had twisted sideways, and the other stretched out its upper hind leg, while Mundry branded and earmarked it, and castrated it if it were a bull calf. After branding 75 to 100 calves at one salt lick, we would move to another and repeat the process.

I had plenty of grief a little later that summer while wrestling calves. I had to leave the first summer roundup in June a few days early in order to look after the haying in Peach Valley. This must have made other cowmen a little resentful, as they did not brand my own calves or those belonging to the various farmers whose stock I was running. When the second roundup came in August, these calves were extremely large. It was up to me to wrestle them, I knew. I said not a word, but whenever one of those young giants came my way, I threw him down even if the struggle almost broke my back. One day I grabbed an extremely large and wild young heifer calf. Just as I exerted all my strength to lift and throw her, she jumped high into the air. Over I went, landing underneath her two hundred pounds of beef. This knocked all the breath out of me, and I was glad enough that the next few calves belonged to other outfits.

One of the wildest rides that we had on this roundup was below the rim rock at the extreme western end of Grand Mesa. This country was largely covered with cedar and scrub oak, with quite a bit of sage brush farther down. The land was so steep that it nearly stood on end. The salt lick, which was slanting and rough, lay far down the mountain side in the sage brush. Three or four men went up into the cedars and scrub oak to chase the cattle down, while several of us remained at the salt lick to hold the cattle as they came out of the trees. Within a short time, I heard yelling up on the mountain side, and down the cattle came. Many of them were extremely wild, for the wilder the country the wilder the cattle. A scared cow came tearing down the mountain right across the lick, and tried to get by me. For a few moments we had a game of dodging back and forth. She finally passed me and started to run. "Turn the cow or kill the horse," thought I, as I threw the spurs into my good horse's flanks. Soon, by jumping rocks and sage brush I came nearer to the cow, and finally overtook her. I gradually got her turned back toward the lick, and kept her on a fast run so that she was not able to dodge me again. One of the cattlemen remarked that this was pretty damn good riding for a "farmer."

From the Mower camp we were to go immediately to the open A bar I camp instead of ours; because our lower camp was not large enough to hold the gang, and our lower pasture was very inadequate. The day before we were to start, someone left open the gate to our pasture, with the result that most of our horses escaped. We made a search for them and found that they had joined a band of wild range horses. When we tried to run them back into the pasture, the wild "broncos" immediately started into an almost impossible country for riding, with ours following them. We jumped on a couple of our remaining horses and tried to catch up with the runaways.

Brownie was a rather fast horse, and I rode him like the devil over brush and stones and in between scrub oak trying to turn the deserters but to no avail. Suddenly I felt Brownie limp. I got off to see what was the matter but could find no bruises anywhere. He immediately became so lame that we had to go back to the Mower camp. We could find nothing the matter with him, but turned him into the pasture for rest. Several weeks later I caught him to examine his legs. Just above his front left hoof I saw a sore spot, from which was protruding a piece of stick about half an inch in diameter. I tried to pull it out with my hand, but it would not budge. We got a pair of blacksmith's tongs and started to pull it. Brownie could not stand the pain and began to strike and rear. We threw him down and with difficulty pulled out a piece of oak wood nearly three inches long. Evidently it had gone into his hoof on the underside and had gradually worked through. After the cause of his lameness had been removed, he was soon as well as ever.

When Brownie turned lame, and the other horses strayed, I was in serious trouble. In the language of the range, I was "afoot," and yet I had to help on the other end of the range. Moore came to the rescue. "I have lots of horses over at the L—I camp. You can use them, but of course some of them may be a little bit wild," he said, with a twinkle in his eye. I knew I was up against a tough proposition, for I believed that Moore would enjoy nothing better than to give "the farmer" all of his wildest horses to ride.

That afternoon we rode over to the L—I camp. I was on one of Moore's horses that had been pretty well worn down from the strenuous riding of the past few days. After breakfast the next morning we went to the corral, which was filled with thirty or forty cow horses wildly milling about as though they had never seen a man. Moore pointed to a beautiful large bay horse. "That's your pony for today. Better be a bit careful, for he hasn't been worked much." I tried to go up to the horse but could not do so. Finally, I threw my rope and caught him around the neck. When I tried to put the bridle on him, he objected most strenuously, but I finally succeeded. I threw on his back the thick Navajo blanket that my uncle had given me. Next came the saddle, which he tried to avoid. I finally got it on him, pulled the cinches rather tight, led him out of the corral and let him stand for a moment while I put on my gloves and forced my hat down on my head as tightly as possible. He hunched up his back and dropped his tail between his legs, which is a pretty good sign that "hell's a-poppin," or may pop soon!

All the cowpunchers were now on their horses and were looking at me, expecting to see some fun. I turned the bay horse's head uphill, took an extremely firm hold on the reins so that he could not easily get his head down, and jumped on his back. Holding tight rein on him, I patted him on the neck a time or two, spoke a few low words, and he started off without any bucking at all. "Hell fire," said Moore; "you're the first man that has been able to ride that damned horse this summer!"

The morning was clear and sparkling. The mountains were beautiful. Among the white-barked quaking aspen trees were herds of red Shorthorn and whitefaced Hereford cattle standing nearly knee deep in the grass and columbines. I felt like a conqueror. The horse behaved beautifully until about midday, when in trying to turn a bunch of cattle, I got excited and threw the spurs into him too hard. He immediately started to buck, but as I had his head rather high, he could not get it far enough down to do a thorough job. I suppose also that he was a bit tired after his strenuous morning. At least, he did not get me off, and this served to give "the farmer" a better reputation with the cowboys.

Each morning for a week, I was given a new horse—always one that seemed very wild at first glance. I had no trouble with them. Horses seem to know instinctively who are their friends. I have been able to ride several bad horses by means of a friendly approach. One of the strangest things about cow horses is the fact that they will often snort, buck, rear up on their hind legs, run away, and otherwise act like fiends incarnate, and yet when they get into action on the range, they will behave perfectly. They will hold the rope taut after a critter is lassoed, stand still when the only thing that keeps them from running away is the bridle reins thrown on the ground, and cooperate as if they were full partners in cutting out cattle from the bunch.

A good cow horse will chase a critter that the cowboy decides to rope, or to cut out of the bunch, with no need for the master to touch the bridle. The horse will weave from one side to the other as the beast tries to get away by dodging. He will watch the throw of the rope, and if he sees that it is going over the animal's horns or neck, he will sit back on his haunches braced for the shock when the rope suddenly tightens. The cowboy may get off his horse, leaving the end of the rope tied to the saddle horn. Whichever way the cow turns or whatever it does, the horse himself always manages to face it and hold the rope taut. This is the result of a lesson given to him when he is first broken. He is tied by a rope to a wild critter and left to shift for himself. At first, he may get tangled up or even turned over, but he soon learns his business: "Self-taught," Mundry would say. To break him to stand hitched only by the bridle reins lying on the ground, a colt may be left with a bridle with a J.I.C. bit in his mouth and the reins lying loose (such a bit, also called a "scissor" or "loose ring" bit, is really a jawbreaker). If the horse starts to run away, he will almost immediately step on the reins and give himself a jerk that nearly takes his head off. He soon learns.

Teaching the colt to obey the slightest touch of the rein on the opposite side of the neck from the direction in which you want him to go is accomplished by use of the hackamore rather than the bridle. The hackamore is a kind of halter, with a tight band around the horse's nose, but no bit. A rope or "cheek straps" attached to the nose band will be run over the horse's head just behind its ears, in order to hold the contraption in place. Below the jaw on the nose band, two ropes are attached. One is looped to form reins; the other is a long rope which can be used for leading the horse, or for snubbing him to the horn of a saddle on another horse, or for tying him anywhere. By pushing a part of the looped rope against one side of the colt's neck, and jerking a little on the other side, it is possible to teach him in a few days that when he feels a rope or a rein against his neck, he must turn his head away from it. If the rider touched the left side of his neck, he moves right, and vice versa. It is this trained response to slight rein pressure that makes a cow horse able to turn and dodge when his rider is cutting cattle out of a bunch, or roping. It is probably this strenuous method of breaking a cow pony that accounts for the inconsistency between his apparent wildness and his perfect training.

Between the first and second roundups I went down to Peach Valley to help the boys. How frightfully bare, hot and dismal this country seemed, compared to the Grand Mesa range!

Just before returning to the range, I stopped at the Stevens place and happened to mention to Mrs. Stevens how lonesome it was on the range at times. She said: "Why don't you take a cat up there with you? They are very companionable." That appeared to be a good plan, particularly since we had been bothered by mountain rats, which would run along the ridge poles at night and sometimes even scurry across our beds. At times we would lie in bed firing our six-shooters at them in the dark, but so far as I know we never hit one.

Mrs. Stevens led me out to the wagon shed where there was a litter of half-grown kittens. She gave me my choice: a yellow and brown tiger cat. I put it in a gunnysack and tied it on the back of my saddle. No sooner had I jumped on my horse than he began to buck, almost throwing me off. When he stopped bucking, I found that the kitten had been scratching the horse with its sharp claws. I then tied the gunnysack, hanging down, under the neck of the pack horse that I was leading, and away we started for camp.

During the afternoon, the poor kitten became tired, lonesome, hungry, and thirsty, and mewed piteously. As soon as I reached our shack, I put it in a box while I went out to get some milk from the cow we kept in the camp. The calf, which we had turned loose with the cow when we were away, had sucked most of the milk, but I got enough for the little kitten. I named it "Missouri" because the Stevens family were Missourians. The cat seemed to feel at home immediately. That evening, when I sat before the fire in the woodstove, Missouri crawled up on my lap and began to purr.

Missouri would follow me out to get the horses, just as if he had been a dog. He was a great mouser, and would pounce on mountain rats nearly as large as himself and kill them easily. One night I was awakened by fierce spitting and snarling on the part of Missouri. I lighted the candle and there was Missouri, standing on the edge of the wood-box with back and tail bristling. I went over to see what was the trouble and found to my consternation, a large skunk between the box and the wall. I feared that at any moment he would squirt his unholy fluid. Taking Missouri in my arms, I lit a piece of paper and threw it down on the skunk behind the wood-box. He made a hasty exit through the door. I shot three or four times in his direction, but did not hit him. Luckily, the burning paper did not set the wood or the cabin on fire.

Missouri became a great favorite. When we went away from the camp, either to ride on other parts of the range or to go to town, we left things for him to eat until we returned. Whenever we came back, we would find him sitting on the bars of the gate about a quarter of a mile from the cabin, waiting for us. He was overjoyed when we picked him up and carried him back to camp on our horses.

Between roundups, as we had a few days to spare, Harry and I decided to build a large corral at our upper camp. We started to cut quaking aspen logs and to "snake" or drag them in with our saddle horses. We had only worked one day when Horsewrangler cut his hand badly and thought he might be developing blood poisoning. He got on his top horse and started for town and a doctor. As he was unable to use his hand, he did not return for about a week. Meanwhile, I worked at cutting and snaking, and putting up logs, and so completed a fine corral about seven feet high. It was during that week that I first started to smoke a pipe in the evening. Horsewrangler had left one or two of them lying around, and a large can of tobacco. I think it was the lonesomeness of working there without any other person within miles that made me feel the friendly comfort of a pipe. With Missouri purring in my lap and the smoke from the pipe slowly drifting in the air, I felt quite contented.

By fall, Missouri was a very large cat and was much admired by all the cowboys. One day late in the fall we went to town, and when we came back to camp we could not find him. I never knew whether he was stolen, whether the coyotes killed him, or whether he wandered away and was lost. None of us ever saw him again.

One day that summer, I rode my old horse, Koppy, to town, bent on trading him off. He was not only vicious, but had never seen fit to take the proper training for a cow horse—or at least I had never been able to make a good cow horse of him.

Downtown I met a cowpuncher from the Escalante, riding up the street on a pretty strawberry roan. We exchanged greetings and he asked me how I would like to trade horses. I gave the customary reply that I would trade for $10 to boot. He said he would trade even, if my horse was sound. We stripped off our respective saddles and blankets and looked the horses over. Both of them appeared to be perfectly sound, so we traded.

The next morning when we went out to saddle up, Horsewrangler asked me how I would like to trade my roan for a bay that he had just acquired. I replied that I would have to have at least $10 to boot, as my horse was larger than his and was worth at least that much more. After protesting for a while, he consented to the trade. Afterwards, he remarked rather casually that he hoped I liked the bay, admitting that he had learned after getting him that the horse was damned near to being an outlaw. He had thrown a man off the day before and had broken his ribs. I remarked that the roan might be a trifle hard to handle for the first mile or so, too, and that he had killed a man a few days before. We did not indulge in the usual recriminations, since neither of us had a case!

I started to approach "Chub," as Horsewrangler said the bay was called. He gave a snort and ran around the corral, his eyes fairly protruding from his head. I finally had to rope him. Horsewrangler's roan likewise appeared frightfully wild. We saddled our respective horses after a bit of trouble. The roan stood there with back humped and tail between his legs. He did not look too good. My bay started bucking as soon as he was saddled, until the stirrups clicked together over the top of the saddle. "I reckon," said Horsewrangler, "that we had better write our obituaries before we start off." We got our pencils and wrote memorials to ourselves on the door. I do not remember mine, but I admired and memorized Horsewrangler's, which was as follows:

Alas for H. E. Horsewrangler!
He's passed through death's dark door.
He used to ride the snaky bronchs;
He ne'er will ride them more.

He jumped upon a horse one day,
It was a strawberry roan.
The horse went higher than the trees,
And then they packed him home.

They packed him home upon a mule;
He was hanging down each side.
No more through trees and underbrush
Will this poor cowboy ride.

His folks they wept, his folks they wailed,
It was so very sad.
For with all his faults and cussedness
He wasn't so very bad.

And now to heaven he has gone,
And on celestial plains
He rides upon those heavenly broncs
With their shining tails and manes.

And now old Peter leads applause,

And Moses shouts for glee,
For a western cowboy riding
Is a wonderful sight to see.

After writing our obituaries, we had to return to our horses. "I reckon," said the Horsewrangler, "that is it my turn to let down the bars, and I'll lead my horse out to them to save getting on twice." I answered, "Well, I never knew you to be so damned pious before, but just to show you that I appreciate your society I will walk along with you." Although we pretended great coolness, both of us were shivering in our boots, and were just about as happy as men being led to the electric chair. After we got the bars up, we jumped on. Neither horse bucked. I have always believed that giving those horses a little time to let the saddles warm their backs had much to do with our luck. Horsewrangler's roan proved not to be too bad, and the obituary did not come true.

Very soon, however, I discovered what a really dangerous horse I had. A little twig hit his flank. He leaped ahead about fifteen feet without any warning, almost breaking my back. Shortly after this a grouse whirred up with a great noise. The bay jumped ten feet to one side like a streak of lightening. A cow that we were chasing started into a thicket. As I did not want to be caught there, I pulled the reins. The bay stopped as if on a dime, almost throwing me over his head. Once during the day, he bucked. What a horse! He was made of spring steel. But he never was able to buck me off, and in time he became my favorite saddle horse. He was very valuable for cutting out cattle from the bunch because of his great quickness.

I used him, also, for another purpose. When someone who had come up from town with only one horse wished to borrow one, I would very kindly offer him Chub. After hearing the bay snort and seeing his wild eyes, the visitor would decide to ride his own horse again.

Between the time of the second roundup and the third, which took place in the latter part of August, I helped my brothers put up the second cutting of alfalfa in Peach Valley.

The third roundup was held for the purpose of gathering the fat cows that did not have calves, as well as the steers that were to be shipped in the fall or sold to farmers as feeders, and putting them up in the big pasture on rim rock. The top of the range was gorgeous at this time, with bunch grass nearly a foot high.

One day after we had driven a number of steers into the big pasture, we were eating our lunch above the precipitous southwest end of the rim rock. Several of us began to pry large rocks off the top. They would drop down the almost vertical rim rock nearly a thousand feet, strike in the scrub cedars, often cutting several trees off short, and then bounce over the grey adobes with enormous jumps which we could follow only because of the clouds of dust raised by the rocks as they sped along toward the Gunnison River Canyon, some five or six miles away. It never seemed to occur to us that there might possibly be a cow in the cedars, or that a rock might hit a person on the lonely road to Grand Junction!

Mort Beckley saw an unusually large rock that looked as if it could be pried loose. As he worked on it, the rock loosened much more easily than he had expected, throwing him forward over the edge of the precipice. By luck he caught a little sapling and held on tight. The sapling began to come out by the roots and was nearly gone by the time we got to him and drew him up. We gave him the name of "Rimrocker" as the result of this episode.

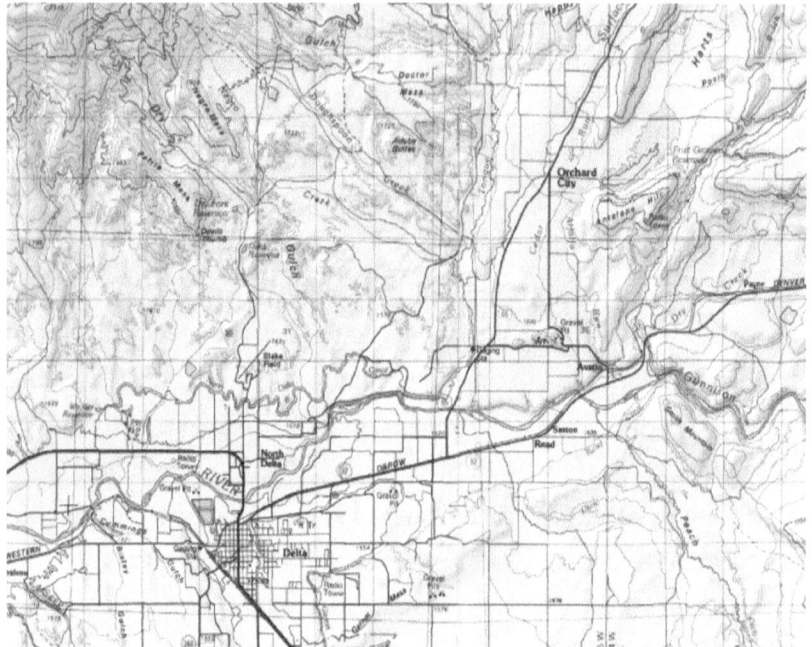

This 20th century topo map of Delta with one-mile-square grid lines, shows much of the region described by the author. Melvale Farm on Oak Creek is at the very top in the foothills of Grand Mesa. Peach Valley is at the bottom right. Garnet Mesa is to the right of the town. Getting around by wagon or on horseback was a slow and arduous process.

Early in the spring we had bought a little team of brown mares, as we no longer had use of the Blair horses. With Topsy and Jess, they made a fine four horse team. Later we bought a nice two horse buggy. The little brown mares hitched to the new buggy made quite a striking outfit. Howard and I figured that now we would be able to take out girls in style, but so far as I can remember, we never did.

Toward the latter part of the summer, Uncle Cornelius paid us another visit. With our fine little team of mares, which I had curried until they shone with more than oriental splendor, I went down to meet him at the train. I expected that he would be highly enthusiastic to see how we had come up in the world since his last visit. But he said not a word. I felt deeply hurt, but thought: "Perhaps he is just ignorant of good horse flesh." Later in the day, Mother informed me that what really troubled him was the fact that the boys smelled of the stable. At this time, his world and mine were miles apart.

CHAPTER XIII

Tough Winter

Early in the fall, there were cold rains and a little snow in the mountains. The cattle, as usual, started down the creeks toward the ranches. For a good many days we had to ride the creek bottoms and drive the cattle back again, as we did not wish them to come off the range until the first of November, or even later if possible. Every day on the range meant just so much hay and farm pasture saved for the winter. It was far from a pleasant job, sitting on a horse in the rain all day, driving cattle where they did not wish to go. As soon as the rain ceased, however, the cattle were glad to stay up on the range.

After the cattle had been driven back, I had some time to spend at the Peach Valley ranch and at home, putting up our third cutting of alfalfa. We had large crops on both places, about 300 tons if I remember rightly. As hay was again low, I made a deal with Mower to winter 300 head of his yearling steers at $3.00 per head. Ordinarily, with pasture and straw stacks, half a ton of hay was ample to feed each critter. To be sure we had enough feed, I purchased a half dozen fields of grain stubble and ten or twelve straw stacks, beside the four or five on our Peach Valley place. Counting our own cattle, we had about 500 head of cattle on our hands for the winter.

About the end of October or the first of November, the cattle began to pour off the range again, coming down the several creek bottoms. As they descended, the cattlemen and cowboys would gather them into large herds and would slowly drive them homeward. At each ranch where cattle were to be left, we had the job of cutting those out marked by particular brands and driving them into a designated field. At times this job was difficult because the cattle did not like to leave the herd, and also because of the inherent cussedness of some critters. I have spent a quarter of an hour racing a steer or cow back and forth in front of an open gate through which it refused to go.

One day, I was riding a rather wild colt. At a place where the road made a right turn, there was an open gate leading into a farm. Nearby was a telegraph pole to which was attached a "dead man" wire, that is, a strong bracing wire running from the top of the pole into the ground, where it was fastened to a large block of buried concrete. Two or three cattle insisted on going into the farmers field instead of making the turn to the right. I raced my horse down toward the gate to turn them. As I neared the dead man, several chickens flew out of the brush. My horse jumped forward and sideways very rapidly, and in come unaccountable way, got his front leg entangled with the wire. He stopped so suddenly that I was thrown fifteen or twenty feet away into an irrigation ditch filled with water. When I crawled out, I saw that the colt was in a rather dangerous situation. I had to go to the farm house, borrow a hammer and cold chisel, and cut the wire to free him.

Although most of the cattle had come down from the range on their own accord, it was necessary to ride the range just below the rim rock for any that might have been caught in the snow. So we returned to Mower's upper camp for a few days. One evening, a farmer named Mangus came to hunt for deer. He was welcomed at camp, as was everyone; but we thought it strange that a man nearly 70 should be hunting on the mountains alone at this time of year. During his first night at camp, there was a snowfall of three or four inches.

We started out early to ride below the rim rock, leaving Mangus at the cabin. When we returned to camp about three o'clock, we saw on the door a crude picture of a bear, with a notice which read about as follows: "Come down the trail to Dirty George Creek. Have killed the damnedest biggest bear in the world. Bring pack mules. Mangus." With a couple of pack horses we started down the trail as the old man had directed. At a crossing of the creek, in a bunch of willows, was the dead bear. Old Man Mangus was at work skinning him. The bear must have measured 24 inches between his ears, and he had a foot about fifteen inches long and nine or ten inches wide. The great toe of his right back foot was missing. Here was the bear that we had seen and tracked when we were small boys! Here was the bear whose traces we had seen so often on the range, the bear that killed so many cattle, and on whose head the cattlemen's association had placed a bounty of $300!

We skinned the bear and packed the skin on a trembling horse. We then cut off large pieces of meat and fat and placed it on the other horse. We had bear steak for supper that night, and at other meals for several days, but I did not really enjoy it.

That evening we heard Old Man Mangus tell his story. He left camp, it seems, shortly after we had gone. Not far from camp he sighted the bear crossing the nearby trail that ran down the mountain. He shot twice at it without having, as he thought, any success. As the bear went down the trail, Mangus followed its tracks, and soon found blood on the snow. He traced the beast down the mountain until he finally came to a crossing on Dirty George Creek, which was fringed by young quaking aspens and small willows. He had hardly reached the creek when he looked up

The pelt of the "great bear", shot at close range by old man Mangus. The Blachly boys had tracked the huge beast many years earlier, and were on hand to help Mangus skin it and trim the meat. (photographer unknown)

and saw the bear only thirty feet away, in the willows, standing on its hind legs with bloody froth running from its mouth. As soon as the great beast saw Mangus, it started toward him. Mangus began to shoot at it with his 45-90 repeating rifle. He poured thirteen shots into this monster before it fell, almost at his feet. He ran off a few steps, reloaded his gun, and took two more shots at close range to be sure that the bear was really dead.

Mangus received the offered reward of $300, and was said to have sold the bear's skin for almost as much. It was reported that the skin was later exhibited at the St. Louis Fair, where it took first prize.

This same fall a large bunch of Mower's "long yearling steers" and some other stock had been left up in the Big Pasture as late as possible, since there was plenty of grass there. The fat stock had been taken to Delta and shipped. About the latter part of November, the weather suddenly became very cold and we could see that it was snowing on the mountains. I had just returned home from the Gunnison River Valley about eleven o'clock one night, when I was notified that all the cattlemen who operated on the western end of Grand Mesa would start at four o'clock the next morning to bring down the cattle from the Big Pasture.

After a few hours' sleep, I went out to the corral, saddled my horse and started to get on him. The horse had a different idea, and do as I would, I could not mount him. Finally, in desperation, I led him into a corner where I ran a pole from side to side, placing the ends between the logs of the corral, and shutting the horse into a little triangle. I was then able to mount him. It was easy to dislodge the pole by a kick. Finally, I started for Delta, where we were to assemble. The weather was bitterly cold. After we had gone a short distance, our feet in our high-heeled boots began to

Cattlemen gathering in town for a roundup of the herd from summer feeding grounds on Grand Mesa. (photo by FF Blachly, c. 1934)

freeze, and we had to walk a mile or so to keep them warm. (It is impossible to wear overshoes while riding; for in case the horse should fall or should buck off his rider, they might not slip out of the stirrups, and the rider might be dragged to death). When I tried to get on my horse again, he objected, and one of the men had to snub him to his saddle horn before I was able to crawl on.

Just as the sun was rising over the mighty Elk Mountains toward the east, we reached the top of the rim rock and the Big Pasture, where the snow was nearly a foot deep. We were almost frozen. We rode to the western end of the pasture, separated into three groups, and started rounding up the cattle and driving them toward the downward trail at the eastern end. It was well toward the latter part of the afternoon that we finally got all the cattle off the mountain and started down the trail, and nearly midnight before we got them to Tom Mower's ranch on Tongue Creek.

The next morning Mower decided that all of these steers would have to be dehorned before he drove them up to our Peach Valley

Ranch for winter feeding. The dehorning was a bloody mess. One by one, the steers were driven and pushed into the dehorning chute, and their horns were shaved off. The job took all day. Tom Mower had provided a barrel of cider for the hot and thirsty men and they imbibed it freely. We did not know it at the time, but the stuff had been "spiked." Toward evening, as we started to our respective homes, some of the men were so happy that they were racing their horses and yelling and singing like Apache Indians.

The next day we drove the bunch of cattle up on Surface Creek Mesa to get them to Peach Valley over the Gunnison River Bridge. From the Mesa down to the bridge was a long narrow grade. In order that too many cattle should not be on the bridge at the same time, and in order that they might be restrained from running across the bridge, the herd was broken up into four or five sections, each headed by one or two cowboys.

I was in front of the second section. Just as the first section started across the bridge a couple of dogs from a nearby farm house ran out barking as loudly as they could, and started into the bunch of cattle. Immediately there was a stampede. We could not hold our sections back, though we waved our ropes in front of them and tried to stop them. When I was forced upon the bridge, two or three times as many cattle were there as should have been, and they were running as fast as they could go.

The bridge, which was quite long and high, began to sway back and forth. A few of the cattle fell down. My horse staggered time after time as though he would fall, but always kept his feet. I thought that at any moment the bridge would give way, and we should be thrown down into the water thirty or forty feet below, amid a surging mass of cattle. At last, however, both men and cattle reached the farther side in safety.

Mower, who was in the rear of the whole bunch, roped one of the dogs that had started the stampede, jerked him over a beam of the bridge, and broke his neck. Out came the farmer with his shotgun, ready to shoot Mower. "Shoot ahead," said Mower, "but if you do it will be the end of you." Finally, the farmer thought better of the situation and went back to the house with his gun.

Things appeared to be prosperous for our family at this moment. We had the contract to winter the Mower cattle, which seemed to guarantee us over three dollars per ton for the hay and a reasonable return for the pasture that we had to spare. We had sold a large crop of oats at a good price. The orchard on the home place was beginning to bear. We had about 200 head of cattle nearly all paid for. The mine in which we were interested looked better and better as drilling went on. And we had several hundred dollars, earned by caring for farmers' cattle on the range. I treated myself to a good heavy suit made by Delta's best tailor.

Practically all of our own cattle had been collected by this time, except a few stragglers and renegades that often stayed out all winter. We let our herd roam over the Poverty Flat and Peach Valley country, where we had bought all the straw stacks and pastures for a song. We figured that the cattle would live well on the salt weed, wild grass along the large ditch banks and stream beds, stubble, and straw stacks, until sometime in January (1904) when we would start to feed them alfalfa hay.

Toward the middle of November we woke up one morning at home to find a foot or more of snow on the ground and the flakes still coming down. For two days the snow fell, until it was about two feet on the level. When the sky cleared, the temperature suddenly dropped. It was bitterly cold. The morning after the snow stopped, I rode Brownie over to Peach Valley to see how the cattle were getting along. As I crossed toward the valley, the adobe hills shone with such unbearable glitter in the clear Colorado sunshine that I thought that I might get snow-blindness. When I came to the larger and steeper hills, I found snow on the eastern sides piled in drifts several feet deep. At times, Brownie would have to take great jumps just to get through these drifts at all. I had to spur him cruelly in order to make him do so. Once I had to get off and break a short path through an extraordinarily deep drift.

When I arrived in Peach Valley, I found that the cattle had all flocked around the three or four straw stacks on the place and had eaten what they wished and trampled down the remainder. Here was a mess: the pastures all covered up with snow, and the straw stacks that should have lasted a month or more, gone. I did not feel too badly discouraged, however, for I believed that warmer days would soon come, the snow would melt, and the cattle would still have the pasture and the straw stacks which I had purchased. It seemed, also, that I had a safe margin of hay.

Howard and I debated as to whether we should hire a man to feed the cattle in Peach Valley while we hauled coal, or do the feeding ourselves. About this time, an old Irishman who said he was almost starving for lack of work, applied to us for a job and we hired him. His name was O'Brien. "The Last of the Kings of Ireland," we called him, because of his claim of descent from the former Irish sovereigns. We gave him a dollar a day and "found." He was supplied with a team and a hay rack, plenty of warm bedding, canned goods, flour, bacon, coal, and so on. One of the little shacks in the Valley was assigned to him as living quarters. His work was not very strenuous, for all that he had to do was to pitch a couple of loads of hay on the rack each day, then pitch it off to the cattle as the horse went slowly down the field. He also had to break up the ice in the pond. We would ride up every few days to see how he was getting along and how the cattle were doing.

He found it a frightfully lonesome job up there in the Valley, with nothing to see but snow in every direction. I sympathized with him but did not see that we could do anything to help him. One morning as I rode up to the ranch at feeding time, I noticed from the hill overlooking the valley that the cattle were scattered over the different fields and that no hay was being hauled. I rode up to the camp house to see what was the matter. Though I knocked on the door loudly, there was no answer. I opened the door and walked in. There lay O'Brien in the bed, apparently asleep. I started to shake him, when to my horror, I found that "The Last Kings of Ireland" was dead. He was buried by the county.

Upon the death of O'Brien, Howard went to live in the Valley and feed the stock for a time. It was agreed that a little later, I should take his place.

Almost immediately after the big snow, I started to ride the range with other cattlemen, looking for any cattle that might not yet be in the winter pastures. We knew that they could not live long on the open range with the snow so deep. It was bitterly cold and our feet nearly froze. One morning Dr. Stockham, as a joke, suggested to the Horsewrangler that he should put a little red pepper in his boots to keep his feet warm. Harry took his father's advice seriously, and carried it out. At first, he said that the pepper made his feet feel nice and warm. As the day progressed, however, they felt as if they were burning up; and he was suffering severely before it was possible for him to take off his boots.

Most of our riding was done toward the western end of the range, between the cedars and the Gunnison River below Delta, where we judged (correctly, as we found) that some of our cattle had drifted during the storm. It was difficult to ride over a wide expanse of rough country, round up the few cattle remaining, and drive them through the deep snow. The weather stayed so cold that we thought our feet and ears would freeze. One evening, just about the time we were beginning to feel that we were freezing to death, we stopped to spend the night with a farmer named Hutchison who had a large potato farm down on the Gunnison below Delta. We told his family of the danger to our ears, since we had no way of protecting them. One of his daughters immediately said that she and her sisters could soon remedy this. They took some of their old stockings, cut off the tops, sewed them together at the smaller end, and lo and behold, we were supplied with warm caps that could be pulled down over our ears. Several years ago, at the Grand Mesa Lakes, I met one of the Hutchison sisters and reminded her of this kindness. "It could not have been me," she said. "I never did a good deed in my life!"

After all the cattle that we could find were in, Howard and I took turns at hauling coal and feeding cattle in the Valley. Teaming was very difficult that winter. The roads became a glare of ice, making it necessary to use rough locks—chains around one of the wagon wheels to keep it from skidding downhill—nearly every day. Even with these, teaming was dangerous work. The horses had to be sharp shod to keep from falling, and most of the time we could use only one wagon, as the danger for a four-horse team and a trailer was too great.

A circumstance that distressed me greatly was a serious injury to one of my favorite horses, Jess. In coming down from the Rollins Mine, where Howard had driven her with another horse to haul a load of coal, she apparently stepped on a round stone in some way and threw out her hip joint. Not knowing that a veterinarian might have been able to pull the leg back into place, I traded her off to serve as a brood mare. This not only broke my heart, but also broke up my best team.

I had several narrow escapes while riding the pastures of farmers to get our stray cattle together. I was attempting to drive one of our cows out of a pasture on the Uncompahgre River, when she suddenly turned into a rather narrow path leading through some underbrush. I started after her on the run. She came to a ditch about five feet wide and several feet deep that I did not know was there. In trying to jump the ditch she fell down on the other side. As I was not more than ten feet back of her, I could not possibly stop my horse. I threw the spurs into him. He rose to the occasion and jumped over both the ditch and the cow. I got the cow turned back, but she made a break for another opening in the brush, and I tore after her. Quickly she dodged to the left. There in front of me was a pool of ice about thirty feet wide, caused by overflow from an irrigation ditch. I thought I was gone, as my horse was running so fast that I could not turn him quickly enough to miss the pond. He hit the ice with all four feet, and strange to relate, slid the whole way across without falling.

One morning about the middle of December, I started for Peach Valley. Northeast of Poverty Flat I had bought a one hundred-sixty-acre pasture of wheat and oats stubble, with the straw stacks. I was saving these fields and straw stacks until the snow should be off the ground. In coming to the top of a little hill, I looked down over the field and saw there two or three thousand sheep with a shepherd and his dog. I rode up to the Mexican Shepherd, told him that this was my property, and ordered him out. He drew his revolver from the holster and said he would shoot me if I did not leave him alone. I looked at his revolver and said

"Remember, if you take a shot at me, the cowboys will hang you as high as Haman tonight." I do not know whether he appreciated the scriptural allusion or not, but he lowered his gun. "I will give you just twenty-four hours to get entirely out of this country," I said. He picked up his little tent and provisions, put them on his burro, called his dog, and started his sheep. I do not know where he went. It seemed a crime to drive him off into the snowy hills, but I was feeling rather desperate about our own situation and could not waste too much sympathy upon a person who was appropriating the straw needed for my cattle.

The early snow did not melt off the ground as we had anticipated. On the contrary, it lay there as a foundation for further snowfalls, which came only too plentifully. I had just started back from Peach Valley one day, when the wind began to blow furiously in my face, carrying a sharp cutting sleet. In order to reach home, I had to hold my horse into the storm. He tried to turn away from it and I had a hard time holding him there. The blizzard finally became so bad, that I could not see the road. Though I felt that we had gone astray, I could not tell in what direction we were moving. Presently my horse stopped. When I looked for the reason, I found that he was standing against a barbed wire fence. I got off the horse and led him along the fence until we came to a gate, through which we passed. We followed what seemed to be a road. Within a few minutes, I saw a little shack a few feet ahead of me, and realized that I had drifted nearly a mile to the south and was at Tim Sullivan's place. A warm fire and a cup of coffee made life look brighter immediately. The storm broke in the late afternoon, and I rode home.

The snow continued to fall every few days, and the weather grew colder and colder. The feet of some cattle began to freeze.

All of the poor critters began to grow painfully thin, yet we did not dare feed them more than barely enough hay to keep them alive. As soon as we started the wagon across the fields to the hay stacks, the cattle would begin bawling. We would keep the wagon with a large load of hay, and going slowly, would pitch it off to the cattle, who followed the wagon hopefully. It seemed that the hay hardly touched the ground before it was eaten up. We soon found that we had to separate the weaker stock from the stronger and feed them from another field, if they were to get anything at all to eat. The hay stacks grew smaller day by day, and yet there was no end to the snow and cold. The piteous bawling of the half starving cattle, the knowledge that we might lose all of them, the frightful cold, and the bitter desolation of Peach Valley covered with snow, drove Howard and me almost to despair.

Several cows became so weak that they would lie down, evidently to await death. Unless we could get them up immediately and start feeding them a little better, they would grow worse, bloat up, and die. We had to adopt a strenuous method of making them get up. We would find two heavy sticks a foot or more long, take the tail of the prostrate cow between the sticks near her body, hold the sticks as closely together as possible, and pull them down her tail very rapidly. This would make even a weak cow so furious that she would get up immediately. It was well to have a horse handy in case she attempted to avenge the insult. After her temper had cooled, special feeding and extra care would be given.

At the turn of the year (1904) we rented the Peach Valley ranch again, and then re-rented it to the Thompson boys on shares. We were to farm with a certain number of horses and some equipment, and were to receive one-half of the oats and hay crops. I figured that by having the ranch operated on shares, we would have enough hay for our cattle with little cost to ourselves. By running the cattle of others on the range, as I had done the year before, I could use my time to advantage and obtain some badly needed cash. Although the older boys were now leaving in order to obtain some education, the younger ones could easily operate the Garnet Mesa place.

Toward the latter part of March, Mower, fearing that he would lose all his steers that were in our care, drove them up to his father's place where there was a little hay left. He refused to pay me a rather large balance still due. About this time, the weather became a little warmer and the snow started to melt. The starving cattle ate every green thing on the ground, including Russian thistle that had been softened a bit in the snow. Cows began to have calves. Some of these cows were so weak that we had to rig out slings and hold them on their feet by means of the hay derrick for a day or so, before they were strong enough to stand alone and eat hay. Several cows died in giving birth to their calves. The poor little calf would stand beside the dead body of his mother, needing food and help but finding none, until we came. We hauled a number of these calves home and fed them milk.

After the snow was off, everything was mud. The weak cattle could hardly drag their feet through it. One cow got stuck in the ditch in the center of the Valley. I roped her by the horns and dragged her out. While she was still lying on her side, I took off the rope and started for my saddlehorse. The cow, all covered with mud, rose up suddenly and ran toward me. The apparition scared my horse, and he started to run away before I could reach him. The cow nearly had me when I jumped the ditch. She jumped after me, but luckily got stuck in the ditch again! I caught my horse and dragged her out once more; but this time, I held the horse's reins and jumped on his back just as I let her loose.

One day early in April, I drove up to Peach Valley in a buggy. When I got toward the lower end of it, I saw a cow stuck so deep in the alkali seep ground that nothing showed but her head, horns, and a little bit of her back. I went up to the Thompson boys to get aid. They had just returned from an expedition on which they had purchased two pigs about eight weeks old. The pigs were in the wagon. As soon as I told the boys of the trouble with the cow, they unloaded the pigs into a little temporary pen that, as it proved, was not very secure. The Thompsons got the long cable that was used on the hay derrick and started down with their team to rescue the cow. The mare I was driving was one of the horses for which I traded the black colt. I unhitched her and tied her to the buggy. The cow was so far out in the mud that we had to hitch the horses to the derrick rope about forty feet away from her head. The team pulled her out of the mud to dry land without much difficulty.

As we started toward the cow to free her from the rope, the team happened to turn enough to see the cow. Her extraordinary appearance alarmed them so much that they started to run away, with the long rope dragging and the double tree pounding at their heels. My mare became frightened and pulled the buggy upside down before we could stop her. We caught her, righted the buggy, hitched her to it, and started after the team. Before we had gone far, we struck a little ditch where, seemingly reverting to her former instincts, the mare balked. There in the distance was the team streaking across the hills, while we were helpless until the mare suddenly changed her mind and started to run. We finally came up with the runaway horses, which had suffered a good deal of damage to their heels because the double tree had been striking against them. When we finally got back to the house, the pigs were gone. We never saw them again. I suppose the coyotes had a good meal. However, I had to pay the boys for the pigs.

A short time after this adventure, I rode over the brow of the hill that separated the two parts of the ranch. About half a mile ahead, I saw two coyotes running after a calf. The mother cow was trying to keep them off as best she could. I yelled at the top of my lungs, and setting spurs to my horse, rode like fury. Before I could reach the calf, however, the coyotes had downed him and had eaten a hole in his side. The poor little fella was barely dead when I arrived. After this I carried a revolver with me for the benefit of the coyotes, but I could never get near enough to shoot one. Coyotes seem to know when a person has a gun, by instinct or perhaps by smell. At any rate, a coyote will let you get within one or two hundred yards of him when you have no gun, but will stay half a mile away when you carry one.

Toward the middle of April, the situation became desperate for the cattle. One night the starving animals broke down the wire fence around the last hay stack and ate up or trampled all the hay which might have fed them for a few days more. Unless something were done immediately, all the cattle would die. There appeared to be no hay for sale anywhere. And even if there had been, were could I raise money to buy it?

I finally located 15 tons in the Gunnison River Valley, but had to pay $20 a ton for it—just about ten times the price of hay the preceding fall. In order to buy it, I was forced to go to the First National Bank and borrow $300 secured by a chattel mortgage. After this hay had been eaten, we had to turn the cattle loose on the range, regardless of the weather or the condition of the pasturage. There was no grass as yet—only a little salt weed, sage brush, grease weed and cactus. With much fear and trembling, we drove the cattle up to the edge of the range to fend for themselves. Most of the animals were so thin that their hides appeared to be merely hung on poles. The fresh salt weed acted as a laxative and the poor beasts were further weakened by the "scours." Cold rains increased the discomfort of the cattle and caused many of the weak ones to die. Luckily, however, the weather soon turned warm and the grass began to grow rapidly. The cattle followed the receding snow and the new grass up the mountain. By the time of the first roundup in June, no one would have recognized the beautiful, sleek fat cattle standing amidst the grass and columbines as the living skeletons that had started up the bare range two months earlier.

CHAPTER XIV

Hitting Bottom

I SPENT THE REMAINDER OF 1904 and the early part of 1905 trying to climb back from my financial troubles. There were many discouraging aspects to the situation. As I have said, we had no way of knowing how many of our cattle—which we had been compelled by necessity to turn loose in an almost starving condition on a practically naked range in the spring—would survive. Because the melted snow made the ground very soft, some of the hungry animals were pulling up larkspur by the roots and eating it, and were dying from the poison which it contained. Quite often when riding the range that spring, we would see dead cattle, or smell the odor of death.

The notes that I had given to obtain money for buying cattle and to purchase shares in the Cleveland Mine, had found their way to the First National Bank. In order to borrow enough more money to obtain the last few tons of hay in the Gunnison River Valley, so that the cattle might not all starve to death, and as a condition precedent to having my other notes renewed, I had been compelled to mortgage to the First National Bank all my cattle, teams and equipment. As was its custom in dealing with cattle owners, the bank would lend money for only ninety days. At each renewal, interest had to be paid at the rate of 10% per annum. I was completely at the mercy of the bank, for I knew that if the price of cattle should fall, they would probably refuse to renew my notes and I would lose all the cattle and other property.

The miners who were working the Cleveland Mine had struck a fault and could not find the vein again. The ore, just before the fault was struck, had been very valuable, and the price of the mine's stock had risen well. But, upon the discovery of the fault and the announcement that the vein could not be relocated, the price of stock dropped to almost zero. There was no telling in what direction or at what depth it was necessary to mine in order to strike the vein once more, or whether it would ever be found within our company's claim.

Probably the most discouraging feature of all was the fact that my "force" was so weakened. Arthur was finishing his medical course in Boulder, and Clarence had gone to Grinnell College Academy. Howard—as the result of his bleak experiences in Peach Valley during the winter and the deadening monotony, danger, and hard work of hauling coal—swore that he was through with the Valley forever. He found some work that made it possible for him to save a little money, and he now planned to join Clarence in Iowa, enter Grinnell College Academy, and then work his way through the college. I hated to think of losing him. Howard was a mighty man. He was over six foot three inches in height, weighed about 190 pounds, and was extremely strong. Moreover, he was a very hard and competent worker. He was an excellent rider, an able teamster, and a man afraid of nothing. And he knew farming and the cattle business—at least from the day-to-day operational side.

Hal, who was just below Howard in age, was also well over six feet in height. However, he was not very strong and he lacked the drive and daring of Howard. Furthermore, he had been going to school steadily, so had not gained all around experience with farming and cattle. He had a dreamy, artistic nature, ill-fitted for the type of life which ranching and the cattle business required.

Hal had a magnificent bass voice nearly an octave lower than mine. He had taken a few vocal lessons from Miss Botsford, and hoped someday to become a great singer. He was a charming person, but nature had not intended him for the life that we were leading.

Ralph, now sixteen, was bothered by some stomach trouble. Like Hal, he was of an artistic temperament rather than a driving, aggressive disposition. The refinement of his nature was not adapted to the rough and tough life of cattle wrestling and coal hauling. Louis, at fourteen, was very energetic and capable, but was too young to assume heavy responsibilities. Edward, of course, was far too young at twelve, to do much. Furthermore, it was essential that all the younger boys remain in school.

In short, my attempt to claw my way back from the brink of financial ruin was undertaken under severe handicaps. My assets were greatly depleted. I was uncertain how many cattle I had left. The mining investment was a disaster. I had exhausted my credit and owed the bank a considerable amount, which was borrowed at a high rate of interest on a ninety-day basis. The large labor force, which alone had made it possible for us to handle extensive ranching operations, had dwindled so that I was now the only one who could work full time.

There were nevertheless certain factors that led me to believe that I could come back. I still might have nearly two hundred head of cattle, if Providence had been kind. Judging by the prices that cattle usually brought, I had an equity of about half the value of the herd after my debts were paid. We had one more year's lease on the Peach Valley farm, and as we had planted most of it to alfalfa and had rented it to the Thompson boys on shares, we seemed to be assured of enough hay for our cattle at very little expense. Further, the Thompson boys were to plant about 25 acres to oats, of which we were to receive one half. As heavy snow still lay on the mountains due to the extraordinary downfall of the past winter, there was every prospect of a large crop of hay and grain.

Although the smaller boys were not able to carry out extensive farming operations, they were able to look after the home place and to attend school at the same time. We had plenty of horses and equipment for any operations that we might undertake. The groceries could largely be paid for by eggs, which Mother sold by the case to Mr. Finney, who shipped them to the mining camps. I could wait until fall, as was the general custom, to pay for the groceries that I needed on the range.

After considering the situation in every way, I decided that I should ride the range again, and help with the work of the home place when there were no roundups. I was able to secure about as many of the neighbors' cattle to take care of on the range as I had managed during the previous summer. Things might yet work out advantageously, it seemed.

In May of 1904, I went with a trainload of cattle to Denver, shipping with it several of our bulls, which we had wintered at the home place after they were deemed too old for service on the range. Again, I visited Arthur, who was just about to be graduated from the University of Colorado Medical School at Boulder. As the boys could easily look after things at home in the spring, I took time to look around again for a possible opening. I soon found that I had no training for the kind of work that I wished to do. As I looked for positions, it began to dawn on me forcibly that it was one thing to drive horses, punch cows, and farm for oneself, and quite another to be a hired man, particularly in a city. To drive a beer wagon or a milk truck was in no sense comparable to teaming on one's own account. Nonetheless, in order to fill in the time between my arrival in Boulder and Arthur's graduation, I found a position with a farmer on the edge of town for two or three weeks.

A day or so before Arthur was to receive his degree, the president of the University held a reception for the graduates and their friends. At this reception, most of the young men and women wore evening clothes. Arthur had a plain black suit, but all that I had was my heavy business suit. I felt ill at ease in the presence of the young people, who seemed so happy and so much at home with themselves and all creation. My embarrassment was all the greater because in walking from the little shack where Arthur and his friends "bached," my feet had become covered with mud. Although I had tried hard to wipe it off before entering the reception room, it still showed in dirty streaks.

For two or three Sundays I went with Arthur to a little Sunday school he conducted among the coal miners' children, eight or ten miles southeast of Boulder. The miners lived in wooden hovels near the mouth of the mines. There were no trees, no flowers, no beauty in the surroundings. Everything spoke of wretched poverty. Had no one any interest in the lot of these people, or any incentive for helping them to better it? Twenty years later I passed through the same place. My questions were answered. The place was exactly the same.

Arthur did a good job in leading the Sunday School. I helped in the singing. It is still an enigma to me how Arthur found time to cover his expenses while doing his medical work, and still look after this little Sunday School.

I was proud to see Arthur receive his diploma, and to know that he had already secured an appointment as physician on an Indian reservation. The salary that he was to receive ($1,000 a year, if I remember rightly) seemed quite grand to me, for it represented the value of over 300 tons of hay, which would take our crew of several boys much of the year to produce.

As soon as graduation was over, Arthur and I started for the train to Delta. As we were on our way to the station, a person was knocked down by a passing automobile, right in front of us. Arthur, forgetting that he was a doctor, ran to the nearby drug store and called for a physician to attend the victim. We caught the train, and were welcomed by the family. Arthur spent a few days at home, and then left for his new position with the Rosebud Indian Reservation in South Dakota.

From time to time I rode up to the range to see how the cattle were getting along. They were still so scattered throughout the lower cedar and oak country that I could not make any estimate on the total number that had survived. Most of my time until the first roundup started was occupied on the home place: plowing, sowing grain (for we always raised about five acres of wheat on the home place for Mother's chickens), cultivating the orchard, and planting the garden. Because of the heavy snows, we felt assured of good crops. The orchard appeared to be in fine condition. The trees, which by this time were quite large, were in full bloom and promised to bear well.

Just before the first roundup, Howard and I took the opportunity to trade for one or two wild horses, with plans to break them. A colt for which I had paid about thirty dollars was so very wild that in order to tame him at all we were forced to keep him hobbled by one front foot, so that we could throw him down at any moment. One day when this colt was being driven with old Topsey on Surface Creek Mesa, I met a farmer on horseback who was leading a small black mare. "How will you trade that colt for the black mare?" he said. "Give me forty bucks and the colt is yours,"

I replied. "O.K.," he replied, and wrote out a check. "Just take the mare along and leave the colt in the corral as you pass my house." "By the way," I said, "is the mare broken for driving?" "Damned if I know," he answered, "I just traded for her."

Howard and I drove the colt down to the farmer's ranch, put him in the corral, and hitched up the little mare with Topsy. We were glad to get rid of the outlaw colt. The mare went along well enough through the adobes, until we came to a place where we had to ford the Gunnison River in order to reach our destination, a neighbor's farm. The River was rather full when we reached it, but we started across. Right in the middle of the stream where the water was about three feet deep, the black mare balked. She would not budge a step, despite fervent persuasion with the end of the heavy rein. I finally hitched the stay chain back of the doubletree so that Topsey could pull the whole load, spoke gently to her, and she started right off. The little mare tried to hold back. In a moment, Topsey had pulled her off her feet and she was being dragged through the water. This was too much for her. She got up and started to run as fast as Topsey would let her go.

Shortly after this, Howard left on a cattle train for Grinnell, to try his fortune in the world of learning. I was greatly downcast. Not only had I lost my bosom companion and chief helper, but I realized as never before that all of my brothers, as well as my friends, were leaving me far behind in the matter of education.

As soon as Howard had gone, I went to the range for the first roundup. The range was beautiful that summer. The heavy snow had made the grass unusually good. The quaking aspen belt was glorious with columbines. There was much lupin, and on many south hillsides near the top of the range were lovely blue gentians. There were also many wild berries: red raspberries, strawberries and gooseberries. The mountain streams were filled with water. The creek near our camp was filled with fish that had been stocked there during the previous years and were now big enough to eat. Nothing gave me more pleasure than to see the cattle, which a few weeks before had been mere skeletons, standing among the white quaking aspens, knee deep in grass and columbines, literally rolling with fat. One could not remain sad too long in such an environment.

The work of riding the range went on about as it had the previous summer. Sometime in June, one of Harry's girl cousins and a friend of hers came up to camp to visit us. They were very nice girls indeed. Harry bragged one morning of my ability to flap pancakes in the air. I made up the batter and started a pancake nearly a foot in diameter. When I had loosened it from the pan, as I thought, I started to flip it. This was not my lucky day. The pancake was still soft in the center, and a bit stuck to the pan, so instead of turning over gracefully as it should have done, it dribbled down my boot, much to my discomfort and confusion. Its successors were better, however, and I redeemed my reputation.

We spent one or two pleasant evenings in singing. The girls knew several songs that I had never heard. For a day or so I rode the range with Harry's cousin. Harry swore that I was the only damned man on the range with whom he would trust a female relative. I have forgotten her name, but she was a good sport and a remarkably good rider. Sometimes, I rode fast over very rough places, but she always kept up. She also appeared to be very well educated, and again, I felt that sense of inferiority which always bothered me when I was with persons who had gone to college—or even high school.

For several years past, the water in the Gunnison River, when

CHAPTER XIV: *Hitting Bottom*

low in the summer time, had been very unsatisfactory. It had a fishy odor, and had become more or less alkaline because of seepage from all the lands of the North Fork under cultivation, including Surface Creek Mesa and other nearby highlands. The town of Delta, seeing that something radical had to be done about the situation, decided to secure water from springs and creeks far up on Grand Mesa. A large force of men were employed to dig the ditch and lay the pipe to Delta. Upon the completion of the new pipeline from the Grand Mesa, Delta had a supply of clear, pure mountain water. Best of all, the water was plentiful and had sufficient pressure to make it unnecessary to use the tank on Garnet Mesa any longer.

One day, while this work was still underway, the Horsewrangler proposed that we go over to see how it was progressing. He suggested that I might like to ride a roan mare that he had not ridden for two or three months and which was a bit wild. I consented. The mare bucked just a bit when I got on her but was soon all right. Near the ditch camp we looked over the undertaking until supper time approached, when we started to leave. I do not know whether Horsewrangler had told the men at the camp that the mare was a bit mean, but the moment I got into the saddle he and all the others started to whoop and yell. My horse became excited and started to buck. Off came my hat, and off came my glasses, but I stuck on. "Ride her, cowboy!" they yelled. I suppose it was a good show for them. When the mare stopped bucking, I looked for my glasses but could not find them anywhere. Probably the mare had jumped on them and trampled them into the damp ground. I never found a trace of them and I did not wear glasses again until I went to college.

One of the hardest rides that I ever made in my life took place that summer. We started out early one morning for the Kannah Creek country, some fifteen or twenty miles west of the Mower camp and around the point of the mesa, toward Grand Junction. This part of the range was extremely wild and was somewhat beyond our habitual jurisdiction. However, we found several head of our cattle down there. Among them was a great Lazy H Box steer that must have weighed 1,200 pounds. He had not been seen by our cattlemen for two or three winters. Like all the other cattle in this region, he was so frightfully wild that we had a hard time keeping him in the bunch with the other animals. Instead of driving the cattle that we had just collected around the point of the Grand Mesa, which would have been a long trip, we decided to take them over the top of the Mesa, up a torturous steep track known as the Shirt Tail Trail. In places this trail went up over rim rock so high that the cattle and horses had to be forced to jump from level to level.

One of the calves had become separated from its mother in the cedars at the foot of the trail and we could not find it. We got all the cattle except this calf started along the trail quite satisfactorily. About half way up, the trail became merely a narrow path along the side of the cliff. Just as we reached this narrow point, the bawling cow whose calf had been left behind suddenly turned and started down the trail toward me. I was leading my horse at the moment. Down came the cow, turning to neither right nor left. I seized a stick lying in the trail and just as she was upon me I struck her over the nose and dodged back against the side of the cliff. Her horn touched my chest, but she went on her way to her calf without doing me any harm. It was growing so late that we did not return for her.

In about a quarter of a mile we came to some stone steps

nearly three feet high. The cattle managed to scramble up these, and the horses and the other men jumped up. The horse I was riding that day was the gaited one that I usually rode when going to town. He refused to make the jump. I spurred him severely, but he still refused. I got off and tried to lead him up. He would not move. It was late in the afternoon, and to get back to camp in any other way than by following this trail would have meant a fifteen or twenty-mile ride through a country that was almost a stranger to me. In desperation, one of the cowboys tied a rope under my horse's tail, fastened it to his saddle horse, and started to pull my horse up the steps. For a single moment my horse hesitated. Then with a snort of rage, he jumped up the steps quite easily.

It was just before dark when we reached the camp. I looked down toward Peach Valley and saw smoke. It was obvious that the threshers had arrived at the ranch, and that my interest in a share of the crop demanded my presence there the next morning. After eating a bite, I got on a farm horse that I had left at the camp and started for Peach Valley. Had I been riding a regular cow horse I would have had no difficulty in going down at night. Cow horses know the range so well that on the darkest nights I have simply turned the reins loose and they have taken me to my destination.

This night, with my farm horse, I became lost—or at least carried off the trail. I finally made up my mind to head as straight down the mountain as possible, since in this way, at last I would be sure of reaching the Gunnison Valley. After going through trees and brush country I came to a creek. The horse went down the steep bank, but could not get out the other side. When I tried to guide him down the little stream in the hope of finding an opening, we ran into a waterfall. Then I rode him up the stream, only to be stopped by enormous boulders. There was a thicket of scrub quaking aspen on the side where I wished to get out, so dense that I had to cut several very small trees with my pocket knife before I could get through.

About four o'clock in the morning, I came to a little ranch in the lower edge of the cedars. Here I put my horse by a hay stack to eat while I took off the saddle, turned it upside down to make a pillow, and took an hour's nap. I then rode home, arriving there about seven. After eating a bite, I saddled another horse and rode to Peach Valley, where I threshed all day. We finished threshing about seven o'clock in the evening.

After supper at home, I mounted a fresh horse and rode back to camp, which I reached about three o'clock in the morning. At six, we started out again on the roundup, and rode all day until five o'clock. It did not take me long to go to sleep that night!

The fall of 1904 proved full of discouragement. A big crop of hay was made in Peach valley, as elsewhere but there was little demand for it. The price dropped to a ruinous point. Then there were fewer cattle on the Western Slope than there had been before, because of the previous frightful winter and the larkspur poisoning. Several cattlemen had been compelled to sell yearling steers to pay notes at the banks, instead of holding them over to ship as two or three-year-olds. Another reason for the very low price of hay was the mild fall and winter, which enabled the cattle to graze much longer than usual.

The price of hay did not concern us as much as it formerly had, since we could use much of our share to feed our own stock, but the inability to sell the marginal amounts that we did not need added to our difficulties. The hay crop had not been mortgaged, and we were free to dispose of it as we saw fit and to keep the proceeds, rather than applying them on the mortgage. The

Thompson boys were forced to bale and ship their part of the hay in order to sell it. For the first time, I think, I began to realize how little surplus it takes to cause over production, and to see that production is only one part of the game of money making. The other economic lesson—that great scarcity coupled with high demand increases prices—had been burned into me in the previous spring when I had been forced to buy hay at $20 a ton. But there was an element which I did not understand at that time in respect to the price of hay in general on the Western Slope. As I now see it, this was the fact that the open range could not support during the grazing season, enough cattle to eat up all the hay that could be produced by the farms for winter feeding. In general, this always assured an excess of hay, and the resulting low prices.

Our Peach Valley oat crop, which also was not mortgaged, was a great disappointment. Some sort of green insect with long wings had attacked the growing crop, which otherwise would have been magnificent, just at the time it was in "milk." The horde of insects had sucked most of the milk out of the kernels so that little was left but the husk. A sack of oats that normally would weigh 100 pounds would now weigh only fifty or sixty. This crop was of such poor quality that we could hardly get rid of it at any price.

There was a rather good crop of apples on the home place, for a change. But they brought almost nothing. Unfortunately, a great number of our trees were Ben Davis or Arkansas Black. While the former bore large crops, the apples were of such poor quality that there was little demand for them and they brought a very low price. As noted earlier, the Arkansas Black was an apple for which there was almost no demand. They were as hard as rock until about the middle of April or the first of May, when they began to soften up a bit. Since they had to be stored so long before it was possible to use them, they were considered undesirable and had to be sold cheaply. So far, the orchard, although now ten years old, had never begun even to pay expenses, due to late frosts in the spring, late summer droughts, and the wrong varieties of apples. Even Mother's optimism in regard to orchards began to wane, and the dream of an orchard to support the family began to fade. I might add that within a very few years after this, not only our apple orchard, but almost all others on Garnet Mesa, were pulled up and never replanted.

As the new branch railroad, which ran up to Somerset, had not yet been fenced, the cattle coming off the range and wandering into the Gunnison River Valley were in great danger of being run over. This happened to four or five of our best cows. They were worth at least $35 each, but the railroad offered me only $15. I went down to talk to an attorney about bringing a suit. "There is no use in doing so," he said. "If the railway company loses such a case, it always goes to the higher courts; and the cost of fighting the original case and the appeal would be far more than any extra money which you might receive."

Like most cattlemen, I had intended to sell all fat cows which had not had calves, and all steers, even the yearlings, in order to pay my notes at the bank and meet the interest that was eating me up. But now cattle prices were so low—while freight costs, commission rates, and feeding charges at the stockyards were so high—that I did not feel justified in shipping, particularly when we had such an abundance of hay we could not sell, but that might convert into beef.

I rode the range that fall, driving the cattle back up the creeks after cold rains had made them feel the compulsion to move down to homeward pastures for good hay. I also returned the cattle of farmers that I had cared for during the summer. Each day the pressure of creditors became heavier. No longer was Howard there to take care of the cattle while I hauled coal to make some money, or vice versa. None of the younger boys could take on such work. Since I had been on the range during the summer after Howard had left, we did not have our usual adequate garden. As we had to depend almost entirely on egg money for groceries the family larder was extremely slim.

After less than 150 cattle, instead of the 200 that I had hoped for, finally came down from the range, it was necessary for me to look after them in Peach Valley. At first, I had only to inspect them once or twice a week. But later it was necessary to ride to the Valley and feed them daily. This prevented me from either hauling coal or getting a job. I was, as a milkman once said, "Tied to the tail of a cow."

About the first of December the idea was given me by John Lance—a man living in the Gunnison River Valley, who was a combination of ex-cattleman, horse trader and butcher—that it might be a good plan to slaughter fat cattle and sell the meat by the quarter in Delta to individual customers. He convinced me that it would be possible to secure almost twice as much for the cattle in this way rather than if they were shipped to market. We rigged out a place on his farm where we could do the butchering, hauled several loads of hay down from Peach Valley, and drove down about a dozen animals that were to be sacrificed. Before we started operations, however, it was necessary to secure the consent from the bank to which the cattle were mortgaged. This was given, but only on the condition that all my proceeds from the undertaking be turned over to the bank to reduce my indebtedness. I might, however, keep the heart, liver, and hide of each animal.

This was one of the most unhappy times in my life. I knew all my cattle personally by the shape of their bodies, the look of their faces, their markings, or otherwise. It was tragic to see these cattle, some of which I had cared for since they were born, shot or struck in the head with an ax, and to see the light fade out of their eyes. I hated to skin them, take out their entrails, and hang them as beef. It was also humiliating for me to go from door-to-door peddling beef. However, by selling the front quarters for about five cents a pound and the hind quarters for about seven cents, I was able to make a little more than if I had sold them on the hoof, and I was able to reduce the bank debts by a few hundred dollars.

There were several reasons why I could not continue in the beef business. Not only was the market limited, but the method of selling beef by the quarter could not continue as the weather became warmer toward the spring of 1905. By the first of the year, we were near the end of our line of credit. I could neither haul coal nor take any kind of paid job, since my time was effectively mortgaged in caring for cattle.

There appeared to be only two ways out. One was to borrow a few hundred dollars more at the bank to pay past-due grocery bills and cover unavoidable expenses. We could then get along until about the middle of May, when we could let Charlie Mundry take the cattle to the range, thus freeing me for getting a job. By the time fall came I could sell enough fat cows and steers to reduce the bank indebtedness quite materially. In this way we could retain a large part of our herd. The other possible alternative was to sell most of the cattle at once in the hope of obtaining a fair sum beyond the amount of the mortgage. However, it was a very poor time to sell cattle, since the price was extremely low. If we could keep them for a few months, we could greatly add to their value at almost no cost to ourselves since we had so much feed for them in Peach Valley. Moreover, by fall, the calf crop would increase their numbers and value quite considerably.

I went to the First National Bank and put the borrowing proposition up to Dr. Stockham, the cashier. But he refused to lend me another cent. About the first of February, things at home were desperate. I told the bank that unless I had a few hundred dollars to live on, I should have to let the cattle fend for themselves while I looked for work. The cashier refused me any money, but said I would have to carry on in caring for the cattle. Within a few days, however, whether or not because of some suggestion from Dr. Stockham I did not know, Mower offered me $16 a head "round" for the cattle, that is, counting both the young and the old animals. This would not have been bad two or three months later when all the cows had calves, but at the moment it was absurdly low. However, since I had no time to shop around, I accepted it, believing that when all my cattle were brought together from Peach Valley as well as from the range, the returns would be enough to cover my notes at the bank and to leave a margin for other debts. Thus, I would be nearly clear of debt and would have my time free to earn a living for my family.

My belief was ill-founded. Only the cattle that were in Peach Valley were immediately available for sale. Those on the range were widely scattered and could not be found and accounted for until the fall roundup. The sale of the cattle in the Valley did not quite pay all the notes at the bank. Stockham refused to renew the balance, and insisted that I turn over all the rest of my collateral—horses, wagons, harnesses, etc. I tried to explain to him that if he took away all my equipment, I would have no method of getting out of the hole in which I was placed. But he was adamant. If I had had more business experience, or had known a little about law, I might have saved something from the wreck. As it was, I lost everything.

When Mower took the cattle, I almost wept. Now, through no fault of my own, as I thought, they were taken from me, because a damned old bank would not help me in a pinch. I was learning through bitter experience that the producer, who generally is and must be a debtor, may be helplessly in the grip of nature's blind forces and at the mercy of the creditor, who is usually able to secure himself so that no matter what comes, he is protected. I was also beginning to realize that it was basically wrong for the cattle business, which requires several years to develop its product, to rest upon such precarious foundations as ninety-day loans, which could be refused at any time and carried high interest rates. With just a little more cash in hand, and a slight extension of credit, I believe that I could have come out ahead, for not only were the cattle increasing, but the price was almost sure to rise.

Even more painful than the losing of my cattle was the act of turning over to the bank all my horses and equipment. Slowly, down the Gunnison road went the little procession of work horses, saddle horses, wagons and other equipment. Hal and I took them to a vacant lot in back of the bank, where I had been told to leave them. As I said goodbye to the faithful work horses and cow horses, hot tears of rage and frustration came to my eyes, for I was parting with friends. As for the wagons and equipment, I had worked every day and night to get them together, and they were essential to my life as a farmer. Without equipment and horses, I would be reduced to the position of day laborer. For more than ten long years I had worked sixteen hours a day under adverse conditions, trying with all my might to get ahead, and this was the result. Finally, I mounted the one horse that belonged to Mother, with Hal seated behind me. As a crowning humiliation, we had to ride bareback because my saddles were among the mortgaged property.

CHAPTER XV

Transition

When Hal and I reached home after leaving all my property at the bank, I told Mother that I did not know which way to turn: that I felt like an old man, and a broken one at that. All of my hard work, worry and privation had finally seemed to affect my health. A week or so before, I had developed quinsy, as we diagnosed it, but had kept working anyway. One day while I was riding with Harry Stockham, the ulcers inside my throat broke and out came blood and matter. Harry swore that I had tuberculosis. "You had better buy a Bible and a hymn book and start reforming," he remarked. Although I did not believe him, for the first time in my life I realized that my body might not be equal to whatever demand I might throw upon it. Physical illness and distress of mind now worked together to fill me with despair.

Mother tried to cheer me up. Sometime that day, Miss Johnson came to see us. I told her what happened. "Now you are free," she said, "why don't you plan to go to Oberlin, as you have often thought of doing?" "How can I possibly go there without any money?" I asked. She assured me that many young men had covered all their expenses by working while going through college. "But," I said, "you forget that I have never even finished the eighth grade in school, and that I am now nearly twenty-five years old."

She replied that she knew of several students who had started late and yet had been successful in college and in life. Further, she assured me that I was not quite so uneducated as I thought I was. She felt confident that I could obtain credit in Oberlin Academy for the English literature I had studied with her, and could pass examinations in two or three courses in history. The English teacher in the Academy was a close personal friend of hers, as was also Professor Peck, the Principal. Mother said that Professor Peck had been a bosom friend of her brother Dwight while both were in college, and that she was sure he would do all in his power for me.

"But," I objected, "how about the family?" "Hal and Louis and Edward can operate the ranch," said Mother. "Since Arthur now had a good position as a doctor on an Indian reservation, he can help a little. For the rest, with the milk cows, chickens, and garden, we can manage."

Although I always intended to obtain more education, I had planned to have enough money from our various undertakings to pay my expenses and those of the younger boys. With no money at all, despite the encouragement of Mother and Miss Johnson, the future looked dark. I still owed several hundred dollars for taxes, groceries, dry goods, and various purchases. There was no possibility of paying these sums, now that I had nothing left to work with to make money. At day labor I could not save enough in years to meet the bills.

In desperation I went down to see an attorney about going into bankruptcy. He prepared the papers and sent them to Montrose, where the referee in bankruptcy was located. I heard nothing regarding the matter for several weeks.

In the meantime, I learned that Mr. Hartig, who had bought the large McGranahan fruit farm near our place a year or so before, had decided to pull out the peach trees that grew between his apple trees and graft most of the apple trees, the majority of which at present were of summer and fall varieties. With the closing of many mines, there was little sale for this fruit. Mr. Hartig proposed to graft the whole forty acres to varieties that would keep and sell well on the central and eastern markets, such as Jonathan, Winesap, and Rome Beauty.

I went to see him and immediately got a job. We spent several days pulling out the peach trees, which was accomplished by means of a four-horse team hitched to a large cable that ran through a triple set of pulleys. After the peach trees were removed, we had to cut the limbs of the apple trees and make a place for the grafts. This was hard work. The trees were fourteen or fifteen years old, and the branches, which we had to cut off at a height of about five feet, were two to five inches in diameter. Sawing off those branches at shoulder height was a severe strain on the muscles. After the first two or three hours, I thought that I could not finish the day, but I did. The next morning, the muscles around my chest and shoulders were so sore that to move them made me wince in pain. It seemed impossible to start sawing those trees again, but there was nothing else to do. After an hour's sawing, the pain ceased, and within a few days my muscles had become accustomed to that unusual working position.

After we cut off the limbs, the grafts had to be put in. This was accomplished by sawing a little notch in the stump of the cut limb, inserting a twig or scion, and then covering the place well with grafting wax.

I had been working at this job for about two months when Mrs. Comings, who was a graduate of Oberlin College, and whose husband owned the chief bookstore in the town of Oberlin, came to visit us. She was related to my grandfather Bradley's first wife and was, I believe, a sister of Mr. Royce, who ran the general store in Paonia where my brother Arthur had once worked.

I consulted her about the possibility of going to Oberlin. She encouraged me a great deal. In fact, she said that she would give me a position in the bookstore, if I could come by the middle of April. I immediately began to interview cattlemen to see if one would hire me to take charge of animals that were being shipped to the Missouri River on a cattle train, as this seemed the only way in which I could afford to go. At last, I found a man who said that he was going to ship a trainload at least as far as Denver, and if the markets were not good there, on to Kansas City or Omaha. He would be glad for me to go with the cattle. I began to make definite arrangements to go to Oberlin.

In the meantime, I received notice from the referee in bankruptcy that there would be a meeting of the creditors in Montrose on a certain date. I rode there but no one showed up. My attorney said that he thought there was no use in trying to continue the proceedings, and advised me to let the matter drop. Apparently, my creditors realized that it was futile to try to obtain payment from a man who had lost everything.

A day or so before the cattle train was to leave, Mr. Wolbert, the cashier of the Farmers' and Merchants' Bank, told me that the bank held a note I had given to the grocer, and he thought that if I intended to act honorably, I should not leave until this had been cleared up. I took the one-month of wages I had saved, and made a payment, but he still insisted that I ought to remain and work until the whole debt was paid. Finally, I agreed to stay for a short time, although this meant that I would miss my chance to go east on the cattle train, and might not obtain a position with the Comings' Bookstore in Oberlin.

It soon became evident that I could not escape from the whole crushing situation in Delta unless I made a fresh start somewhere.

I believed that I had done everything that could be reasonably expected toward paying off obligations. At day labor I would be of little use to the family and could not save anything to pay creditors, for wages were only $1.50 per day. Moreover, if I continued at day labor, I should never be able to obtain an education. There seemed no reason to go on in this hopeless round. Hence, I determined to leave for Oberlin at the earliest opportunity.

About the first of April, much to my surprise, one of my horses that had strayed or been stolen two or three years earlier, was found and returned to me. Thank God, it had not been mortgaged! This at least would make us a team. As the grafting had now been completed, I borrowed a plow from one of our neighbors to plow up the five-acre alfalfa field on the southwest corner of our place, with the intention of planting it to sugar beets. It took me only a few moments to see that the light team was not strong enough to make the plow cut through the thick, leather-like roots.

Therefore, I agreed with a farmer to help him plant his spring crop, if he would lend me a powerful team for a few days. How painfully different was my ability to do things now that all my teams and equipment had been lost! Still, I got the field planted to sugar beets. Mother thought that these would bring in enough cash to pay the taxes and interest on the place in the fall, since a sugar beet factory had just been established at Grand Junction, about forty miles away by railroad.

The plan looked plausible. The sugar beet company claimed that one could raise from 10 to 20 tons per acre, and agreed to pay five dollars a ton for good beets. We talked the matter over and decided that the work of chopping, thinning, weeding and harvesting could be done by the boys outside of school time. Little did we realize the enormous amount of labor involved in this crop. The beets came up in a good stand before I left, and we were able to get them thinned in the proper way. It began to appear that Mother could make a little money on beets. Although it was getting ahead of my story, I must tell what happened to the crop after I left. One day toward the latter part of June, a sky-blackening cloud of grasshoppers alighted on the field, obviously intending to eat the plants down to the roots. As if by a miracle, within a few moments a great flock of blackbirds descended upon the insects, and by nighttime not a grasshopper was left. The beets yielded 20 tons to the acre, which at the guaranteed price, brought the family about $500.

Again, I looked for a chance to take a cattle train east. At last, near the first of June, 1905, I found that a trainload of cattle would be leaving in a few days, bound for Omaha or Kansas City. To my joy, I was able to arrange to have my fare paid in return for sharing with another man the management of the cattle. I felt a little better by this time about leaving Mother and the younger boys, as Louis had secured a position with a large apiary. The work was light, would not take too much of his time, and would give the family some badly needed cash. Hal seemed to be able to take hold of things on the home place. However, I worried a great deal about Ralph, and sometimes even feared that he might die from his stomach trouble. Like most worry, this was mistaken.

A day or so before the cattle train was to start east, I purchased a few dollars' worth of clothes, had my heavy tailor-made suit pressed, and bought two large old-fashioned, flimsy telescoping hand bags. Mother mended all my old clothes. Finally, I packed up everything ready to go, except the rough shirt and corduroy trousers I would need on the cattle train. The $35 of wages that I had in my pocket, I thought, would take me from Omaha or

Kansas City to Oberlin. If not, I would stop on the way somewhere and work a few days to earn the necessary amount.

The next morning, I said goodbye to Mother and the boys with a heavy heart. Despite all the good reasons why I should go, I felt that I was deserting them. Mother insisted, however, brave heart that she was, that she and the boys would be all right. Since, for years I had regarded my brothers as "the little boys," I did not realize that they were older than I was when I had to assume heavier duties than they were facing, and with even more handicaps.

Louis drove me down to the stockyards where the cowboys had already started to load the cattle train. He told me goodbye and started home. When the train was about half loaded, Mower reminded me that I had not yet transferred to him my M Lazy Eleven and other brand certificates, and asked if I would ride home and get them. He was sure that I would have time before the train started.

Of course, I should have told him that I would write and ask Mother to give them to him, but I was too excited to argue, or even to think. He loaned me a top horse, and away I flew the two miles up home and back. As I reached the stockyards the second time, what was my consternation to find the train already starting. "Your bags are in the caboose," said Mower. "Ride alongside and jump on." I rode the horse as fast as I could beside the train, which was just beginning to gain speed. I pulled my feet out of the stirrups, leaned over and caught hold of a handle bar on the caboose, swung on and let the horse go. From the back of the caboose, I waved goodbye to the cowboys and to my home town, which I was not destined to see again for more than thirty years.

Slowly we climbed the divide. During the night the other cowboy and I took turns sleeping in the caboose bunk. Early the next morning we stopped at Salida, my birthplace, to feed and water the cattle and transfer them to the wide gauge railroad cars. While the cattle were eating, we went to a nearby restaurant for breakfast. As we had had nothing to eat since the previous morning, we both ordered steak and potatoes at the high price of sixty cents a portion. When the steaks were brought in, each one covered a large platter.

By dusk on Saturday, we arrived in Denver, where the cattle were placed in the stockyards to await sale on Monday morning if the market were favorable. Otherwise, they would be shipped to Kansas City. Just before reaching the city, I put on my best suit, and that evening called on Miss Johnson who had recently moved to Denver. On Sunday afternoon we went to the zoo. I had never seen a zoo before and was quite thrilled by all of the animals. At night I went to the Presbyterian Church, where Ed Tucker, a former member of our double male quartet in Delta, was singing in the choir.

The next morning, I went to the stockyards with my large bags. I was informed that the owner of the cattle had not been able to get a satisfactory price in Denver and was shipping them to Kansas City. The train would leave in a few minutes. Remembering my experience of having nothing to eat on the way from Delta to Salida, I stepped into a stockyards restaurant and ordered sandwiches enough for three meals. While the food was being prepared, I suddenly heard the train whistle and saw it starting to move. It was my fate to go without food again.

I rushed out of the restaurant. The engine was about a quarter of a block away from me. As the train was fifty or sixty cars long, I decided that it would be going too fast for me to jump on if I waited until the caboose reached me. With both heavy bags in one hand, I seized the ladder of a freight car with the other, and managed to climb on top. Quite a strong wind was blowing. Burdened as I was by the bags, I found it difficult to reach the caboose by way of walking over the tops of some fifty cars. At times I thought that I might be blown off. However, I managed to keep my feet and to climb down into the caboose at last.

The next morning, we arrived in Omaha, where the cattle were to be fed and watered. During the night I had been considering whether it would not be better to go straight from Omaha to Grinnell, Iowa, and visit Clarence, since Howard and Uncle Dan Bradley were also there, rather than go on with the cattle to Kansas City. I shared the idea with my companion and explained that if I went on with him, I was not at all sure of being able to reach Oberlin with the little money in my pocket. He said he could easily handle the cattle alone on the short distance to Kansas City. I thanked him, shook hands, and took the train to Grinnell.

It was a great pleasure to see Clarence and Howard again. They encouraged me about the possibility of earning my expenses in college. Howard was doing this by running a small clothes-pressing establishment. Clarence was pumping the pipe organ in one of the churches, caring for lawns and furnaces, and chopping wood.

I had arrived, I learned, just a few days before commencement. Uncle Dan, the President of the college, was far too busy to see me very much. But what a noble soul he was: kind, encouraging, warm hearted and cheerful! Of course, he said, I could make my way in college. He himself had had a rather late start, due to helping his mother with the printing business in Siam; but that had not hurt him. Experience was just as valuable as book learning. I went to chapel once or twice and enjoyed seeing the students. Uncle Dan spoke at one of the services, in a sincere and impressive manner.

As Clarence and Howard had planned to leave before commencement in order to begin work for the summer, I had only two or three days with them. One evening Clarence and I went down to see Howard off for the North Dakota wheat fields, where he was going to work for money to pay his expenses during the next school year. As the train pulled out of the station, Howard "jumped the blind baggage."[10]

The next morning, I left by train for Oberlin and arrived there about five-thirty in the evening. My pocket contained exactly thirty-five cents. The rest of my money had gone for food and carfare. I left the little station and walked up South Professor Street carrying my unwieldy bags. The day was exceedingly warm, and with my heavy suit I was red-faced and perspiring. College students were strolling about or sitting on wide verandas talking or singing. They all appeared light hearted and free. The girls in their soft bright summer dresses, walking under great elm trees, looked almost like angels to me, and the pleasant college town of Oberlin, in comparison with Poverty Flat and Peach Valley, seemed a veritable heaven. A new and different life, which I could dimly foresee but could not yet apprehend, was opening before me. My first life was ended.

---

10   An old hobo expression referring to the "blind" space between the train engine and the baggage car.

Appendix I

In the Years Since 1905

Those who have seen the manuscript insist that I must satisfy the curiosity of any who may read the book, by giving them some idea of my own later life and the careers of my brothers. All eight of us were able to do some work at the college level, and several worked their way through college. I received a bachelor's degree from Oberlin College and a doctorate of philosophy in public law from Columbia University. All my years since have been spent in research, writing, and university teaching, with an occasional period devoted to administrative work. Arthur, who died a few years ago, became a well-known physician in Portland, Oregon. Clarence, after his graduation from Grinnell College, received his doctorate in sociology from the University of Chicago. For many years, he was an economist with the United States Tariff Commission, and he edited and largely wrote a Tariff dictionary published by that agency. He has also published several volumes of poetry. Howard, before his death in 1934, was a prosperous contractor in California. William Harold went to Oberlin, but died before finishing his education. Ralph went to the State Agriculture College of Colorado, and later became an engineer. Louis, who is a graduate of University of Wisconsin, was an officer in the First World War, and afterward a commission merchant in New York City. When the Second World War occurred, he became purchasing agent for the United States Army in North Africa, and later economic advisor to the occupation administration in Germany. He has spent a great deal of time during the past several years in securing and preserving many annals of the old west, as told by the lips of aged settlers and their descendants, to his tape recorder. Edward, due to ill health, was not able to finish college. He now lives in New Mexico, where he is engaged in writing.

We were able to make the later years of our own dear Mother's life easier than the years which this book describes. At the urgent suggestion of her sons, she sold her remaining property in Delta and moved to Boulder, Colorado. Here Edward lived with her, and several of the other brothers visited her from time to time. She was provided with a pretty little house, a piano, and other comforts. Since she was a member of the Eastern Star and the Presbyterian Church, she had pleasant social contacts in Boulder, and many acquaintances there soon became her friends, drawn by her personal charm and intellectual vigor. She died on Washington D.C., as the result of an accident, while visiting Clarence there in the spring of 1926. "The righteous shall be in everlasting remembrance."

Appendix II

Context of Time, Place & Circumstances

The first twenty-five years of my life were spent in the southwestern part of Colorado.

This is perhaps the most fantastic part of the United States with its towering mountains, deep and narrow canyons, fast rushing rivers, and many creeks and waterfalls. Let us examine the nature and surroundings of this area a little more in detail.

Most of my story takes place on the so-called "Western Slope" of the Rockies. On the North this region is bounded by the Grand Mesa and the West Elk Mountains, on the East by the Sawatch Range, on the South by the San Juan Mountains, on the West by the Uncompahgre Plateau and on the Northwest are adobe formations, extending up to the cedar line of the Grand Mesa.

A spur of the high Sawatch Range, crossing over the West Elk Mountains, continues as Grand Mesa and bends down in the southwestern direction to a point fifteen miles Northwest of Delta. The Grand Mesa is the highest and largest plateau in the United States. Extending about fifteen miles around the western end is a perpendicular rim rock, composed of lava from an extinct volcano located at the southeastern end of the bottom of the rim rock. At present this volcano bed forms a deep lake called, "Crater Lake," which is connected with about thirty other little lakes and reservoirs. One of the most interesting features is a bed of coal at the height of about eight thousand feet, extending almost from the western end to the West Elk Mountains where they join the great eastern range.

This bed of coal was formed millions of years ago by huge ferns and trees. During some great convulsions of the earth, they were covered with a thick layer of sandstone on top of which the volcano had thrown its hot lava, thus compressing the ferns and trees into coal. This coal bed is soft bituminous at its western end and gradually hardens as the height and width of the mesa increases, up to the far eastern end where it is extremely hard, almost anthracite.

To the East is the Sawatch Range, containing some of the highest mountains and peaks on the North American continent, such as: Mount Elbert (14,431'), Mount Harvard (14,420'), Mount Massive (14,418'), Mount Princeton (14,197'), and Mount Yale (14,196'). These mountain peaks stand on a base of some thirty-two thousand acres. The prevailing westerly winds from the Gulf of Mexico and the Pacific Ocean, scorning the hot deserts of California and Arizona, flow high, and congealed by the extreme coldness of these mountains and peaks, they deposit their moisture in rain or snow.

The snow is very often thirty to forty feet deep, and in low places forms perpetual glaciers. This combination of high peaks, lofty mountains, and wide base creates a kind of refrigerator system that usually keeps the snow from melting too early in the year. In spring, when the snow starts melting, the water flows down through the Taylor River into a natural storage basin. This 'Blue Mesa Lake' has been enlarged and is now called 'Blue Mesa Reservoir', having a huge capacity for water storage.[11]

To the South are the San Juan Mountains, also containing several peaks also well over fourteen thousand feet high: Uncompahgre Peak (14,309'), Mount Wilson (14,246'), Mount Sneffels

---

[11] now called 'Taylor Park Reservoir'

(14,150'), and Wilson Peak (14,017'). Unlike the highest eastern mountains, these mountains are extremely steep and have practically no base to absorb and hold moisture. There are only a very few places in this area where small water reservoirs have been made.

Furthermore, much of the timber on these mountains has been cut off to be used for mining purposes, thus enabling great avalanches to form and rush down the mountains. As a result of the very small base and the effect of avalanches, the snow, although as deep as in the eastern mountains, usually does not last long. The rivers hiding in these mountains swell with great floods in the late spring and early summer but are often almost dry in the late summer and early fall.

To the eastern end of these mountains are numerous small peaks, which we locally called the 'Sawtooth Range'. To the Southwest and West is the Uncompahgre Plateau, only about nine thousand feet high. The eastern part of this plateau slopes gently down towards the Uncompahgre River. The middle part through deep and narrow gorges leads down towards the Gunnison River, the only outlet for the entire water system of the area.

This encircling system of different kinds of mountain formations surrounds four hundred million to five hundred million acres of mesa and valley land of various descriptions. The mountains are very steep and rugged above the height of about 6,500 feet, where mesa land begins, gently leading down towards the numerous rivers and creeks. The peaks of the mountains are bare due to strong winds. Just below the peaks are treelike formations, lying flat, hugging the scanty soil in desperation. Further down, at an elevation from 13,000 to 10,000 feet, is a band of spruce that often grows in groves—at least on the Grand Mesa. In several places these trees stand stark naked, without any bark, almost like white ghosts, due to the fact that they had a soft inner bark, which in high and dry elevations disintegrated, causing the outer bark to slip off.

On the Uncompahgre Plateau, pine trees take the place of spruce. These extend down until they reach a belt of cedars and piñons, at about 6,500 feet. Below the spruce is a band of quaking aspens, the leaves of which turn yellow in the fall. Below the aspens is a line of scrub oak, whose leaves turn bright red after the first fall frosts. Below the scrub oak that there is a band of mixed cedars and piñons. In the fall the color combinations of these different bands gives the impression of a vast flag.

The central land portion, surrounded by all these mighty mountain formations, is an area of mesas, river bottoms, and valleys. The mesas as a rule are partly covered by sagebrush, and in part of the year with a considerable amount of salt weed. Some places are largely covered with stalks of cacti with sharp needle leaves. The flowers of these cacti are of various shades of red, pink, yellow, and mauve, forming a vast beautiful carpet in spring and early summer.

The largest and most important of the alluvial soil mesas is the California Mesa, which is a lower extension of the Uncompahgre Plateau and slopes gently down towards the Uncompahgre River. Separated from this mesa, evidently cut off from it and gradually raised by the Uncompahgre River, is Garnet Mesa. North of the Gunnison River are several mesas, which as a rule break off to adobe formations or else to creek bottoms.

Important mesas are: Negro Mesa (covered with cinders from the extinct volcano), Doughspoon Mesa, January Mesa, Surface Creek Mesa, and Rogers Mesa (this mesa has little or no water irrigation). The rivers and creek bottoms are usually covered with greasewood, a plant with little round leaves (about one inch long) and hard spurs. When dry, the stem of the wood is so hard that it is almost impossible to cut with a knife.

Between the Uncompahgre and Gunnison rivers, except for in the Garnet Mesa, is an old sea bottom below the surface of which is a layer of alkaline sea salts. East of the Garnet Mesa is a ridge called the Vernal Mesa, about six miles wide, the top of which drops almost perpendicularly down into the Black Canyon.

Such was and is the country of which Escalante, a Spanish priest from Santa Fe, said, "It is only an area fit for savages." He and his party had explored this region, forded the Colorado river, and then headed South back to Santa Fe in 1776, the year of the Declaration of Independence.

Although the Taylor and Gunnison rivers arise in the eastern mountains and the Uncompahgre in the southern mountains, they flow for a good many miles only five to fifteen miles apart before merging about 10 miles northeast of Gunnison. Another strange paradox is the fact that although the eastern part of the Uncompahgre Plateau (California Mesa) has a great deal of land capable of irrigation, it has a relatively small amount of water, whereas the Taylor-Gunnison river system, with a very large amount of water bursting out from Black Canyon, flows through a narrow valley that contains a very small amount of land. The Uncompahgre River flows into the Gunnison west of Delta and then, flowing northward, joins the Colorado River near Grand Junction.

Several creeks are important in this story. Beyond the western tip of the Grand Mesa, flowing down towards Grand Junction is the Kannah Creek. Near the western tip of the Grand Mesa, flowing south towards the Gunnison is Point Creek. This creek is dry most of the year, but by a ditch and a rather large pond, it supplied water to the 'Halfway House' between Delta and Grand Junction. From the point of the mesa in the following sequence are those creeks: Doughspoon Creek, Bluenose Creek (changed by my father to Oak Creek), Dirty George Creek, and Surface Creek.

The North Fork River and the Smiths Fork River, Minor River, both rise in the West Elk Mountains. Several small rivers near the Gunnison and a complex of creeks and rivers rise in the Sawtooth Range and flow into the Blue Mesa Reservoir.

Although several rivers arise in the eastern part of the Sawatch Range, we only mention the Arkansas River here. This, because the Arkansas flows through a very deep and narrow canyon, 'Royal Gorge', which at the time was the sole eastern entrance to the western part of Colorado north of the San Juan Range, both by wagon and railroad. This gorge is about one thousand feet deep.

One would well ask why anyone would desire to live in this region. The answer is that the Mormons of Utah, through their missionaries, had demonstrated that these mesa and valley lands, with irrigation, could be made to blossom as the rose.

During the era of this story, some great national issues arose: Exclusion of Chinese, women's suffrage, federal monetary policy, and the opposing forces of isolationism and expansionism.

In 1869, the driving of a golden spike fastened the last rail in the railroad connecting California and the West with the eastern part of the United States. With the completion of the Transcontinental Railroad in 1879, many branch lines running North and South were established, thus opening up millions of acres of land for settlement. This, with the free immigration policy of the United States (which admitted practically all members of the Caucasian race) and coupled with the Homestead Act of 1862 resulted in a rapid settlement of the country by millions of farmers. This led to a constant overproduction of agricultural products, which could only be sold at extremely low prices. Corn became so cheap in Kansas that it was used as fuel.

The farmer's dream 'of a little wife well willed, and a little farm well tilled, and a little barn well filled, give me, give me' became almost a nightmare. Although they got the land for $1.25 an acre, they found that fencing it, building a house and barns, and stocking it with horses and cattle required quite a large expenditure of money. As most of the immigrants were extremely poor, they were forced to borrow this money from representatives of eastern capitalists at a 10% or 12% rate of interest. The situation in Colorado was made even worse by the monetary policies of the federal government.

The situation in the East was quite different. As millions of immigrants from Europe remained in the East, there was created a surplus of labor. Food prices could be kept low as there was a very large supply of cheap beef (grown on the free grass of the open ranges and "finished" with cheap corn) and cheap agricultural products. This enabled the eastern industrialists to keep their laborers alive on very low wages for long 12-hour working days.

The severe panics of 1873 and 1893 added to the misfortune, not only in our family, but also for millions of businessmen, farmers, and laborers all over the United States. The results of the panic of 1893 were particularly disastrous in Colorado, since they coincided with the establishment of the gold standard and the demonetization of silver.

As a result of the situation described, several organizations were formed attempting to alleviate the abuses, such as the Farmers Alliance, Populist or People's party, and the gradual establishment of labor unions.

In the western states, politically the most important one of these organizations was the Populist Party, which in Colorado became so strong as to practically wipe out the formerly predominant Republican Party. In 1893, the Populist Party elected their first governor in Colorado, Davis H. Waite, known as "Granny Waite."

Shortly after the Civil War, great herds of cattle from Texas were driven into the grasslands of all the Rocky Mountain States. As soon as railroads were constructed, these drives of cattle from Texas ended. This was followed by a number of large cattle barons with tens of thousands of heads of cattle running on open ranges —a vast area of land owned by the federal government, but not as yet committed to any purpose such as Indian reservations or homesteads.

Branding and shipping required the work of thousands of cowboys. Beginning about 1870 arose the so-called cowboy robber, in which bands of cowboys stole cattle and horses. They were protected by the fact of roughness of this region, particularly by what was called the 'Outlaw Trail', which extended from old New Mexico to Canada. The nearest point of this trail to Delta was at Fruita, not far from Grand Junction. Most important features of this trail were the holes in the wall: Brown's Hole and Robbers Roost. The holes in the wall consisted of a very narrow opening between two almost inaccessible formations, through which stolen cattle and horses could be driven into a large area, capable of supporting several hundred head of cattle for a short time. Brown's Hole was a little settlement composed of outlaws and in some cases, their families. Robbers Roost was a very high and small tableland, so well protected that is was almost impossible to enter it, except by those well acquainted with it. Officers of the law dared not enter. Robbers Roost was on the outlaw trail only about 90 miles from Delta.

The most ambitious and brightest of these horse and cattle stealers soon graduated into robbers of stagecoaches, bank-robbers, train-robbers, and robbers of payrolls of mining companies. Famous cowboy robbers of the time were: Matt Warner, Mike Cassidy, Butch Cassidy, and the McCarty gang. The peak of their operations was between 1870 and 1893, when the McCarty gang was partly eliminated in its attempt to rob the bank at Delta. Butch Cassidy finally committed suicide in Mexico while fighting the law officers. The remaining robbers were gradually eliminated by two factors: being drafted in the army in the Spanish-American War, or being unable to carry on in their operations because of a rapid settlement of the country.

During this period, the Indians on the eastern slope of the Rockies had been moved from eastern Colorado to the western slope. They had been established in a reservation consisting of three parts: The northern part on the White River at Meeker, the central part in the Uncompahgre valley with headquarters near Montrose, and the southern branch south of the San Juan Mountains at Ignacio.

The Meeker Massacre by the White River Indians, in which the Indian agent and a good many others were killed, served as an excuse for driving all the Uncompahgre and White River Indians across the hot and waterless adobes to northern Utah.

Most important and far-reaching events of this period occurred during the Spanish-American War, in McKinley's term of office. Theodore Roosevelt as Assistant Secretary of the Navy had managed to secure the building of a large number of warships.

After the blowing up of the Maine in Havana, the United States declared war against Spain. Theodore Roosevelt organized a group called the 'Roughriders', composed of college men and cowboys. Marching up the San Juan Hill, they outflanked a Spanish garrison and captured the capital of Cuba. In the battle of Manilla Bay on May 1st 1898, the American fleet defeated the Spanish fleet. In the Peace Treaty the followed, the Philippine Islands were surrendered to the United States with a proviso that they would be granted freedom, as soon as they were capable of governing themselves. The Hawaiian Islands followed shortly after.

After Spain surrendered the Philippines, Emilio Aguinaldo led a rebellion against the government established there by the Americans, but was defeated after two years. Aguinaldo, former leader of this group, rebelled against the government of the Philippines, established by the United States, but was defeated after two years. It is interesting to know that many of the former cowboy outlaws either joined the Roughriders or were drafted by the Army and became a very valuable part of the army against Aguinaldo. They came home as heroes and settled down. This as well as the fact that the open range empires were being settled up, led to the end of the cowboy-outlaw era.

As a result of the Spanish-American war and the defeat of Aguinaldo, the United States became one of the great naval powers in the world.

In this period, the federal government began an investigation of the Green and Colorado Rivers as a source of irrigation water and electric power, under John Wesley Powell and his group. Also, the federal government investigated and helped finance the Gunnison tunnel and financed and established the Salt River irrigation system in Arizona.

In the most general way, this era nationally marked the end of the frontier agricultural economy and the beginning of the present great industrial age.

The main source of power in Colorado was the horse, the mule, and to lesser extent the patient burro, which carried the prospector's kit. Many operations, now performed by electric power, were done by manpower. Travel was largely by the farm wagon or buggy, or for longer trips, by the railroad.

Our domestic facilities were equally simple. Heating was done by cooking and heating stoves instead of central heat. Washing was carried on by the rubbing board instead of the electric washing machine. Wax and tallow candles and kerosene lamps supplied the lighting.

Several improvements in farming operations developed during this era, such as the grain binder instead of the cradle, sulky plough or wheel plow, wheel scraper and blower threshing machines.

It was the time of small individually owned businesses, instead of great chain corporations that exist at present. Several great mail-order houses existed, i.e. the A & P, Montgomery Ward, and Sears & Roebuck. The end of this period saw the beginning of great monopolies and trusts and of an attempt by the federal government to cure their evil practices.

Appendix III

History of the Uncompahgre Tunnel Project
(Continued from Chapter XI)

As the result of the Fellows-Torrance expedition, the Reclamation Service decided that the tunnel was, indeed, practicable from an engineering viewpoint, and they fixed the location for the project. The Service also concluded that bringing the waters of the Gunnison River into the Uncompahgre Valley would result in the reclamation of about 100,000 acres of desert land in addition to the acres already farmed; that the cost of the tunnel would be about $850,000, and that the cost of the distributing system would be approximately $650,000. Its engineers stated that water could be supplied at $25.00 per acre foot, or less. Since the lands already cultivated in the valley provided large crops when adequately watered, and since it was assumed that most of the desert land would prove equally fertile under irrigation, the estimated costs did not seem excessive.

It is necessary to go back for a moment and explain how the Reclamation Service came into the picture, since this agency was finally responsible for the Uncompahgre Project. For years past, Congress had discussed reclamation but had done nothing toward its achievement. After nine so-called "irrigation Congresses" had talked about the matter, in 1901 President Roosevelt strongly recommended Federal reclamation as a part of his conservation program, and a Reclamation Act was passed in 1902 (32 Stat.388). This law established a Reclamation Service headed by the Director of the Geological Survey. One of the first projects taken up for consideration by the Service was the diversion of the waters of the Gunnison into the Uncompahgre Valley. In March, 1903, the Director of the Reclamation Service found the project feasible, and it was conditionally authorized by the Secretary of the Interior.

At the suggestion of the Reclamation Service, a meeting of persons who might come under the project was held on May 5, 1903, at Olathe, Colorado. I attended the meeting and was greatly impressed by the way in which the business was handled. As I learned afterward, Mr. Fellows was there, but since he was not introduced while I was present, I did not recognize him as the same battered, ragged and exhausted man whom I had seen in Peach Valley. Various speakers from the Reclamation Service stated in a general way the scope of the project, what it would probably cost, when it might be completed, what kind of organization would have to be established by the land owners concerned for dealings with the Federal government, and what methods of paying for the project would be required. So far as I could see, the whole plan had been worked out by the Reclamation Service to a high degree of perfection. Nobody appeared to have any particular objection to the proposed plan, and after a little discussion it was generally agreed to by the land owners. The meeting proceeded to establish an organization called the Uncompahgre Water Users Association, as an agent for dealing with the Federal Government. A board of eleven directors was elected and given full power to make decisions for the members of the association. I knew several of these men very well, especially A. H. Stockham, George Conklin and W. O. Stevens. The board of directors met at Delta on May 11 and adopted articles of incorporation for the Association.

Among the more important provisions of the articles of incorporation were: (1) that the Association, rather than private individuals, should treat with the Federal Government with respect to the tunnel project and allied matters; (2) that the capital stock of the Association should be $100,000 and should be divided into 100,000 shares; (3) that for every acre of land which was to come under the project, the land owner might purchase one share of stock and no more; (4) that the ownership of each share of stock should carry as an incident thereto "a right to have delivered to the owner therefore, water by the Association, for the irrigation of the lands to which such is appurtenant"; (5) and that revenues necessary for the construction of the project should be raised by assessment upon the stockholders, to the total of not more than $25.00 per share, spread over a period of ten years. Every subscriber for stock was required to sign a contract which included acceptance of the articles of incorporation attached hereto.

Things moved slowly in Washington. It was not until February, 1904, that the present tunnel site was officially recommended. In May of that year a consulting board approved the location, and in June, after sufficient stock had been subscribed, the construction was finally authorized by the Secretary of the Interior.

Meanwhile, the board of directors of the Association had been informed by the Secretary of the Interior that the articles of incorporation were unacceptable in several respects. By the fall of 1904, after long correspondence, the articles were amended to meet the requirements of the Reclamation Service. A contract was signed between the Federal Government and the Association on December 3, 1904. This contract made the Association liable not merely for $25.00 per share, but for *the entire cost of the project,* which should be payable in ten annual installments after the work had been completed. A share of stock obligated the purchaser to pay his proportionate part of the total cost of the tunnel and the irrigation system. Revenues for the construction of the project were to be raised by assessments from time to time as required, "upon and against the shareholders." Each stock owner must also pay annually his proportionate part of the operation and maintenance costs. In other words, the Association and the shareholders were liable for an entirely unknown amount of various possible costs for each share held. The assessment and other charges became a lien on the land, and the shareholders were made jointly and severally responsible for all payments.

Before construction work was to begin, the Government required that 85,000 shares of the stock of the Association be subscribed. It was thought that this would guarantee the cost of the project. Considerable difficulty was experienced at first in finding enough subscribers, for various reasons. A good deal of the land in the valley was owned by individuals or companies who had obtained it by foreclosing mortgages. They did not intend to farm it, but only to hold it until profit could be made by selling it, and they had no intention of investing more money into it. Other land had been purchased subject to "guaranteed water rights" upon the existing irrigation systems, and some of the owners felt that they did not need water from the new system, as they had early priorities. However, the required number of shares was finally taken up within a few months, and more subscriptions came in later. The official list of stockholders, published in 1907, includes my mother's name.

In January, 1905, more than twenty months after the organization meeting, the tunnel work was started by contract. It was presently abandoned by the contractor, who had used up seven percent of his time in making only two percent of the tunnel, at its easier end. After some delay, the Reclamation Service itself undertook the work. This and other unexpected delays caused a good deal of dissatisfaction among the people who lived in the valley.

In connection with operations on the project, a number of difficulties arose. Wagon roads had to be constructed to the site of the work, over what had been described as the wildest country in the United States. Little camp towns had to be built at each end of the project to house the workmen. Troubles developed in respect to the crew. Due to the isolation of the site and the dangerous nature of the work, it was hard to secure labor and there was an enormous turnover. Often men would not remain on the job long enough to pay the cost of their transportation to the site. The eight-hour day law had come into effect and it was claimed that this greatly increased costs. Workmen's compensation certainly added to the costs of construction, as there were many accidents and at least eleven deaths on the job.

Extremely hard rock at the Black Canyon side of the tunnel made drilling slow, difficult and expensive. In places, faulting of the rock was encountered. One fissure permitted a flow of water that reached seven cubic feet per second and greatly delayed the work. Pockets of gas were opened at times, that drove men from the tunnel. On the western end, where most of the drilling was through shale, the sides and top of the tunnel disintegrated and had to be shored up and ultimately cemented. The adobe soil, through which the canals leading from the tunnel to the valley had to run, was found to erode easily. Some of the deposits of alkali dissolved in water, causing certain areas to settle below the general level. The alkali in the soil also had a bad effect upon the cement, so that it disintegrated within a few years.

Troubles and misunderstandings arose with respect to water rights already in effect. The Federal Government finally bought most of the existing canal systems, along with their water rights.

Further troubles grew out of the fact that although some of the land served by the project was already provided with irrigation canals and ditches, much of it did not have these facilities. Apparently, the Reclamation Service had originally assumed that when water was made available in the main canals which were a part of the project, running only a few miles from land to be irrigated, the farmers would cooperate as they had formerly done by constructing minor canals and ditches to bring water to their fields. This the farmers did not do, since their contract stated that the Government was to deliver the water to the lands of subscribers. The many canals and ditches that had to be built in fulfilling this contractual clause added a good deal to the overall costs. Moreover, it was found that in completing the project several small tunnels had to be dug. A number of flumes had to be built in order to carry water over arroyos, chief among which was the flume across the Uncompahgre River that carried water to the lands of the western mesas. Several siphons also had to be constructed, to lead water to lands too high for gravity flow. A good example of these was the long siphon that brought water to the upper Garnet Mesa. This particular siphon soon disintegrated because of alkali and had to be replaced.

Building the large canals proved to be an expensive matter. The constructions of the South Canal, 12 miles long, the East Canal, 35 miles long, and the West Canal, 30 miles long, required a good deal of money. Moreover, when to the newly constructed waterways were added several hundred miles of earlier canals that had been purchased, the undertaking had more than 500 miles of canals and ditches to maintain and operate.

A few years later it was found that even after the union of the two river systems, there was not enough water running in the late summer and early fall to irrigate all the land adequately. Hence, a reservoir of great capacity had to be constructed.

Due to the numerous difficulties, many of which had not been foreseen by the Reclamation Service or the Association, the tunnel was not completed until June, 1909. At 5:18 p.m. on September 23, 1909, President Taft touched a golden plate with a silver bell, closing an electric circuit that opened the headgates of the Gunnison Tunnel. Thereupon, the released water flowed through the long bore and ran upon the dried-up valley of the Uncompahgre. The dream of Larzun had come true! Through the Vernal Mesa had been driven a tunnel nearly six miles long, with a bore of 10 ½ feet by 11 ½ feet and a carrying capacity of 1,300 cubic feet of water per second.

Unfortunately, the project had already cost nearly three times as much as was originally estimated, and the Water Users' Association was charged with a staggering burden. Although I was in College at the time, my family was still involved in the hopes, fears, trials and difficulties of the project. Hence, I hope that I may be pardoned for telling briefly how it worked out.

The completion of the Uncompahgre Project did not immediately bring the farmers of the Western Slope the golden age so confidently expected. The long time required for getting the project started and completed had been disastrous to numbers of persons who had taken up land, graded it and improved it, in the expectation that within two or three years, they would have an abundance of water. Many were forced to leave after having used up all their available capital.

The building of the tunnel had led to much land speculation. The prospect of an unlimited supply of water, particularly near the time when it appeared that the tunnel would be completed, caused land to soar in price. The upward trend was reinforced by the prevalent delusion that a great deal of irrigated land would be ideal for orchards, from which high returns of $500 or more per acre were to be expected each year. It was widely advertised that one of our neighbors, Mr. Sweitzer, had made $1,300 per acre from his peach orchard on Garnet Mesa. As a result of such expectations, bearing orchards were being sold for as much as $1,000 per acre. About one year after the tunnel was opened, Mother sold seven acres of her land for $400 per acre. But the bubble soon burst. For five successive years after the completion of the project, there were heavy frosts over the valley in the late spring, that ruined the fruit crops. The result was that most of the orchards in the region were pulled out by the roots, and land was planted in ordinary crops such as sugar beets, potatoes, onions, corn and alfalfa. As these crops sold at the low prices then obtaining, and therefore could not be grown profitably on land for which high prices had been paid, farm property values in the area dropped sharply. Land prices on Garnet Mesa fell almost immediately to $150 per acre or less.

Another fundamental miscalculation had been the Government's assumption that all of approximately 140,000 acres which would come under the project would benefit from irrigation. Such was far from being the case. Areas suitable for irrigation must have two main characteristics: they must be fairly level, but gently sloping so that water will run through all the ditches; and they must have fertile soil. Much of the land under the Uncompahgre Project did not meet these essential requirements. Except for a few places, such as the land bordering immediately upon the Uncompahgre River, Garnet Mesa, Peach Valley, etc., the area east of the Uncompahgre consists of rolling hills and ridges whose irregular contours make irrigation impossible.

Even the flat lands in this part of the Project, are largely unsuited to irrigation because of poor soil. There are a few fertile areas here, but much of the soil is permeated with alkali, and most of it is very shallow, with hard impenetrable shale not far beneath its surface. If the percentage of alkali is extremely high, the soil will not support any crops. If less high, it will grow only relatively small amounts of certain crops, notably sugar beets. Shallow soil, even when non-alkaline, such as that of Poverty Flat, will yield a few good harvests and then will be practically exhausted. Irrigation will not remedy these deficiencies of the soil itself.

Because so many areas east of the Uncompahgre are either totally worthless, or far less productive than the best lands within the Project, they should not have been included on the assumption that they would bear a proportionate share of the costs, nor would they have been included if the facts had been taken into proper consideration by the Reclamation Service. It is true that the Service had ordered a soil survey to be made as a condition precedent to undertaking the irrigation project, but this had been so superficial in nature as to be useless. It had not indicated that most of the eastern adobe lands would have to be written off as unable to pay their part of the cost of the project. Yet, such was the case.

The land west of the Uncompahgre River, as well as that on Garnet Mesa, is very different. Here are large mesas with sandy loam covering the basic shale for depths up to fifty feet. Since the land, in general, is gently sloping and smooth it is well adapted to irrigation, and when adequately watered it produces large crops. After these lands were served by the project, however, an unfortunate circumstance developed. As the higher parts of the mesa were irrigated first, the lower lands were filled with seepage water having a strong alkali content, so that they became waterlogged and unfit for farming. To redeem these lands required large and costly drainage systems. Not until such systems were built, could the lower lands pay their share of the project.

The net result of failure to take these facts and probabilities into consideration was that the costs of the project were three times as high as had been contemplated, and yet had to be borne by only about one-half of the 140,000 acres originally supposed to be capable of improvement by irrigation. Since there had not been any agreement regarding the maximum charge per acre, and since those who joined the project had signed contracts binding them to joint and several responsibilities, each member found the costs per acre almost prohibitive. Ultimately, a long series of amended contracts had to be worked out.

Furthermore, it appeared that in developing the reclamation plans, too little attention had been given at first to certain basic factors, such as the productivity of different types of soil and the kinds of crops that could be raised. Costs were to be distributed as if all the land under the project would be equally productive. Such was far from being the case. Yet the poorest part of the irrigated soil, despite its general unproductivity, had to pay the same amount per acre as the best.

Another matter which had been overlooked was the fact that the land to be served by the project was a large isolated valley far from centers of population. Even if good crops were raised, they could be sold only by shipment over the high Rocky Mountains on a little narrow-gauge railroad running from Grand Junction through Delta to Salida, and transported on a wide gauge railroad to market centers. Apparently, nobody had considered that the high freight rates, which were often from $4.00 to $7.00 per head for shipping cattle to market and from forty to fifty cents per box for apples or pears, might make it impossible for the valley to compete with other regions of the country, even under irrigation.

In planning for the project, the Government had made no provision for the generation for electricity by water power, although the matter had been considered, and reports had declared it feasible. The plain fact was, that the Reclamation Act had not provided for such water use. The costs of constructing and maintaining the project would have borne much less heavily upon the shareholders if a substantial part of them had been paid by the sale of electric current to neighboring communities.

Insufficient attention had also been given, evidently, to the probable costs of upkeep and maintenance. Such costs soon amounted to much more than $100,000 per year.

Because of these numerous factors, almost immediately after the tunnel began to deliver the life-giving water, there was profound dissatisfaction among the subscribers to the project. Instead of obtaining water for their land at a capital outlay of $25 per acre, they found themselves required to pay several times as much. The construction cost alone, divided among the acreage that could actually be tilled, amounted to more than $100 per acre. This was payable in ten annual installments; and the annual upkeep and maintenance costs amounted to about two dollars per acre more. Thus, in effect, the yearly outlay for water was twelve dollars per acre. No ordinary crop could stand such water cost, under the other disadvantages that I have mentioned. Many water users could not possibly pay, and others indignantly refused to pay the high yearly installments. Soon there was much delinquency in payments.

Things dragged along for nearly two decades, in a fashion that was unsatisfactory to all. After much pressure, in 1927 Congress authorized the Reclamation Service to make several adjustments. The project was then declared to include only 128,770 acres. Of this land, 25,357 acres, largely in the region east of the Uncompahgre River, were classified as permanently unproductive; 27,629 acres as temporarily unproductive, due largely to seepage and waterlogging; and 75,784 acres as fully productive. The Government assumed $1,365,427 of the construction costs of the project. Payments on the temporarily unproductive areas were suspended. The care, operation, and maintenance of the project were transferred to the Association. Construction charges were to be paid in thirty-five equal annual installments instead of ten.

Even these adjustments were insufficient to meet all the difficulties. The dissatisfaction continued, and the Association was unable to meet its obligations as required by the Government. There appeared to be a need for still further modification of the payment contracts, and for more accurate determination of the amount of irrigable land.

There was even greater dissatisfaction from the beginning of the depression in 1929 and later. The prices of crops and cattle were so low that they did not meet freight charges to markets. A Department of Agriculture man was sent out to look into the situation and to decide whether the solution might be greater productivity. The Association wrote back to the Department: "If we cannot sell the one blade of grass we now produce, what in the hell is the use of trying to produce two blades?" A conference was held in Denver and a conference committee was set up. This committee found that there were many adverse factors in the situation: high taxes, limited feeding and pasturage areas for livestock, marketing difficulties, high transportation costs, non-resident ownership, tenant farming, bad soil, and faulty irrigation conditions such as seepage and waterlogging. They also found that the contractual conditions regarding the blanket mortgage and the joint liability of the shareholders were very objectionable.

Largely as a result of this committee's activities, in 1931 Congress passed an act postponing payments until the land was on a profitable basis. Once profitable, owners would be assessed $52.00 per acre in forty yearly installments. The government undertook to expend not more than $500,000 for drainage. This sum was to be repaid from funds raised by the Association in installments, the last of which should fall due in 1961.

I have already mentioned the fact that even the Gunnison and the Uncompahgre Rivers together were not sufficient to supply irrigation water in late summer and early fall. To remedy this situation, the Federal Government built a large reservoir toward the head waters of Taylor River, a branch of the Gunnison, as a cost of $2,000,000. According to a contract dated May 31, 1934, this sum was to be paid by the Association in 40 annual installments. The total cost of the project had now risen to $10,000,000, or more than six times the original estimate.

Pursuant to the new Reclamation Act of 1939 (53 State.1187), the Association asked for an amended payment contract and a reclassification of the lands under the project. In accordance with this request, the Bureau of Reclamation made a careful investigation, which included a reclassification of the lands and of the ability of water users to repay construction costs to the United States. As a result of this study, it found an irrigable area of only 70,828.4 acres, which it divided into three classes and several subclasses, according to productivity. The Bureau made an important recommendation to the effect that the Water Users Association should be permitted to establish a schedule of differential annual assessments.

As a result of this study and recommendation, with the consent of Congress, a new contract was drawn up dated December 13, 1948, to supersede any and all earlier ones. This contract provided, among other things, that the indebtedness of the Association to the United States was reduced from $7,692,329.61 to $5,957,912.95, which should become a general obligation of the Association. The adjusted indebtedness was to be paid in annual installments of $60,000 per year, subject to increases from year to year according to the gross crop returns per acre under cultivation. Thus, instead of the initial ten-year period for payment, the Association now had about one hundred years to liquidate the debt. By this contract, the Association agreed to make levies, assessments and charges to meet all payments due to the United States. The annual payment of $60,000 was to be met from assessments upon the shares of stock of the Association. These yearly assessments must be "apportioned to the various classes of land of the project based upon their respective abilities to pay," according to schedules contained in the contracts, as follows:

Class	Assessment
Class 1	$1.50 – 2.00
Class 2 "mesa"	1.00 – 1.50
Class 2 "adobe"	.60 – .90
Class 3 "mesa"	.45 – .75
Class 3 "adobe"	.20 – .50
Class 3 "sandstone"	.20 – .50

The power to reclassify land for repayment purposes was vested in the Association, subject to the consent of the Secretary of the Interior. The Association agreed to care for, operate and maintain the project in such manner that it shall remain in good and efficient condition.

As a result of this and former contracts, the Federal Government wrote off nearly $3,000,000 of construction costs. The final contract did away with the blanket mortgage of the land under the project and the provision for the joint liability of the stockholders. It extended the time of payment to virtually 100 years, thus making each year's payment relatively small. It placed the classified lands of the project on a basis of ability to pay. By thus looking at the project from a broad economic viewpoint, the government was able to place it upon a workable business basis.

With the adoption of new methods of farming, the cultivation of certain different types of crops and a great increase in demand, the productive land now irrigated by the project has become a veritable garden spot. The cost of water is well within the ability of the farmers to pay. Many of the formidable difficulties that faced the early shareholders had been overcome, and the waters that once flowed through a deep canyon in their own wild way now served mankind. The struggle for water had ended.

Andrew Trew Blachly **Mary Adelle Bradley**
(1847 - 1893) (1854 - 1927)

Frederick Frank Blachly (1880 - 1974) *[plus 7 siblings]*
Miriam Eulalie Oatman (1887 - 1962)

Frederick Johnson Oatman Blachly (1917 - 2016) *[plus 2 siblings]*
Elisabeth Macdonald Haughwout (1911 - 1973)

Peter Macdonald Blachly (1949 -) *[plus 4 siblings]*
Janet Lynn Circosta (1951 -)

Sat Hari Khalsa (1978 -) *[plus 1 sibling]*

www.ingramcontent.com/pod-product-compliance
Lightning Source LLC
Chambersburg PA
CBHW030611100526
44585CB00032B/225